The Digital Humanities Coursebook

The Digital Humanities Coursebook provides critical frameworks for the application of digital humanities tools and platforms, which have become an integral part of work across a wide range of disciplines.

Written by an expert with twenty years of experience in this field, the book is focused on the principles and fundamental concepts for application, rather than on specific tools or platforms. Each chapter contains examples of projects, tools, or platforms that demonstrate these principles in action. The book is structured to complement courses on digital humanities and provides a series of modules, each of which is organized around a set of concerns and topics, thought experiments and questions, as well as specific discussions of the ways in which tools and platforms work. The book covers a wide range of topics and clearly details how to integrate the acquisition of expertise in data, metadata, classification, interface, visualization, network analysis, topic modeling, data mining, mapping, and web presentation with issues in intellectual property, sustainability, privacy, and the ethical use of information.

Written in an accessible and engaging manner, *The Digital Humanities Coursebook* will be a useful guide for anyone teaching or studying a course in the areas of digital humanities, library and information science, English, or computer science. The book will provide a framework for direct engagement with digital humanities and, as such, should be of interest to others working across the humanities as well.

Johanna Drucker is the Distinguished Breslauer Professor in Bibliography in Information Studies at UCLA, USA. She has published widely on topics related to visual design in digital and print forms. Her publications include: *Graphesis* (2014), *Diagrammatic Writing* (2013), *The Visible Word* (1994), and *Visualization and Interpretation* (2020).

The Digital Humanities Coursebook

An Introduction to Digital Methods for Research and Scholarship

Johanna Drucker

LONDON AND NEW YORK

First published 2021
by Routledge
2 Park Square, Milton Park, Abingdon, Oxon OX14 4RN

and by Routledge
52 Vanderbilt Avenue, New York, NY 10017

Routledge is an imprint of the Taylor & Francis Group, an informa business

British Library Cataloguing-in-Publication Data
A catalogue record for this book is available from the British Library

Library of Congress Cataloging-in-Publication Data
Names: Drucker, Johanna, 1952– author.
Title: The digital humanities coursebook : an introduction to digital methods for research and scholarship / Johanna Drucker.
Description: First edition. | Abingdon, Oxon ; New York : Routledge/ Taylor & Francis, 2021. | Includes bibliographical references and index.
Identifiers: LCCN 2020044897 (print) | LCCN 2020044898 (ebook) | ISBN 9780367566661 (hardback) | ISBN 9780367565756 (paperback) | ISBN 9781003106531 (ebook)
Subjects: LCSH: Digital humanities. | Humanities—Research. | Digital media.
Classification: LCC AZ105 .D783 2021 (print) | LCC AZ105 (ebook) | DDC 025.06/0013—dc23
LC record available at https://lccn.loc.gov/2020044897
LC ebook record available at https://lccn.loc.gov/2020044898

ISBN: 978-0-367-56666-1 (hbk)
ISBN: 978-0-367-56575-6 (pbk)
ISBN: 978-1-003-10653-1 (ebk)

Typeset in Sabon
by Apex CoVantage, LLC

Contents

Tables

Figures

Preface

This book is meant to provide an introduction to digital methods for research in the humanities. The text is guided by the principle that technical expertise and awareness of critical issues are inseparable. Every section of this book weaves ethical and critical concerns into the application of technology in the belief that *digital humanities methods* are a combination of these.

Other approaches to teaching digital humanities exist. Some are close to critical media studies, others shift toward data science or computation. Still others focus on digital editing and writing practices, online exhibit design, and community activism. Some put more emphasis on critical and theoretical issues while others attend exclusively to hands-on skill-building. This book takes the approach that unless you have *tested theory with making* you cannot understand a medium or process—and without critical reflection, making becomes an unexamined technical activity.

Every field of cultural activity currently engages with digital methods and these approaches provide useful foundations across a wide array of creative and professional arenas. Many of the tools and platforms used for digital projects were not developed exclusively for the humanities. Humanist scholars have many perspectives on knowledge production. But one of the threads running through this book is the question of how humanities research meets digital methods, many of which were designed to serve empirical approaches in social science disciplines. Humanists have, in general, taken more *from* these approaches than digital methods have absorbed from the humanistic fields. One role of humanistic scholarship is to keep ambiguity, complexity, and the capacity for contradiction present in the face of techniques that privilege efficiency and problem-solving. Humanists do not approach their research as problems to be solved, but as investigations of the cultural record. The digital humanities have the potential to put instrumental technologies into dialogue with interpretative activities.

Background

This project builds on an earlier course book, *DH101: Introduction to Digital Humanities*, that I created in 2011–12 for use at the University of California,

Los Angeles (UCLA). That book remains available online and its outline undergirds this new text.[1] That original course book has an even longer history which I will go on to explain, and the fact that it has been used, cited, and adapted by others for their teaching is what prompts this new iteration.

I owe a significant intellectual debt to my colleagues at the University of Virginia for introducing me to much of what I now know about digital humanities. When I arrived there in 1999, a vibrant intellectual community had been created around the Institute for Advanced Technology in the Humanities (IATH) under the (truly visionary) leadership of John Unsworth. Other initiatives, mainly fostered by the Alderman Library, such as the Electronic Text Center and Virginia Center for Digital Humanities, along with outstanding projects—the Tibetan and Himalayan Digital Library, the Rossetti Archive, Valley of the Shadow, the Blake Archive, and others—had attracted a cohort of gifted and dedicated scholars. Daniel Pitti, Worthy Martin, Thorny Staples, and Kim Tryka provided expertise and experience from which I learned immensely. Many visitors and distinguished scholars—Harold Short, Marilyn Deegan, Willard McCarty, Susan Hockey, Laura Mandell, and Susan Brown—were part of the more extended community whose ideas informed my work.

In the early 2000s, I was the recipient of a newly established grant offered by the National Endowment for the Humanities to support curricular development in the digital humanities. The colleagues we assembled under the auspices of that grant contributed generously to the initial conception of a digital humanities curriculum: Jerome McGann, Stephen Ramsay, Bethany Nowviskie, Andrea Laue, and Geoffrey Rockwell. The full network of persons with whom the exchange of ideas has proliferated over time is far too numerous to list. None of those individuals wrote this book, or crafted this syllabus, or formulated these principles, but I could not have done these things had I not been immersed in the intellectual community they provided from 1999 through the mid-2000s. Their imprint on the development of these ideas remains. I thank them all profoundly.

At UCLA in the 2010s I was able to develop the syllabus on which this book is based. Colleagues Jan Reiff, Lisa Synder, Francesca Albrezzi, and Lisa McAulay have been stalwart supports. Former students David Kim, Anthony Bushong, and Iman Salehian were substantial contributors on the first version of *DH101 Coursebook* (Drucker 2014). In the final iteration, Dianne Weinthal and Nick Schwieterman contributed invaluable research and expertise. Many more persons than I can name have contributed to the generative dialogue from which this project springs. As to my Digital Humanities colleagues at UCLA—they know very well what role they have played in making this book a reality.

Current approaches

Every field of cultural life is now mediated in some part through digital environments and platforms. Knowing *how* they shape *what* we know is fundamental for navigating contemporary life. An understanding of digital methods is crucial for informed citizenship, the production of fair and equitable communication, and for knowledge production.

The humanities face many urgent challenges.[2] The digital humanities cannot save the humanities from institutional extinction or cultural marginalization. Nor should digital methods be taken as the new humanities, as if *reading* can be replaced with *data mining*. Digital and traditional methods are complementary. Also, it behooves us to remember that all significant digital humanities work has been produced by scholars with a deep knowledge of their fields, not by individuals simply using a tool or creating a platform. The additional challenges of sustainability faced by digital methods are substantial and sobering. We have to consider all of the costs involved—human rights, ecological abuse, and labor practices.

When digital methods were first introduced into the humanities, they stretched our minds—trained on close reading, critical theory, and other methods—through the experience of new disciplines. The encounter was dizzying, exhilarating. At present, digital humanities has become codified into standard practices, which is what makes it possible to write this course book. An ability to use digital methods in an informed and responsible way is a now crucial part of any scholar's intellectual toolkit, as is a capacity to reflect critically on the ethics and values in these systems.

A note about scholarship in this field is in order. While peer-reviewed publications remain the standard for research work, the rate at which conversational exchange generates ideas and information outstrips both the timeline and mode of these conventional formats. Much useful commentary, pedagogy, and critical insight occurs on blogs and websites and is cited throughout.

The book addresses a series of topics. Each section introduces a digital method and critical considerations, accompanied by examples. Exercises and recommended readings appear at the end of each section. References cited and resources (tools, platforms, tutorials) are grouped at the end of each full chapter. The book can function as a stand-alone introduction or be integrated into a course structured on the fundamentals of digital humanities concepts and methods.

Notes

1 See: dh101.humanities.ucla.edu

2 The debates about the value of digital humanities range broadly in tone. Attacks from outside the field tend to align it with neoliberalism and an entrepreneurial emphasis in the university. Criticism from within tends to point out its limited demographics in terms of participants and early emphasis on first-world western cultural traditions. See references by Adam Kirsch, Tanya Clement, Alan Liu, and others in the Recommended readings and References cited in each chapter.

References cited

Drucker, Johanna. 2014. "DH 101 Coursebook: An Introduction to Digital Humanities." http://dh101.humanities.ucla.edu.

Resources

Syllabi for Digital Humanities https://otago.libguides.com/digitalhumanities/teaching and https://wiki.commons.gc.cuny.edu/DH_Syllabi/.
Tools https://guides.nyu.edu/dighum/tools.

1 Digital humanities overview

1a What is digital humanities?

Definition

Digital humanities work is done at the intersection of computational methods and humanities materials.[1] The research materials may be analog or born digital, and the integration with computational methods depends upon decisions at every stage of a project's design. A few frameworks for how digital humanities research is structured are provided here at the outset. First is a general description of the *components* of digital humanities projects. This is followed by discussion of the *fundamental activities* in the lifecycle of digital work.

Components and activities of digital humanities

The *components* of digital humanities work can be expressed in this way: MATERIALS + PROCESSING + PRESENTATION. In this formulation, digital humanities projects begin with *materials* (images, texts, maps, three-dimensional models, sound and media files, or any combination of these) that are central to the research project. These materials are subject to computational *processing* (data mining or statistical analysis). The outcomes are organized in a *presentation* that may be web-based or offline, depending on the needs and goals of the project. A project can be digital without being online, but all online projects are based on digital files and computational processes. Here they will be explored in detail. Keep in mind that that term *digital* refers to information in binary form while *computational* refers to processes performed by algorithms.

The *fundamental activities* that take the materials through processing and into presentation are mediation/remediation, datafication/modelling, processing/analytics, presentation/display, and sustainability/preservation. Understanding the ways in which each aspect of these activities engages technical as well as ethical considerations helps shape responsible work in digital projects. This assists innovation that brings humanistic values to bear on technological procedures. Technological instruments are never value-neutral but seeing precisely where and how values affect implementation requires understanding the workflow.

Components and workflow

The components of a digital humanities project workflow involve methods that are likely to be unfamiliar to traditional humanists. They need a bit more explanation:

MATERIALS have to be put into digital formats so that they are computationally tractable. This requires mediation/remediation and data modeling, creation of files, development of metadata for description and use, and other decisions that will have implications for intellectual property, access, sustainability, and use. The way in which materials become digital matters.

PROCESSING uses computational methods and tools. Processing is often the black box of the digital humanist's work, since much of it can be performed with off-the-shelf tools whose workings may be invisible or incomprehensible to the user. Having some understanding of these processes allows critical engagement.

PRESENTATION often makes use of online platforms such as blogs, WordPress sites, or those specifically designed for humanists, like Omeka or Scalar. These may be hard to customize and may force a project to conform to a particular argument structure. Project-specific designs involve work and skill. Digital projects often have off-line outcomes in the form of publications or reports. Format has its own force in structuring the impact of a project and reinforcing its argument. Even elements like background color, font choice, and graphic style affect how research is received.

Engaging with any of these components requires striking a balance between ease of use and critical understanding. Digital methods can be learned gradually and build in complexity.

These components and the activities on which they depend are the foundation of all digital humanities projects, from the simplest to the most complex. At each stage of the discussion, issues relevant to implementation and design are combined with their critical implications. The decisions about how materials are made computationally tractable in digital formats have long-term consequences just as the use of processes by the researcher has implications for the way results are understood and interpreted. A presentation hides as well as shows many of these decisions, and documentation is an essential feature of responsible research work in digital humanities so that other researchers can recover the decision-making process that shaped the project. A healthy combination of hands-on, practical, how-to-do-digital-humanities, and critical skepticism is required throughout, particularly if values and methods central to the humanities are to find their way into the technologically driven activities. [See: Exercise #1 Analyzing a project.]

Fundamental activities

The activities fundamental to the design and implementation of research have been mentioned in the previous section.

Mediation/remediation

This work involves either making analog materials—such as maps, manuscripts, archaeological remains, specific editions, or primary documents of historical or recent events—available in a digital format *or* creating and using born-digital materials. Taking information in one form into another is the activity of *remediation.* The information in one medium (paper, film, stone, etc.) is remade in digital form. This creates information in a file format that a computer can process. Born-digital materials are also highly *mediated* and decisions about their formats are crucial to their use as well. Digital humanities projects often engage with both analog materials and born-digital ones, but all are managed in the form of digital assets.

Datafication/modeling

This is the work of abstracting discrete values from a phenomenon or artifact. These values may be expressed in numbers or texts and are necessarily a reduction of complex materials into a form for computation. With data we can automate processes of sorting, counting, comparing, or making statistical assessments. Materials or phenomena of almost any kind (such as the height of churches, the length of edited segments of film, the number of persons in a social network, or a list of names or places) can be turned into quantifiable and/or discrete data. The practice of *datafication* depends upon modeling. What are the assumptions that are built into deciding what can be extracted from an artifact, text, or other object of research? What terms can be used to represent or describe an object? Data modeling will be discussed in depth ahead. It plays a major role in the intersection of values and biases and the interpretative work central to the humanities in dialogue with technological methods.

Processing/analytics

This involves the automation of counting, sorting, or analyzing through computational *processing*. Every computational process involves intellectual models, no matter how automated its operation. To some extent, research questions are shaped by what can be done using automated processes. For example, if a map is generated using only two-dimensional data, its flat image cannot present the experiential understanding that comes from walking through the territory. The arguments that can be made in any process are constrained by its specifications, as will be explored in more detail in discussions ahead of visualization, data mining, network analysis, and other automated processes. The concept of analytics encompasses many aspects of feature extraction (deciding what is relevant in a file) and then processing those features through some activity of contrast or comparison. As in the case of data, these processes contain cultural assumptions that value certain elements of the cultural record over others. In addition, as processes become more sophisticated and engage machine learning and artificial intelligence (AI), they often reinforce biases built into their model.

Presentation/display

The presentation of results often takes digital form, sometimes in an online environment, as visualizations, maps, diagrams, stories, articles, or exhibits, and sometimes in analog or hybrid formats. Every research presentation is structured according to a narrative that organizes the display. Even repositories and collections present an argument or story through the structure of their interface. The simplest interface design embodies decisions about the hierarchy of what is important and what is not, what is to be revealed and what is concealed, in the presentation of research.

Sustainability/preservation

This must be taken into account from the initial design of a project. Initial design decisions will depend on the institutional site in which the project is conceived and will be managed, on the amount of resources and expertise available (costs and labor), and on other factors specific to the project (such as the intellectual property involved, issues of privacy and protections, and regulations to which the work is subject). Sustainability also involves consideration of ecological costs and human rights issues central to digital labor in a globally networked environment. All digital projects are costly to produce and maintain.

Computation and the humanities

Remediation/mediation, *datafication/modeling*, *processing/analytics*, *presentation/display*, and *sustainability/preservation* are the fundamental activities of digital humanities research. Each involves a series of decisions and tasks that will be described in the sections ahead in more detail. These activities make it possible for automated algorithmically driven processes to operate on humanistic artifacts in a digital format. Similar methods are used in other fields and many are drawn from fields far from the humanities. Much of the earliest digital humanities work had its roots in linguistics, where statistical and computational methods were first applied to keyboarded texts. But computational methods are largely discipline agnostic. We can use the concepts just described (e.g. *remediation* or *analytics*) to do work in biology, ecology, history, geography, performing arts, or economics and political work as easily as in the study of novels, poetry, or philosophy.

This recognition should not be used as an excuse to forget that the humanities have their own intellectual traditions. An ongoing question for digital humanists is whether or not these traditions, and their methods, have found a place in the field. Are computational techniques, many of which depend on quantitative methods from the natural and social sciences, appropriate for humanistic work? Digital tools and platforms have greatly augmented humanities work, and in this book, we will be concerned with these as an extension of humanities methods, rather than engaging digital techniques simply as a method in themselves. The question of what cannot be done with such methods—or how they are based on certain assumptions they enact in their use—will return frequently.

Tools and platforms change, but the principles of digital practice have become clearer and more codified over time. Therefore, this book takes a pragmatic approach: how to introduce the basics of hands-on practice in combination with critical principles in a way that can be transferred as tools change. For instance, if you know how to structure data to analyze a network, that data can be put into any platform (Gephi, Cytoscape, Tableau etc.) to generate a visualization. The difference among platforms is that they generally move towards greater ease of use, but greater complexity (more functions), over time. They become harder to customize or understand.

The underlying activities just noted—remediation, datafication, processing, presentation, and sustainability—remain central to digital work and methods in the humanities and other fields. The chapters break these activities into more specific tasks, so they will be referenced throughout in the sequence that follows the workflow from materials through processing to presentation stages. Topics such as mapping, visualization, managing intellectual property, and so on are subsets of the basic activities and will also be addressed within the chapter sequence as it follows workflows.

Debates

Much debate about the dynamic between technological methods and humanistic ones has been generated over the last twenty years, but in essence, the question is whether the capacities for judgment that include ambiguity, contradiction, cultural specificity, and other qualities that involve human beings in their individual as well as collective understanding of the value of expressions and artifacts can be adequately carried out by automated processes (Gold and Klein 2019). Or not. The answer is of course that while digital methods augment our abilities, particularly offering benefits at scale (work on large bodies of material and at accelerated rates), we should not forget that computation depends on models that inscribe values and biases, and mask them through efficiency and the appearance of authority. Thus the digital humanist continues the work of reading, studying, reflecting, and arguing while making use of tools and platforms whose techniques might not be apparent. Making some of those techniques legible is part of the learning process and should also be part of the documentation that accompanies research.

Other debates about the fundamental politics of doing digital work arise from within critical race studies, where links between the larger contexts of digitization and long term practices of exclusion and oppression call for attention (Risam 2015). Other critics have suggested that digital humanities is intimately connected to the policies of entrepreneurial neo-liberalism within higher education. Questions of gendered asymmetries in practice and institutional roles, concerns about credit for intellectual labor, and discussions of marginalization and challenges to enfranchisement, have been raised usefully at micro and macro levels of production.

The course book approach

This book is structured as a course in digital humanities. It begins with basics in every topic to explore the fundamental components of all digital projects. Implementations of these components, and decisions made at the outset, have implications for the longevity and sustainability of projects and research. The course begins with data production and use, file formats, and markup languages. Then it addresses standards for metadata and description or classification, activity that puts digital humanities in dialogue with libraries, museums, archives, and cultural memory practices. After that, it examines ways of working with data in visualizations, mapping, networks, and other diagrams. Other chapters look at text analysis, data mining, and tools of interpretation at the close and distant reading scales (including topic modeling). In shifting towards narrative and presentation, it focuses on interface design and user experience. While issues of privacy and provenance appear throughout as ethical dimensions of design, a section specifically focused on issues of intellectual property addresses communities of practice and use, as well as ownership. Finally, the closing chapters look at project management, documentation, sustainability, credit and attribution, and other factors in short and long-term production of digital assets and their management. Political, critical, and ethical issues are woven throughout.

To make the lessons vivid and concrete, examples of projects whose approaches exemplify features of digital humanities work are used to demonstrate its benefits. Digital projects can age rapidly. Some very valuable intellectual work has an already dated look about it. Separating intellectual work from style features of presentation emphasizes substance over appearance. Intellectual trends also fall out of favor. Authorship attribution was a central question in early textual analysis. Now discernment of racial bias, computation of non-binary gender patterns, and activist decolonization of knowledge are trending. Maintenance is a constant problem. Links go dead, projects no longer function, software features become obsolete, newer browsers do not always read older projects, and so on. These are critical aspects of the work and understanding how to create projects that have optimal chances of longevity is another one of the many challenges in doing digital work. A similar comment can be made about the rapid obsolescence of tools and platforms in an endless cycle of iterative upgrades. But arguments also age as new critical frameworks arise.

The central argument of this text is that the basic principles of digital work have become clear, codified, and standardized in ways that transfer from platform to platform over time. Specifics may change, but the construction of data, knowledge of digital formats, understanding of basic processing techniques and their output as display, and consideration of the ethical issues involved in every decision can be grasped and transferred over time. Similar principles occur in other areas of our experience. If you understand the difference between addition and subtraction, it does not matter so much whether you do it on paper, a chalkboard, with an abacus, or an automated calculator. The principles of addition and subtraction do not change. Likewise, when such calculations are embedded in cultural circumstances, the ethical consideration of what is being subtracted from whom and added to the advantage of one person or group over another cannot be addressed simply by checking the accuracy of the resulting sum.

The core belief of these lessons is that no digital work should be done simply through technical means. All activities should combine critical understanding with hands-on work. To separate critical reflection from methods is to turn human beings into mere instruments of automation, or to make humanists serve agendas at odds with their core beliefs and values. Instead, we should aspire to make automated processes engage more fully with humanistic capabilities for interpretation and responsible judgment in the service of equity across diverse populations and cultures.

Takeaway

This book is meant to introduce the critical and technical principles for doing digital humanities. Digital humanities work is done at the intersection of computational methods and humanistic research. Most digital humanities projects consist of materials, processes, and presentation. Many are built on existing tools and platforms, rather than in customized environments. Remediation/mediation, datafication/modeling, processing/analytics, presentation/display, and sustainability/preservation are the fundamental activities of digital humanities research. Learning how these components and processes work is crucial to understanding the implications of their use in intellectual and critical terms.

Exercise

Exercise #1: analyzing a project

Look at one example of a digital humanities project and see if you can describe it in terms of the basic components of materials, processing, and presentation.

- Historical Photographs of China
  www.hpcbristol.sjtu.edu.cn/
- In the Spotlight
  http://playbills.libcrowds.com/
- Pacific and Regional Archive for Digital Sources in Endangered Cultures (PARADISEC)
  https://catalog.paradisec.org.au/
- Renaissance Lyon: Le Plan Scénographique c. 1550
  www.renlyon.org
- Arqueología histórica de Santiago
  https://instagram.com/arqueologiahistoricasantiago

Recommended readings

Croxall, Brian. 2018. "Taxonomy of Research Topics in Digital Humanities." https://github.com/dhtaxonomy/TaDiRAH/blob/master/reading/activities.md.

Liu, Alan. 2011. "The State of the Digital Humanities." http://liu.english.ucsb.edu/the-state-of-the-digital-humanities-a-report-and-acritique/.

1b Principles and scenarios for digital humanities

What is involved in *doing* digital humanities? How do I take a collection of photographs and turn them into something that can be analyzed with digital tools? Can I analyze texts to see if they are likely to be by the same author or if they have been altered? What methods can I use to extract useful information from a massive collection of recipes in American cities over time? Are interesting patterns to be found in the relation between neighborhoods and online game participation? How do these relate to income, age, race, and education level? These are all examples of the kinds of projects that are enabled with digital tools. In spite of the brief discussion about basic components and activities, questions about how exactly these are done remain. In this section, a few definitions clarify the terms *humanities* and *digital*, and then a set of imaginary examples will be introduced to make the principles from the last section more concrete.

Definitions

The previous section introduced the basic components of digital humanities projects and five principle activities that are fundamental to *doing* work in this field. But both *humanities* and *digital* need explicit definitions.

The *humanities* are those areas of cultural activity that are explicitly concerned with human existence and experience, such as history, literature, the arts, performance, and cultural traditions across geographical realms and time periods. The term humanities was used in Western Europe during the Renaissance by Italian scholars involved in the study (and recovery) of works of classical antiquity. In this context, the term emphasizes the shift from a medieval world-view, to one in which human beings were "the measure of all things." But all cultures across the globe—Asian, African, and Indigenous peoples of all times—have their own traditions of philosophy, literature, history, and the arts. The humanities are the disciplines that focus on these expressions of human culture.

The term *digital* refers to information stored in discrete binary form, as the inscription of positive and negative charges, encoded as ones and zeros, or bits in which one state is absolutely distinct from the other. Digital information is both *discrete* and *binary*. The precise definition of *digital* in media is information stored in discrete binary code. *Digital* does not simply refer to all media and networked communications. Also, information can be digital without being online. But all online information is coded and transmitted in digital formats.

While binary code underpins all digital activity at the level of electrical circuits, the operation of digital environments depends on the ability of that code to encode other symbolic systems. In other words, not code "in-itself" as ones and zeros, but code in its capacity to encode instructions and information, is what makes computation so powerful. Computation is infinitely more powerful than calculation, which is simple mathematics (no matter how complex or sophisticated). Computation involves the manipulation of symbols through their representation in binary code. The possibilities are infinite. The benefits of being able to encode information, knowledge, artifacts, and other materials in digital format is always in tension with the liabilities—the loss of information from an analog artifact or experience.

Common myths about the digital environment are that it is stable, even archival (e.g. permanent) and that it is "immaterial" (e.g. not instantiated in analog reality). Every actual engagement with digital technology demonstrates the opposite. Digital formats are ephemeral, vulnerable, and depend upon elaborate material infrastructures. (Blanchette 2011)

Humanistic approaches

Humanistic approaches can be brought to the study of any field. Historians of science or social institutions can focus on these as objects of study without making use of their empirical methods. Humanists study the forms and expression of human culture and interpret its development and effects. Disciplinary lines blur in digital humanities, where methods borrow many techniques from the sciences (for instance, statistics). However, one distinction between the sciences and the humanities remains. The sciences are rooted in the belief that knowledge is observer-independent. The humanities are traditionally defined by practices of interpretation that are necessarily observer-dependent. When I read a book and you read a book, we each produce our own understanding. But if I identify a frog and you identify the same frog, or I come back to your frog on a different day, our identification should remain the same (unless we have new evidence). Perversely, we can argue that one never encounters the same frog twice, but within the methods in which evidence is used to identify a frog, that argument will find few takers. In the humanities, the standards of evidence are harder to secure. How is Kermit the frog to be identified?

As discussed in the previous section, all digital humanities projects are built of the same basic structural components. The degree of complexity that can be added into these components and their relations to each other can expand exponentially. We talk about the "back end" and "front end" of digital projects, the workings under the hood (files on servers, in browsers, databases, search engines, processing programs, and networks) and the user experience. A few new terms and concepts will be introduced here, such as information architecture, services, and user experience.

To reiterate, the basic components are: *materials:* a repository of files or digital assets; *processing:* some kind of information architecture or structure and a suite of services; and *presentation:* a display of results within an online or offline user experience. This description is deceptively simple, but it is also useful as a way to think about building digital humanities projects. At their simplest, digital projects can consist of a set files (assets) stored in an information architecture such as a database or file system (structure) where they can be accessed (services) and called by a browser (use/display). At a more complex level, they can involve networked repositories of vast size and variety that can be analyzed with high-level algorithms and AI engines that index libraries of terms, code, and data in emergent processes.

Creating a research project

Analyzing a humanities research project to create a digital project is much like doing a word problem in mathematics. You begin with a description of the research problem. Then you have to figure out what materials can be made computationally tractable by being put into digital formats. Then the research issue has to be addressed by processing these data computationally in a manner appropriate to the intellectual problem. The output will need to be presented as an image, argument, exhibit, virtual simulation, or in another format. That is the essence of digital humanities. You begin with a question and/or a collection (files, images, texts, maps, data, field notes, photographs, or any trace or remains) and then work with digital methods to create a research outcome.

Checklist for analysis:

- Define your research question from within your field of expertise.
- List the materials to which you have access and describe their current format.
- Assess the intellectual property, privacy, and ethical use of these materials.
- Determine which aspects of your research lend themselves to quantitative (numerical) and which to qualitative (interpretative) processes.
- Decide what digital formats will aid your research (scanning, imaging, keyboarding).
- Consult with institutional technical support units on developing a workflow.
- Figure out what skills and tasks you can do yourself and which will need assistance.
- Develop a work plan and budget with a realistic timeline.
- Decide what features you want in a prototype project design; revise and repeat.

Scenarios

The following scenarios provide examples of the kinds of work being done in digital humanities and how such work unfolds.

Imagine a Digital Humanities Research Center has sent out a call to faculty and students for very brief project proposals. Five different projects have been submitted and each one is described in a few sentences. The first task is to figure out the digital research components for each in order to decide if it will benefit from this investment.

Some specialized terminology here will become clear in the chapters ahead as text-analysis, topic modeling, image analysis, mapping, network diagrams, 3-D modeling, and other methods are described. For now, those terms are simply introduced, not explained, so the reader should not be alarmed if they are unfamiliar.

These are recognizable as humanities projects. They are rooted in historical research or critical analysis. They make use of documents from the cultural record. They link events to places or times and each has both a thesis and a corpus of materials on which to draw. Listing the steps necessary to turn these into digital projects begins to expose the challenges, ethical concerns, and labor involved. Because these are fictional projects, much permission is taken with supplying specifics that are not necessarily actual evidence or facts.

Scholar A: is studying the history of collecting Indigenous artifacts in a major natural history museum. The research question is how catalog records, descriptions, acquisition records, field notes, and other documentation imposed colonial views.

This is a text analysis and topic modeling project.

Workflow

- First determine what sources are available. Are they digitized? If so, in what format? If not, what format will make sense?
- Find out the acquisition history of the artifacts and who currently has the rights for the cultural property.
- Make a decision about the boundaries of this project in terms of dates and also scale. How many records and artifacts will be digitized?
- Do an initial study of the vocabulary terms for classification of Indigenous objects. How much standardization is there across the records over time?
- Address the cultural property issues and communicate with stakeholder communities.
- Get access to the catalog records and determine what will be required to put them into digital form. Will they be put into a spreadsheet or kept as unstructured text data?
- Run the texts through a text analysis program to identify terms and frequency of data use.
- Decide how to characterize classification terms.
- Check results against a control set of non-Indigenous artifacts for the same dates.
- Create a basic topic-model around terms associated with colonialism and Indigeneity.
- Create a visualization of the frequency of terms across periods.

Discussion

Each step will require definition and clarification. The project uses OCR software, text analysis, topic modeling, and visualization platforms as well as structured data formats that might be aligned with standards in use for the cataloging of cultural objects or other standard vocabularies. In addition, consultation with the communities for whom these artifacts have value is essential. The naming conventions, identification, display, use, and preservation may all be subject to tribal customs or Indigenous laws. Just because artifacts were acquired centuries ago does not mean they are not still subject to considerations regarding cultural ownership.

Scholar B: is assessing the ways characterizations of gender appear in early English ballads and broadsheets with woodcuts. Are crimes and punishments characterized differently along gender lines? How do the terms of moral judgment change over time?

This is both a text and image project. The corpus of materials is clear. The work will involve text analysis and data mining to produce visualizations.

Workflow

- Identify which ballads and broadsheets deal with crime and punishment, including their time period.
- Make a spreadsheet in which crimes and punishments are identified with gendered individuals.
- Determine how gender is being defined.
- Determine how moral judgments are defined and expressed.
- Determine which terms of judgment are gender-identified.
- Decide whether you will rely on tags/metadata descriptions or extract the texts from the ballads.
- Determine which features of the images are significant (clothing, accessories, settings, facial expressions, body language, gestures, etc.).
- Create a vocabulary for tagging images with metadata.
- Enter the data into a spreadsheet.
- Generate visualizations that chart gender by date in relation to crimes and punishments.
- Determine how to chart moral judgments in a meaningful way.

Discussion

The challenges here are the amount of labor involved in creating a meaningful tag set, applying it consistently to crimes, punishments, and moral judgments, and determining a visualization that allows multiple variables to be displayed. Decide if the final project should be static images or a data set to which filters and queries can be applied. If the latter, then the controlled vocabulary should be offered to the viewer. If the full text of the ballads and broadsheets is going to be made accessible, they will have to be remediated (automatically, with correction by hand, or keyboarded). The intellectual decisions by which moral judgments are modeled should be documented.

Scholar C: is examining the role of geography on a Caribbean island nation in shaping the outcome of a slave rebellion.

This is a mapping project, but the available source materials are not evident, and it may need to evolve into a 3-D modeling project.

Workflow

- Locate relevant documents and materials from which to understand the geography of the Caribbean island from the point of view of slaves and colonial military forces.
- Identify locations and knowledge of geography and topography through available documents. This is a challenge on account of the asymmetry between the documentation of knowledge from the two different populations.
  - Some archaeological remains show where different groups were encamped and where battles were fought. These are partial and not well documented.
  - Logs of the military commander's actions exist, but they are in facsimile form. They provide day to day accounts of troop movements and skirmishes.

Discussion

This project will be difficult to execute without more information, but an animated map can be developed that shows the sequence of known events in relation to the geography (barriers to movement, sightlines, and available fresh water supply, among other features of the landscape).

Scholar D: is focusing research on the shaping of queer identities in Peter Ratcliff's private recordings of performance art of the 1960s in New York City and their influence on popular perception of gay culture when they became available online in the 2000s.

This is an audio-visual project, but also involves topic-modeling, social network analysis, text analysis, and data mining.

Workflow

- Identify the videos of the performances that are in good enough condition to be remediated.

- Remediate and add time stamps and other information to the files.
- Automate processing of certain features of the files. This is possible, but custom metadata will be needed to identify voices, instruments, ambient sounds, etc.
- Locate the owners of the intellectual property (the performers) and obtain releases for research use.
- Determine liabilities on the use of private videos of performances that were sometimes only available to invited/closed audiences.
- Create a metadata scheme for describing the performers, locations, dates, and content of the performances.
- Watch and tag the performance tapes (approximately three hundred hours of tapes exist in Ratcliff's collection, recorded on average once a week for six years from 1964–1969).
- Review transcripts for about half of these tapes made ten years ago and tagged in a custom XML scheme that was based on TEI.
- Make a spreadsheet of performers, dates, and other information.
- Identify the materials that constitute "popular gay culture" in the 2000s in New York City.
- Do text analysis and topic modeling of these materials (journalism, reviews, plays/drama, publications, poetry, and other items).
- Create a model of "influence" in terms of social networks, text analysis, data mining, and other materials.
- Decide what kind of argument structure to use in presenting the outcomes.

Discussion

Challenges for this project include addressing intellectual privacy and property issues and potential liability, the time commitment to watching the tapes and tagging them, the difficulty of identifying popular culture reception, and the challenges of modelling "influence" as a concept. This is a project that might be done better without digital tools.

Scholar E: is interested in creating a virtual reconstruction of a medieval pilgrimage site using a collection of three thousand photographs, field notes, drawings, and other materials taken before and after the site was badly damaged in a recent conflict.

This is a 3-D modeling project.

Workflow

- Identify all primary materials and codify their relevant features.
- Make decisions about which of these materials should be digitized and what kind of metadata they should receive.

- Balance decisions about file formats and the costs of storage against access and use.
- Determine whether digitization of photographs and drawings will need to be done in-house or should be outsourced.
- Decide if field notes will be digitized or remediated.
- Perform geo-rectification and identification of updated/outdated place names.
- Determine which features of the photographs can be extracted with automated techniques.
- Geo-locate and upload the site drawings for use.
- Extract information from the field notes to assist in recreating architectural features.
- Decide how evidence in these notes and materials will be embodied in the 3-D model.
- Assess modeling software that supports queries of the model or else creates static images, or animations and decide on a platform.
- Make decisions about how the model will be stored and displayed.
- Upload, tag, and describe primary materials and decide how they will be displayed in a content management system.
- Create a prototype design of an interface that supports access and use.

Discussion

Challenges for this project include the following: some of the materials were created in the 19th century. Place names, identifying features of the landscape, and other references have changed. In addition, the site was partially destroyed by an earthquake in the region in the 1960s and restored for military use. Labor and resource investment in 3-D modeling is considerable.

Each of these scenarios, first stated as a humanities research problem, has been broken down into steps for action. Some of these steps are easy and others are very difficult. The amount of labor involved in such projects is considerable. In addition to the usual scholarly research tasks, implementation of digital methods will be time consuming. Automation is not a time saving device, but involves ever-proliferating tasks. In addition, issues of institutional support, storage, intellectual property rights, privacy concerns, and sustainability come into play. The question of expertise—who has it and what their contribution to the project is—will also require consideration. Work for hire and intellectual credit for contributions need to be spelled out along with expectations. All of these are part of project management and design and will be addressed in the chapters that follow. [See

Exercise #1: Basic components.] [See Exercise #2: Workflow.] [See Exercise #3: Ethical concerns.]

Takeaway

The basic structure of any digital humanities project is a combination of digital assets, a set of services (query, search, processing, analysis), and a display that supports the user experience. The purpose of this discussion is to move from the front-end experience to knowledge of the back end and to get under the hood and make a digital project start to finish.

Exercises

Exercise #1: basic components

Using one of the scenarios described in the previous section, describe the components of the project (materials-processing-presentation) to see if you understand the concepts involved.

Exercise #2: workflow

Using another of the scenarios, describe the ways the activities of mediation, datafication, processing/analytics, presentation, and sustainability need to be addressed.

Exercise #3: ethical concerns

In which of these scenarios are issues of privacy most likely to need consideration? Cultural appropriation and ownership? Intellectual property?

Note

1 The question of whether digital humanities is a single, collective, noun or a plural one depends on context of use. Where diversity of practices is referenced, and multiplicity of approaches, the plural verb makes sense, but when referring to the field of digital humanities, the singular seems appropriate.

Recommended readings

Gold, Mathew, and Lauren F. Klein. 2019. "Introduction." In *Debates in Digital Humanities* Minneapolis, MN: University of Minnesota Press.

Posner, Miriam. 2013. "How Did They Make That?" https://miriamposner.com/blog/how-did-they-make-that/.

Risam, Roopika. 2015. "Beyond the Margins: Intersectionality and the Digital Humanities." *Digital Humanities Quarterly* 9 (2). www.digitalhumanities.org/dhq/vol/9/2/000208/000208.html.

References cited

Blanchette, Jean-François. 2011. "A Material History of Bits." *Journal of American Society for Information Sciences and Technology* 62 (6). https://onlinelibrary.wiley.com/doi/abs/10.1002/asi.21542.

Gold, Matthew, and Lauren F. Klein, eds. 2019. *Debates in Digital Humanities*. Minneapolis, MN: University of Minnesota Press. https://dhdebates.gc.cuny.edu/.

Risam, Roopika. 2015. "Beyond the Margins: Intersectionality and the Digital Humanities." *Digital Humanities Quarterly* 9 (2). www.digitalhumanities.org/dhq/vol/9/2/000208/000208.html.

2 Data modeling and use

2a Making data

The term *data* is so ubiquitous that it seems to refer to information in any form. The word *data* derives from the Latin word *datum*, which means *given*. This suggests that data exist in the world. But in fact, data are made, produced through a process of abstraction that is called *data modeling*. Every stage of this process of making, using, presenting, or repurposing data raises ethical issues related to privacy, ownership, and use. In this section, we will look at data production practices, including appropriation of existing data, to understand fundamental concepts and concerns.

The discussion of data conjures images of columns of numbers and quantitative information. But what does it mean to talk about data in the context of the humanities, where images, texts, dance, music, and monuments might be the focus of research? Quantitative data can be produced from a wide range of sources, not just numerical ones. Anything that can be counted can be used to produce *quantitative* data. The number of words in a text, beats in a measure, pixels on a screen, and distances on a map can all be turned into quantitative data. As already mentioned, these are acts of remediation by which some feature of an already existing phenomenon is abstracted into a value. But what about more subjective values such as rating the actions of a fictional character as "good" or "bad?" Can such assessments be kept standard across different readers, data producers, or even artifacts? The data created from these interpretative judgments are termed *qualitative*.

Humanities "data" are produced by taking documents or artifacts and abstracting from them certain features that can be represented explicitly. Humanists also extract data from the records kept about those artifacts—such as library and museum catalogs or estate and auction catalogs.

Structured and unstructured data

A distinction is made in digital work between structured or unstructured data. Structured data is composed of entities that are explicit, discrete, and unambiguous—like numbers or true/false statements. Unstructured data, like natural language, is sometimes ambiguous and unclear—like a picture of a mother holding a child which can be described in many ways.

Typing on a keyboard "structures" a text as an alpha-numeric (ASCII and/or Unicode) file that can easily be processed as data. The distinction of one letter from another or from a number structures the data at the primary level. But the words that the text contains might still be ambiguous or vague.

Data structures can also be expressed through formal organization. A table, for instance, is a data structure that determines the values of the information according to their position. A spreadsheet is a table (or collection of tables) that is a common way to structure data. Data in a spreadsheet can be saved in specific formats such as. xsl (Excel),. csv (comma separated values), or. tsv (tab separated values). These are all forms of structured data that can be easily imported into and exported from a spreadsheet and used in other programs. Other ways of structuring data will be addressed ahead, such as markup, or use of other file formats designed for particular fields or tasks. Most programs that deal with data will allow save or export functions to produce a variety of standard outputs.

The distinction between structured/unstructured data has ramifications for the ways that information can be used, analyzed, and displayed. The term unstructured data is generally used to refer to texts, images, sound files, or other digitally encoded information that has not had a secondary structure imposed upon it. Analog objects such as literary texts in print or manuscript and historical records on cards or ledgers are generally unstructured data, though they often contain features that can be translated into structured data. The distinction between a poem's title and its stanzas, or the addressee and recipient of correspondence can be specified explicitly. Structured data has an explicit form that has been deliberately designed, generally for a specific purpose (such as managing financial records or keeping track of populations). Unstructured data has implicit form but may not be organized in a standard way. Structured data can be processed and manipulated more readily than unstructured data, but each has features that are of interest and value.

To illustrate the difference between unstructured and structured data, look at these two examples:

Table 2.1 Structured and unstructured data

Unstructured data:

Among the Doe family members, Jane was best known for her affinity for Washington and all things related, including the mementos and archives, some of which had been equally dear to her grandmother, who had cherished her family history, half a century earlier.

Structured data:

Family	Children	Location	Birth year
Doe	Jane	Washington, DC	1978
Doe	John	Seattle, Washington	1982
Doe	Jane	Eternal Rest cemetery	1908
Doe	Washington	Plymouth, MA	1777

In the first sentence of the unstructured example, how would the word "Washington" be identified as a geographical location versus a family name? The context of the word in the sentence suggests that it refers to an ancestor, not a place. But as we see in the structured data example, the word becomes explicit when put into a labeled column. Note, however, that the distinction between city and state is not made clear in the way the table is organized. The *Location* column contains several kinds of information and it is not standardized by type or format. This kind of ambiguity in structured data formats is resolved by data cleaning, to be discussed ahead. With training, AI engines can distinguish place names from personal ones and are used to parse (automatically analyze) unstructured data. When designing structured data, disambiguation and clarity of data type and format should be kept in mind.

Reading a data *model* (as opposed to the specific data) means analyzing the categories into which the information has been organized. Even the small sample of structured data offered above suggests judgments have been made about what information to include and how to classify it. The term *Location* in the third column could mean a place of residence, or birth, or activity. By their proximity, *Location* and *Birth year* appear to be correlated. This suggests that Jane Doe was born in the Eternal Rest cemetery, which would be unusual. Many categories, such as racial identity, gender, nationality, and religious or political affiliation, are specified according to categories that are biased. If an artist was born and raised in Spain, worked in France, but maintained Spanish citizenship, what is their nationality? Are they still Spanish even if they have neither citizenship nor passport but feel a strong cultural affiliation? If someone was active in the Communist Party for ten years, but not before or after, what is their political affiliation? Human lives are of long duration and our identities are not singular, uniform, or consistent. Crucial information about family relations, kinship ties, and other important facts are not present in the table above. Modifying the data model would be necessary if this were a research project about the Doe family and their archives.

New and/or existing data

Digital research in the humanities can make use of existing data or create new data. These have different workflows to them, and each requires some critical attention.

The use of existing data allows analysis of records and materials in a format that lends itself to digital tools. For example, if we take an existing inventory of a museum collection, it will be well structured with categories of artist, location, date, medium, and dimensions. Research questions can be formulated on the basis of this data. We might be able to track certain trends. When were larger or smaller canvases painted? Are they associated with certain artists? Do Western and Asian patterns diverge or run parallel to each other? Are gender or age significant factors in the data or merely incidental?

Work with existing data raises immediate questions about how complete it is or who made it. In the example above, does the inventory reflect the collecting patterns of a particular individual or institutional collector? Can it be trusted for insight into trends in painting over time and across cultures? Painting practices in one cultural and historical location might have been site specific so that works that could not be detached from walls and sold and might not be part of this inventory. Prohibitions against the removal and sale of cultural property might have prevented paintings from one region from being collected in another. Works by female artists might not have been identified under their own names but attributed to someone's studio.

Existing data provide information, but rarely the information about their own making, either as documentation or as metadata. The decisions that shaped the data so that it is presented as if it were a neutral statement of facts cannot be recovered easily. A useful exercise before making use of existing data is to analyze its *model*. What features of the phenomenon have been described explicitly? What might be missing? How are the fields named and what does the classification system suggest? False binarisms and categories of racial or gendered identity may be reductive, simplistic, or abusive in certain circumstances. All of these questions are part of understanding the *data model* of existing data—and of making new data.

Data modeling

As already noted, the creation of data involves modeling. This determines what will be identified as a feature, how it will be made explicit, and what format it will have. All data models embody values that carry implicit or explicit judgment and therefore often include biases. Almost all data are partial and represent some features of a phenomenon and not others. Policies of inclusion and exclusion operate to reify and reinforce biases, making them seem natural.

Here is a specific example of data modeling: begin with a classroom and ask what data is available in the situation. Anything that can be sorted, measured, or counted could be turned into data. The number of chairs, windows, desks, books, lights, pupils, or teachers present are all easily quantified, but some factors will vary at different times. If the data sample is taken at midnight, or during vacations or weekends, instead of during the school day, the population will be different. The model should account for the time of the sample and its frequency. The assumption that certain things actually "belong" to the classroom has been made in the initial list. But the books may be transient, folding chairs might have been brought in to handle an overflow attendance at a special event. These issues expose the fact that even the simplest-seeming act of data production involves a model. Our model might need to be modified depending on the purpose for which we are collecting the data—safety, health, or usage—or to justify new furnishings. Does it matter whether the occupants are male or female, trans or queer, non-binary, and range in age from five to seventy? The specifics of the model for creating data in classroom assessment will depend on the purpose. [See Exercise #1: Creating a data model.]

When we are dealing with concepts or issues that are not immediately quantifiable, then data modeling becomes even more complex. For example, take the statement, "The discouraging climate in the classroom was not conducive to study, no matter how hard the young people worked." Determining the model to get data for assessing this statement is immediately complicated. If we identify the demographics of the "young people" in gendered terms, or in their racial or ethnic identity, we need to know if this is relevant information. The basic assumptions of sentiment analysis suggest that we can code terms as positive or negative—but according to what criteria is the "climate" described as "discouraging"? The interpretative dimensions of data modeling are evident at every turn.

When we are analyzing language, instability of meaning is built in. A word might mean something very different in context: "the mother of all storms" is not the same as "the mother ship" or "the weeping mother." A data model that looks for the term "mother" in a collection of texts would find all of these, but to group them into a single category and suggest that here there were three instances of the same word would be problematic.

Data models are interpretative acts. In standard approaches to data science, the tenets of "good" data practice are clearly spelled out. Data should be valid, accurate, complete, consistent, and uniform. (Elgabry 2019) But in the case of humanities data, this can be very difficult. The materials that remain from the past are by definition incomplete, sometimes ambiguous. Imagine assessing an 18th century collection of correspondence. Modes of formal address might be partial and only include a title, not a name. They might be inconsistent—sometimes dated and sometimes not. Missing data are particularly tricky, since they cannot be measured with any degree of accuracy (Onuoha 2018). Working with cultural materials to extract data requires recognition of these challenges.

Checklist for creating a data model

- Identify information that can be described unambiguously in your sources.
- Create a set of labeled categories that are clear and distinct.
- Decide which categories will be specified numerically, by true/false values, or by descriptive terms.
- Assess the difficulty of keeping your entries consistent.
- Standardize the format for each data type (dates, places, and names).
- Limit the vocabulary for description except in the comments.
- Read the categories you have established to see what the data model will take from the original sources.

- Check for assumptions about categories that may embody bias.
- Check your data model for completeness and accuracy.

When using existing data sets, one of the first exercises should be to "read" the data structure and analyze the model on which it is constructed. What cannot be represented in its scheme? In the example of the classroom above, no mention was made of seating arrangements and preferences, but for a sociologist, such information would be crucial. Different data would be required to assess how pupils chose to position themselves and what information about social identity could be deduced from this.

Parameterization

Data models depend on the concept of parameterization, or what can be measured. Some features of texts, images, recordings, and cultural phenomena lend themselves to parameterization: the number of words, the size of a canvas, the length of a song, the height of a building, or the shape of a pot are easily turned into metrics. But within cultural artifacts, many features that are fully legible to human perception are difficult to parameterize. For instance, we might be able to measure turn-taking frequency in a conversation, but how would we put a metric value on tone of voice, posture, facial expression, or other non-verbal aspects of the exchange? How are such assessments standardized from one researcher to another? We might be able to measure how many minutes a character is on a stage or a screen, but does it matter whether they are seen close up, from the back, or at a distance?

The problems in parameterization extend those of the data model and its value systems (and biases) into very real challenges with implementation. Parameterization comes down to the ability to distinguish something that can be counted according to some metric (quantity, scale, size, direction, frequency, or other quantitative metric). Some forms of human expression, while fully legible to us, are difficult to parameterize. Information in images, for instance, does not lend itself to a simple system of analysis. Language is composed of discrete units (words) governed by rules (grammar and syntax), while images are not governed by such systems. All of these systems of representing cultural phenomena depend upon the position of an observer. How far is it from London to Paris? The physical distance might remain metrically the same from the 14th to 21st centuries, but the length of time required to cover that distance would vary considerably according to many factors (class status, economic resources, gender, weather, time of year, political conditions, size of the party travelling, mode of transport, and so on).

Parameterization always requires judgment about what can be measured and how. Data are generally created for a specific purpose—governing, analyzing, controlling, supervising, or simply managing. In addition, the question of who is doing the parameterization and for what purpose has to come into consideration. From outside of a cultural or historical framework, these judgments may create data that are skewed to the point of inaccuracy, thus lacking any validity. Parameterization relies on knowledge of a discipline or field in order to produce meaningful data.

Tokenization as a feature of data production

Tokenization is a subset of parameterization and is the act of determining what units of representation can be identified in a corpus or artifact. Words, for instance, are easy to tokenize because even in a plain text they are separated by an identifiable element, the space. Again, in images this is a far trickier matter since a figure might be separate from a ground, but it might be partially hidden, incomplete, enmeshed in shadow or otherwise difficult to distinguish as a discrete form. What can be tokenized in sound files and recordings when they are analyzed as wave patterns, instrumental parts, and overlapping resonances?

Parameterization and tokenization both rely on judgments about what is significant and how a feature can be identified and extracted from a work, artifact, or phenomena. In the analysis of a place name, for instance, location will be understood differently in a gazetteer than in a travel narrative. The tokenization of "Washington" as a place, defined as a single word, will not suffice if what is needed is knowledge about whether it was a port of departure or a destination. For this information, at least two words will be necessary, "to Washington" and "from Washington" could be distinguished from "at" or "in" the same place. But this two-word tokenization would miss a phrase like "back to my beloved Washington" whose sentiments might be as significant as the mere fact of its being a destination. These points will be taken up in the discussion of issues like the inclusion or elimination of "stop words" and other matters in the text analysis section ahead.

Data vs. capta: a brief polemic

Given all that has been stated, what should be clear is that data are not "given" but made, or "captured" by a process of making categories and distinctions for measuring, sorting, or counting entities. For humanists, the challenge of finding and using existing data is considerable. One may take an existing data set, like that of a museum catalog or auction inventory and ask relevant questions of it that relate to humanities research. In that sense, the data serve the same purpose as any other primary text, as a document to be read, analyzed, and interpreted. But, as was evident in the earlier Scenarios section, in many cases, the challenge will be to make data, extract it from existing materials that are text-based or consist of other files of recordings, objects, or documents, and through the processes of modeling, parameterization, and tokenization create structured data with which to work. Working effectively with such data will be the subject of the next section, but it should be remembered at every point that the "data" were not given, but "taken," and are actually *capta*, information captured through a process of abstraction and structuring that depends upon decisions that are already acts of interpretation (Drucker 2011).

Data ethics

Because data are always produced through an act of selection governed by decisions, they are necessarily the expression of a point of view and value system. They may not be intentionally malevolent. They are simply part of the process by which data are produced. Whether making data or using existing data, researchers need to be aware of the ethical concerns and also government regulations for use. Ethical concerns are broad and deep, but regulations tend to be local and more specific. From an ethical perspective, data collection has to be carried out in accord with the guidelines that assure that if human subjects are involved, the researcher knows the correct protocols for approval of the work (informed consent, work with vulnerable populations, anonymity, and privacy) (Floridi and Taddeo 2016). Any researcher should also be aware of intellectual property and the limits on cultural appropriation. Whose cultural materials are being used? Who has the right to grant permission for their use and/or publication? How were they acquired? Are there provenance issues and/or concerns that should be addressed in advance of use? [See Exercise #2: Ethics of legacy data.]

The production and use of data are regulated differently across nations and locales. The European Union has strong protections that require notification before data are collected. The collection, repurposing, and monetization of personal data is prohibited or limited in some areas. The California Consumer Privacy Act imposes more stringent limitations on data acquisition than most other states in the US. The "triangulation" or correlation of data sets raises serious issues with regard to individual privacy, since one or two pieces of information, once matched, can violate privacy statutes and erase anonymity. Certain kinds of data, such as medical records, are protected by particular statutes (HIPAA, the Health Information Portability and Accountability Act, and FERPA, the Family Educational Rights and Privacy Act, for instance), but again, these protections can be over-ridden when different data sets are combined. Studying the history of counterculture and underground activities, sub-cultural activities in which individuals participated pseudonymously or anonymously, for instance, can have unintended consequences if identities are revealed and connected in the present.

Data privacy is a critical concern when dealing with any information related to individuals, particularly vulnerable populations (undocumented, trans persons, children, and incarcerated individuals). In addition to understanding restrictions on gathering data or storage of data should be considered as part of research practice. Information stored on a local drive—such as desktop or a flash drive—may be less at risk of being hacked than when stored on a Cloud server. But information that is not backed up regularly is at risk for other reasons (loss or destruction). Back-up procedures, copies, and firewalls for protection are all part of regular maintenance.

Checklist for ethical data use

- Do you know the source of the data—is it authentic and trustworthy?
- Are you aware of constraints on the use of the data (privacy or property issues)?
- Have you obtained proper permission for acquisition or use of this data?
- Does use of the data put anyone at risk?
- Is there personal, financial, or medical information in the data that can be identified through correlation with other existing data sets?
- Is the data biased, offensive, or a misrepresentation of a community or event?
- Are vulnerable populations represented in the data set?
- Document the source, data models, and production whenever possible.

Every individual researcher is responsible for understanding where the data they are using came from, how it was gathered, and what the restrictions are in use. They must work within the legal limits, but even more importantly, perform according to a responsible and ethical code of activity. Risks and consequences are real, and data collected in one circumstance may need to stay secure in order not to be put to a purpose that violates the rights of communities or individuals involved.

Takeaway

Data are the basic units of almost all digital work. They can be manipulated in many ways and also analyzed through a variety of methods, but data drive the world of digital research. This will be even more clear in the discussion of file formats, which are the standards through which remediation of analog materials and production of born-digital ones takes place. Structured data expresses a model of content and interpretation. Structuring data allows analysis, repurposing, and manipulation of data/texts/files in systematic ways. It also disambiguates (between say, the place name "Washington" and the personal name). Structured data is interpreted and can be used for analysis and manipulation in ways that unstructured data cannot.

Exercises

Exercise #1: creating a data model

What kind of data model would you produce to study different musical tastes among your peers? What categories would be essential? Useful? How would you characterize tastes or preferences?

Exercise #2: ethics of legacy data

A research project lists all of the individuals in the diary entries of a famous politician. Many of these are coded to protect the identity of the persons involved, some of whom were the politician's gay lovers. Several of these are still alive and well-known figures. A key to all of these has been provided by a scholar. Where do these belong in the spreadsheet?

Recommended readings

Flanders, Julia and Fotis Jannidis. 2012. "Knowledge Organization and Data Modeling in the Humanities." Whitepaper. https://wwp.northeastern.edu/outreach/conference/kodm2012/flanders_jannidis_datamodeling.pdf.

Elgabry, Omar. 2019. "The Ultimate Guide to Data Cleaning." *Towards Data Science*. https://towardsdatascience.com/the-ultimate-guide-to-data-cleaning-3969843991d4.

2b Cleaning and using data

Quantitative or qualitative data can be made useful in many ways, but one common way to store and analyze structured data is in a spreadsheet. Spreadsheets can be very simple in structure, consisting of just a few columns or rows of information, or they can spread to be enormous and contain elaborate formulae, functions, links, and operations. A spreadsheet is basically a table that can be dynamic (manipulated and changed) as well as static (a presentation). The grid format of the table dates back thousands of years to the ancient Near East and Babylonian system of accounting, mathematics, and management. The basic principle is entities/entries should be classified by type. This separation of entities by "content type" in the row and column structure keeps entities discrete, but also allows them to be manipulated for many purposes. Databases and spreadsheets are not just formal structures, they are intellectual ones expressing judgments and viewpoints through their organization and labeling.

For data to function effectively, a few conditions need to be met, some of which pose their own ethical and intellectual dilemmas. Data will need to be more or less (preferably more) uniform and standardized. For instance, dates should be given in a particular format. This sounds simple enough, but some dates might only be specific to the year, some to the month and day, others to an hour or minute. Methods of recording time and dates are often local, or historical. The start points for the calendar in Biblical, Islamic, and Mayan systems are all different. How are these dating systems accommodated? Simply subsumed into a modern western calendar? Standardization can erase specificity and cultural identity, so immediately, issues arise in making data uniform.

The basic functions of spreadsheets are data cleaning, making reports, and creating pivot tables for comparison of values. Turning data into charts and graphs will be treated later, in Chapter 6.

Terminology and practices

A good way to familiarize yourself with the vocabulary of spreadsheets: cell, row, column, range, function, report, and presentation is to work through a tutorial in any standard spreadsheet program (Microsoft Excel, for instance). In addition to learning this vocabulary, study the basic operations such as order, filter, combine, and so on. Skills for manipulating spreadsheets are essential for data driven work from the simplest to the most complex levels.

One important concept to understand and implement is that of the unique ID. This will be an alpha-numeric ID that is exclusive to an individual entity (like a personal name or publication). Imagine you are inventorying the manuscripts, correspondence, and memorabilia linked to publications by an author. The columns will be labeled as information fields, such as standard bibliographical information about publication date, publisher, length, edition, and so on. The author whose archive this is will remain the same, but authors of correspondence should be given their own unique ID. In the inventory, each item about which information is being entered should also have a unique ID. This will allow the materials to be identified efficiently and unambiguously (for instance, if there are three manuscripts for one book and four letters from one person in the same year, giving each a unique document ID eliminates confusion). The decision about how granular this should be depends on the project. For instance, if there are three manuscripts of the same book, each has a unique identifier and also some distinctive information about its place or date of production. But what about miscellany stuck into the manuscripts at random—a letter from a friend, a holiday photograph, a note relevant to travel arrangements. Should these have unique IDs? Are they separate documents? Or do they "belong" to the larger manuscript?

For whom is this information useful and how will it be used? The ephemeral documents are not, strictly speaking, part of the manuscripts. They may contain information that needs to be structured differently. A manuscript generally does not have a recipient or a sender, and correspondence does, for instance, and so representing this object in the same database (data model) as the manuscript raises questions. If a later process sorts all items in the spreadsheet by date, the additional items will need counting. If the postcard is from a friend, it will have a different author. The purpose of structured data is to make research and analysis possible without confusion. Consider this when putting information into the spreadsheet.

Functions and operations

The functional capacity of spreadsheets is enormous, but simple operations like sorting (on date, location, or other content type), counting, or filtering are fundamental. These operations are structured into spreadsheet software. But for these to work, the data have to be "cleaned" to some extent or entries that are not standardized will fall out of the report or visualization.

Filtering refers to the act of sorting data by characteristics and features. If a feature has not been added into the dataset, it cannot be used. If the manuscripts by an author contain locations that were part of the "North" and "South" in the Civil War, but that information has not been specified, the data in the author's work cannot be analyzed according to these criteria. If housing records do not contain information about demographics for evictions, then activists cannot assess and act on issues of potential discrimination. The way a category is specified will determine its use not only in making data, but in the way it can get repurposed—but also, reused out of context.

Pivot tables are methods of selecting and comparing information in the data set to perform analyses. Some comparisons make sense, but others do not. Pivot tables only work when the comparisons are sensible. Comparing the page length of an author's manuscripts to publications over time might make sense, though interpreting the results would require more than a simple statement to assess the many factors involved. (Was her work edited more or less closely? Did she mature as a writer? Were publishers willing to take more chances after certain marked successes?) But comparing page length to locations cited or to the number of postcards received from friends in a particular period of time might be meaningless. Reading correlations across data requires critical reflection.

Data cleaning practices, intellectual and ethical considerations

The very concept of "cleaning" data suggests elimination and purging techniques that should be approached with caution. Some forms of standardization may be engaged without violence to information, while others impose strong acts of interpretation.

In the example of contrasting date systems mentioned previously, the data might be preserved in their original form and format, referencing the cultural contexts in which they were produced. For instance, one column using a western standard format that includes year 0, but also CE and BCE dates can be used as a shared frame of reference. However, translating all dates into that single format could be seen as erasing cultural identity. When western dates are identified as CE, Common Era, rather than AD (Anno Domini), this shifts the framework from religious to secular references. But that does not change the fact that the birth of Christ is a dividing point.

Imposing these systems on non-Christian cultures imposes a culturally specific framework that is neither neutral nor universal.

The constant trade-off between preserving the specificity of source information and standardizing information for use is always fraught with ethical questions. Validity (is the data accurate and authentic) and security (has the data been altered or changed) are also critical factors. Professional data entry practices in many fields are designed to make data interoperable by standardizing its formats, and in library and museum practices, standards are essential if information from one cataloger is to work with that of another and if catalogs are to integrate across systems. Digital humanities projects often begin with strong convictions about the interpretative requirements of their study and the need for highly customized data and metadata (to be discussed ahead). A researcher might feel every individual named in a lifetime of correspondence, or specialized description of features of artifacts, or esoteric fan-based knowledge of a set of recordings are essential. But when the time for interoperability or cross-project functionality arises, the intellectual investment in elaborate data constructions is often jettisoned, sacrificed to expediency.

Designing data from the beginning of a project to suit research needs and anticipated uses makes sense. But overly customized data structures can pose difficulties for integration with other projects or repositories. Documentation is essential, particularly when categories have been designed specifically for an individual project. Working with artifacts, archives, and cultural materials requires keeping clear understanding of whose intellectual property these are and whose characterizations of their features are being produced. With whom will the data be shared? Where will it be posted or stored? Who is at risk from its characterizations? [See Exercise #1: Creating a scenario.]

Checklist for data cleaning

- Are all dates formatted the same way?
- Are all quantities specified explicitly?
- Is spelling consistent?
- Do fields contain unambiguously unique information, or do they need to be split?
- Is the vocabulary for qualitative judgments consistent?
- Is information missing or incomplete in many fields?
- Is there repetition of information?
- Will the information be able to be filtered and sorted accurately?

Spreadsheets vs. relational databases

A spreadsheet is a powerful instrument for intellectual work in a structured data format. But keeping consistency in a large-scale project becomes difficult. One of the solutions to this is to shift from a flat database structure (spreadsheet) to a relational database. Relational databases separate information into tables so that information that varies can be distinct from that which stays consistent. These will be the subject of a section ahead.

Takeaway

Data models are interpretative intellectual tools for extracting information from artifacts or phenomena. They make use of parameterization (counting) and tokenization (what can be defined as a discrete unit) to produce quantitative or statistical information. Data may be qualitative as well as quantitative, and gathered with subjective criteria, but for purposes of processing, the data must be discrete, distinct, and unambiguous. It must be "machine readable" to be available to be processed computationally. Many data sets are created for a particular purpose or project, but decisions about the data model should be documented. The ethics of data gathering need to take into account possible re-use, discovery, violation of privacy, and liabilities for the repurposing of data for monetary gain. This is particularly true of data associated with individuals or identifiable groups. Data are never neutral, but always constructed from some point of view, with a specific set of values and beliefs.

Exercise

Exercise #1: creating a scenario

What kinds of data can a scholar working with Rare Book auction catalogs use to produce their research project? What materials will they need and how will they structure data from them? Create a scenario in which this occurs. www.rarebookhub.com/catalogues/

Recommended readings

Owens, Trevor. 2011. "Defining Data for Humanists: Text, Artifact, Information or Evidence? Journal of Digital Humanities." *Journal of Digital Humanities* 1 (1). http://journalofdigitalhumanities.org/1-1/defining-data-for-humanists-by-trevor-owens/.

Taylor, Jack. 2016. "Data Cleansing Pitfalls." *Invensis*. www.invensis.net/blog/14-key-data-cleansing-pitfalls/.

References cited

Drucker, Johanna. 2011. "Humanities Approaches to Graphical Display." *Digital Humanities Quarterly* 5 (1). www.digitalhumanities.org/dhq/vol/5/1/000091/000091.html.

Elgabry, Omar. 2019. "The Ultimate Guide to Data Cleaning." *Towards Data Science*. https://towardsdatascience.com/the-ultimate-guide-to-data-cleaning-3969843991d4.

Floridi, Luciano, and Mariarosaria Taddeo. 2016. "What Is Data Ethics?" *Philosophical Transactions* A374: 20160360. http://dx.doi.org/10.1098/rsta.2016.0360.

Onuoha, Mimi. 2018. "On Missing Data Sets." https://github.com/MimiOnuoha/missing-datasets.

3 Digitization

3a Digital documents: formats and protocols

Data can be created offline, as the discussion of the previous sections makes clear. Many analog and digital forms of data in the humanities are used for non-networked purposes. For instance, in cultural institutions, all sorts of records contain data: registrar's lists, acquisition and loan materials, and systems that manage collections are frequently created without a web presence or role imagined for them. So are auction catalogs and estate inventories and many other records related to activities and property. This information can be an object of study without ever being on the Web.

Information on the Web is transferred with a protocol known as HTTP, or HyperText Transfer Protocol. Files used online must meet specific standards and protocols for presentation and display. The language for files that are published on the Web is HTML, which stands for HyperText Markup Language. This "language" is a set of standards that govern the way in which materials have to be structured to be displayed and used. Essentially, all online material is formatted in HTML, even if other kinds of data are embedded in its file structures. Understanding the practical issues of implementation is essential for doing web-based projects. In addition, knowing a bit about the governance and use of HTML standards provides insight into the political and ethical issues involved, as well as into the activity of the World Wide Web Consortium, or W3C. This organization plays a crucial role in keeping the Web working.

HTTP, HTML, CSS, and JavaScript (or other programming and scripting languages) are the main elements that are used to structure web-based documents, determine the way they look, and what functions they can perform. CSS stands for Cascading Style Sheets and consists of instructions on every style feature of a web document. JavaScript refers to the popular programming language that makes web pages dynamic and interactive. HTML documents can contain CSS elements and lines of JavaScript (or other code). But they can also reference these as linked files. The concept of linking is now banal, but in the early days of hypertext documents, the idea of connecting one document to another by clicking a link of text was revolutionary. Be kind to your elders. They had to learn so much that you already know.

What is HTML and why does it matter?

HTML is a descriptive language that identifies the structural elements of a document. All HTML documents are structured with tags—standard terms inserted between angle brackets that are actually instructions. The basic tags, <html></html>, have to be placed at the beginning and end of any such document. This tag tells a browser to read the document according to a set of rules or protocols. While the simple <html> tag is sufficient, technically, every document that conforms to current standards (HTML5) should begin: <!DOCTYPE html>. This tag is called a "document type declaration." In other words, it identifies the kind of document in the file as HTML so that its contents are read according to a fixed set of rules.

Other kinds of document types exist and will be discussed in later sections. Older HTML documents contained a different version of this declaration. Standards change—and understanding who changes them and how is this monitored provides insight into the workings of the Web. HTML5 uses some new tags and retires others.

Browsers must know what to do with HTML documents. To accomplish this, elaborate mechanisms and social practices come into play that are largely invisible to the ordinary user. HTTP and HTML depend on interlocking systems of standards for networks. Every individual web project is part of the complex social system in which standards and protocols are regulated. This social organization is part of a network of global communication that imposes many First World priorities, English-language constraints, and even political agendas through its daily operations (Goldsmith 2018). But without standards, browsers would not be able to read or display HTML files.

HTML basics

HTML files range from very simple to highly complex. For example, a basic HTML file can be made from three tags (and their corresponding closing tags—most tags in HTML must be "closed"). You can try this yourself by taking this tiny bit of code, putting the word "Test" between the body tags, and saving the file as .html. Keep in mind that to make an HTML document you will need to work in an application that supports plain text and allows you to save .html files. (This includes Notepad for Windows, TextEdit for Mac, or the more robust Atom and Sublime Text that display syntax in a clear format that helps reduce errors.)

Table 3.1 HTML basic sample

```
<html>
        <head>
            My file
        </head>
        <body>
            Test
        </body>
</html>
```

This simple file says, this is an <html> document, it contains information about the file in the <head> and the substance of the file in the <body>. The <body> text is what will be displayed on the screen. HTML documents are nested hierarchies. When elements are added to this document, they will also nest, as in the case of the <p> paragraph, which contains an <ul> unordered list consisting of <li> list items:

Table 3.2 HTML second sample

```
<body>
          <p>
                <ul>
                        <li></li>
                        <li></li>
                </ul>
          </p>
</body>
```

This basic structure can become an elaborate document through addition of style sheets and JavaScript, links and references, connections to streaming data and real-time processing, as well as calls to access databases and other web-accessible sources. Every web page is an HTML document. To see this, look at the "Developer" view accessible in any browser. Much of the information in the code appears only as a link <href>. Learning to read code for the structure and workings of HTML documents demystifies these operations and allows greater control over your own work. Many online tutorials for HTML exist. The best starting point is always the W3C Schools. The W3C is the organization that monitors standards. They are the authoritative, open, not-for-profit, source for information about and on the Web. [See Exercise #1: View developer.]

Another approach to creating HTML is called "markdown" which can be written in any plain text editor (Simpkin 2020). It uses a very reduced syntax that does not require tags or expert knowledge. Learning markdown simply requires making use of standard symbols and inserting them in a text as it is written. For example, a text written between two asterisks * like this * will be italicized after the file is converted from plain text to an html-based display. Some people find markdown sufficiently intuitive to simply incorporate it into their writing style. The disadvantage is that it relies on a processor for conversion. Many free processors can be found online and are often included on platforms (as a plug-in in WordPress, for instance).

Creation and regulation of HTML

HTML was developed around 1991 by Tim Berners-Lee as a standard for publishing documents online. Utopian aspirations underpinned early web development and are still present in the way the W3C works as a consortium. Still led by Tim Berners-Lee, it is not a government organization and works solely through participation and cooperation to ensure that the benefits of web access are "available to all people, whatever their hardware, software, network infrastructure, native language, culture, geographical location, or physical and mental ability." The W3C controls the standards for tags, protocols, and other features of the Web. No one owns HTML. It is a non-proprietary standard available for use free of charge, but it is subject to rules that control its use and some entity—the W3C—has to monitor and regulate those rules. The W3C provides educational resources for self-paced training in many fundamental techniques, including HTML, CSS, and JavaScript. [See Exercise #2: W3C Schools HTML tutorial.]

Browsers are a frequently overlooked component of the web environment. Browsers, such as Google Chrome and Safari, are actually applications, packages of software that retrieve materials stored on servers and display them locally, on your laptop, phone, or other device. When a user enters a Uniform Resource Locator, commonly referred to as a URL, in a device or opens a web page, communication occurs to prompt the transfer of information. This call for information retrieval is exchanged using HTTP (the "http" that is displayed in a web address; the HTTPS variant with the "S" indicates that the transfer is *securely* encrypted). Sometimes the information is loaded into the browser and cached, or stored, and sometimes it is loaded in a slow, steady manner—streaming—as an event unfolds in real time. This process is called packet delivery and involves the movement of parts of files through routes through the internet by breaking it into smaller units that get reassembled in a manner that is generally invisible to a user.

A browser can be used to access a search engine as well. Browsers cache material, so they also hold information about users that can be captured and repurposed. This raises questions about who should own such information—and whether users should be informed when they are being tracked. The practice of storing "cookies" allows browsers to track behaviors, store login information, and look at patterns of behavior. As noted earlier, increased regulations for privacy (the General Data Protection Regulation) have been passed by the European Union that are more stringent than those in the

United States. Search engines also make use of this information to weight results and customize them through reinforcing algorithms. Biases and prejudices built into search engines play a significant role in the ways these reinforcing patterns work. Invisible and pervasive, browsers and search engines are far from neutral (Noble 2018). They mediate information—what can be shown, what will be displayed, what is retrieved, and whose interests are served in the process.

Obsolescence risks

While many HTML tags have remained relatively stable, some have been retired as "obsolete." A look through these tags is instructive. As usage changes, older files retain features that may not display properly. Browsers update at different rates. Some may preserve the ability to read older files for some time, but this process of transformation is ongoing.

The history of what are called "deprecated" (no longer supported) tags tells its own interesting story of changes in styles, attitudes towards formal identity and classification of elements. While deprecated tags can still be used, they will increasingly be ignored or produce errors as browsers update. The increasing refinement of tags reflects the expectations of users for more functionality in web pages and puts more pressure on designers to embed finer-grained instructions for display and use. [See Exercise #3: Deprecated tags.]

Giving it style: CSS

When HTML was first developed, the tags were all structural. They defined the parts of the document as a collection of formal elements. Tags for headings in various sizes (generally from 1 to 5, largest to smallest), paragraphs, breaks, lists (ordered with numbers or unordered with bullet points), indents, and a handful of other defined elements constituted the tag set. The original HTML tags did not take graphic features into account. The design community was appalled. How could the brilliant minds behind the W3C standards not understand that the choice of a typeface or font, the colors and sizes of text blocks, the layout and organization of information were themselves part of the meaning of a document? This early decision to overlook style elements reflected a longstanding bias against visual features as important elements of meaning production.

Many humanists who were adherents of text-based work had no problem with this. A "plain" vanilla approach to text display seemed adequate for their work. They were content with default fonts and layouts. Looking at early web projects in digital humanities on the Wayback Machine allows some of this approach to be studied. The work looks very dated.

Style elements were quickly introduced. The refinement of features online required a number of engineering decisions. If a font was to be used in a document, where was the information to reside? In a library accessed by the file? In an accompanying file, usually very large and bulky, that had to be accessed on the fly. Were fonts to be licensed? Controlled? Designers who made web-specific fonts wanted to be paid for their work. They did not want their designs appropriated and used without some recognition and recompense. How was this to be controlled? The production of a font on screen is a non-trivial matter. The amount of information required for each glyph to display properly is substantial. Every letterform is being described as an image, either as a vector graphic, a raster, or a pixel pattern.[1] (These terms will be discussed in more detail ahead, but each is a way to describe a visual form.) If a designer went to the trouble of making a highly refined layout, then the browser had to be able to access the components for this to be displayed. Not all browsers used the same standards. Designers would go through iteration after iteration to see how their work was treated by different browsers.

The solution to the design challenge was the creation of style sheets. Style elements can be specified in several ways: 1) referencing a style sheet; 2) including style sheets in the <head> of the document; 3) adding in-line style features locally inside of the <body> area of a document. CSS derive their name from the fact that their instructions are inherited downward through the document—the instructions "cascade" the way waterfalls do, touching every element in the hierarchical organization of a document.

The advantage of creating style sheets is that they can be referenced by an unlimited number of documents. An entire corpus of files can use the same style sheet. Changes to the way these look and are displayed or work can be made globally. A change to the style sheet changes all of the documents that link to it. If a document has some specific reason to need customization—a particular font or color, for instance, in one section—such a feature can be embedded in the <head> of that document or inline in the <body>.

Table 3.3 CSS sample

```
<html>
        <head>
                h1 {
        font-size: 24pt;
        margin: 0.67em 0;
                }
        img {
                border: 0;
                }
        </head>
        <body>
        </body>
</html>
```

The elements in this style sheet tell the browser to display the largest header, h1, as 24 pt type with a margin of .67 em and to display images with a border of 0 width. Any element in the html file can be given style attributes in the head, inline in the file, or in a style sheet to which the file is linked by an href.

One challenge remains in the use of character-based scripts (Chinese, Japanese, and Korean) in documents, but even more, in urls, browsers, and in code (Choi 2020). Here, too, hegemonic practices prevail. Non-ASCII characters began to be integrated into web addresses in the late 2000s in what are called IRIs, Internationalized Resource Identifiers. The argument for standards quickly collides with issues of cultural colonialism and power when a single writing system dominates the global network.

Providing dynamic functionality: JavaScript

HTML tags describe elements of a document and thus allow them to be styled and displayed. As HTML has progressed, particularly with HTML5, certain functions and dynamic behaviors were built into the way tags would be processed by browsers. However, for higher level and more effective functionality, programming code in JavaScript is used. This is a common scripting language for web-based activity because, like HTML and CSS, it is read easily by most browsers.

Many free tutorials and support materials are online to assist the novice designer in embedding JavaScript in an HTML document. As with CSS, these instructions can be put into a file that is linked in the <head>, or they can be put into the <head> as <script> instructions. They can also be inserted in-line in the <body> between <script></script> tags. The script tag simply tells the browser to read this bit of text as a script—something that does something. Many tutorials embed bits of JavaScript that contain links to style sheets or libraries (collections of code) that must be referenced by your file. This makes your work dependent on the maintenance of these files on someone else's server—and also means that customization of these files is difficult. Being aware of how you are building in dependence on other work or references is important. However, being able to make a site dynamic and interactive depends, largely, on JavaScript. Whether you can learn the basics, or simply copy code to embed basic functionality in your site, you want to have a reading level understanding of the code.

If every line of code, every tag, and every instruction in your site is something you wrote yourself, you will always be able to update, fix, and troubleshoot your work. One rule of thumb is to design with hand-written HTML, CSS, and JavaScript until you need functions or features you cannot write yourself. Then expand. [See Exercise #4: JavaScript examples.]

Accessibility and access: two fairness issues

The notion of *ableism* calls attention to the blind spot of individuals with full use of their bodies to the challenges faced by those who do not enjoy that advantage. Web-based materials can be made available to sight-, mobility-, and hearing-impaired individuals through attention to design features. Individuals who are limited in their tactile/manual mobility need devices that are voice activated and directed. Delivering materials in an online environment so they are accessible to these populations means building in text-to-voice capabilities and roll-over text that describes visual features to the sight impaired. This is done using the "alt" attribute within an image tag to provide a verbal description of the image.

Many websites and their contents are subject to legal regulations as areas of "public accommodation." The Americans with Disabilities Act was put into law in 1990 before the Web was fully operational. The Act could not have anticipated what would be required to guarantee that access to content online is "full and equal" for all users. Now it is interpreted to mean that the content, navigation, and other functions must be accessible. How, for instance, would a visually impaired individual work with drop down menus or know how many tabs are in the top-level menu bar?

The WCAG, or Web-Content Accessibility Guidelines, contain detailed and specific recommendations for making sites accessible. Different levels of conformance are specified as well, and criteria for meeting these are an essential aspect of design for many institutional sites. Private or personal sites are not required to be ADA compliant, but government, financial institutions, housing agencies, and educational institutions generally should be. The actual terminology of "Public Accommodations and Facilities" in the ADA refers to services that have a physical site for business or transactions. Because these must be accessible and ADA compliant in physical space, they must also be compliant in virtual space. You can install a plug-in called WAVE in your browser that monitors accessibility. [See Exercise #5: Guidelines for accessibility.]

In addition to accessibility issues, consideration of access involves social justice and fairness concerns. Infrastructure determines bandwidth and data download capacity. Designing for the lowest level of capacity, imagining that access might be through a phone or other device connected by Wi-Fi or cellular technology, rather than a laptop, desktop, or wired connection takes into account digital divides that disenfranchise whole portions of the local and global population. Keeping the size of files small is one way to make your site download efficiently and make it more available to more varied populations.

The phrase responsive design refers to design for multiple platforms—phone, tablet, or laptop—within the same website and its specifications. Because in many areas of the world and under diverse circumstances individuals access web content through a range of devices and networks, taking these access points into account is another critical aspect of ethical work. Taking a minimal approach that engages low level design and implementation makes use of the most modest means of production, only adding features and complex functionality when necessary. In general, the simpler your technology, the greater the access it provides and the more sustainable it is (e.g. a site made in HTML is more sustainable than one made in Flash, which is no longer supported in most browsers).

Copying code and using templates

Software programs for creating web-based materials have been around for decades. These programs make it possible to prototype web functionality, make design mockups and functional sites, and to put materials online that have features through a drag-and-drop or graphical design interface. They make it easier to create sites with advanced functionality, even without sophisticated skills, as do standard platforms like blog, wiki, WordPress, and others. The trade-off is that customizing and maintaining such projects can be difficult. The CSS and other components that support the functions may or may not be accessible. Software programs for web design often include code that will be hard to read and may be part of proprietary materials that are referenced by a link, but not accessible to the individual user.

Copying code from others is a questionable enterprise since it means taking the investment someone else has made and appropriating it for one's own use. While new content may be put into the design, using someone else's work is still an act of appropriation—possibly even plagiarism. A good exercise is to see what happens in a classroom when students "borrow" code from each other—with and without permission or acknowledgment.

Takeaway

HTML is the standard for publishing documents on the Web. The standards are governed by the consortium that maintains the protocols and also provides free tutorials and instruction for use of HTML, CSS, JavaScript and other basic tools for design of the style and functionality of web-based materials. Considerations of access, accessibility, and other issues of fairness should be taken into account as part of the design process to ensure "full and equal" use of materials.

Exercises

Exercise #1: view developer

For examples of HTML, see W3C consortium lessons, but also, view these same pages in the "View>Developer" or "View>Source" option in your browser.

Exercise #2: W3C schools HTML tutorial

Work through this tutorial and its exercises: www.w3schools.com/html/

Exercise #3: deprecated tags

Look at these tags and see if you can figure out why they were abandoned. www.w3docs.com/learn-html/deprecated-html-tags.html

Exercise #4: JavaScript examples

Look at these JavaScript examples to see if you can read them: www.w3schools.com/js/default.asp

Exercise #5: guidelines for accessibility

Look at these guidelines and consider steps for implementation: www.w3.org/TR/WCAG20/

Recommended readings

For description of Character-based scripts scripts and iri, idn, and urls, see: www.w3.org/International/articles/idn-and-iri/.

Raggett, David. 1998. "A History of HTML." In *Addison Wesley Longman*. www.w3.org/People/Raggett/book4/ch02.html.

Zhang, Sarah. 2016. "Chinese Characters Are Futuristic and the Alphabet is Old News." *The Atlantic*. www.theatlantic.com/technology/archive/2016/11/chinese-computers/504851/.

3b Digitization and file formats

When digitizing analog materials or in creating born-digital resources, decisions about the process will have implications for the life of the project. Choices about file formats have implications for access, accessibility, and sustainability. As just noted, *access* is what makes material available to users across a range of technological and cultural circumstances. *Accessibility* is concerned with making digital materials work for sight-impaired, hearing-impaired, or individuals with a range of abilities. *Sustainability* issues touch on energy use, human rights, costs, and liabilities in every aspect of production, preservation, and use. Each file standard encodes information differently. In some cases, this will matter and in other cases, this may not be an issue. The time to make an informed decision is at the beginning of a project since some file formats cannot be changed without losing information.

One of the myths of digitization is that making information digital is a form of preservation. Digital files are not archival—they are neither stable nor permanent. They deteriorate in a process called "bit rot" that begins as soon as they are made. Every access and download risks further degradation, and files are rarely perfect copies. Though the average user will not notice the difference between an origin and a copy, files are never exactly the same one to another. Even if they were, the additional problems of file format obsolescence would need to be factored into decisions about digitization. Some file formats are more likely to survive than others because they have larger communities of support.

A file's format determines what can be done with it. Conversion of primary sources into digital forms needs consideration from the point of view of what will be preserved and what will not. An image file of an oil painting created with a raked light source will show the dimensionality of the brush-strokes, paint, and surface, while one taken with diffuse lighting will not. "Bit-depth" (the number of bits per pixel) and resolution (pixels per inch) are crucial factors in digital imaging since they constitute the stored information. Time-based media have unique requirements if their display depends on mechanical or electronic features of projectors. If a text document is going to be OCR (optical character recognition) readable, it cannot be scanned simply as an image. While many kinds of information can be compressed during capture or original remediation, secondary considerations come into play when considering transmission across the Web. Even if bandwidth has expanded, it is not an infinite resource. Like all other digital infrastructure, it has costs associated with it.

For our purposes, two major issues need to be considered. Are file formats chosen for a project proprietary or not? And are they lossless or lossy? These two distinctions will be examined for their implications. Other considerations about size and functionality should be weighed at the beginning of a project's design with factors about use, long-term maintenance, and cost factored into the decision.

Proprietary and open-source formats

Proprietary formats are ones whose specifications are owned by private corporations or businesses. These formats are often only able to be used and accessed on platforms from the same companies (think of Apple products). Proprietary formats include those generated from within specific programs and platforms, Microsoft's XLS or PPT formats for Excel and PowerPoint. An Adobe InDesign file cannot be opened in a simple viewer window, it must be opened using the company's platforms. When using platforms, checking on the export and save functions is crucial to see if non-proprietary formats are also available. Some proprietary formats are so ubiquitous that they are widely used as industry standards in digital work such as Photoshop, PSD.

Many common formats are open source. This does not mean the file standards are available to be changed and modified, but that they can be used by any platform or individual. Their specifications are not protected by private companies, and they are not subject to copyright. Formats like GIF, PNG, SVG, FLAC, MP3 (only recently), CSV, Plain Text, HTML, and many others are open source. PDF, which began as a proprietary format, has become open source for many purposes, but remains proprietary for others that are exclusive to the Adobe platforms. Open-source formats tend to have large user bases and communities of practitioners.

Many format standards are used widely and maintained by non-commercial entities. For instance, the ubiquitous JPEG standard is maintained by a small working group that is part of the International Standardization Organization (ISO) known as the Joint Photographic Experts Group. These behind-the-scenes organizations (like the W3C) play crucial roles in ensuring continuity of the massive amount of material that has been produced in digital form. Imagine what would happen if such a group disappeared and the standards were changed. Whole inventories of image files would cease to be readable. Decisions about when and how file formats change have enormous economic and political implications. JPEG is an open-source standard, and it is written in a programming language called C which means that the way the data are structured is governed by procedures that will remain readable for the foreseeable future. Most digital file formats are barely half a century old. Predicting their longevity is difficult at best.

Lossless and lossy formats

When a file is created—such as a scan or recording—a decision about what kind of information it contains needs to be made based on factors such as use, preservation, and resources available. Though storage has become relatively cheap, it has other costs associated with it, and increasingly cultural institutions are realizing that having massive amounts of data stored that is not being used is a liability. In other words, the file format with the largest size may not always be the best.

The terms *lossless* and *lossy* are used to distinguish between formats that preserve all of their information and those that compress information for efficiency. A high-resolution file—audio, visual, media, or 3-D—might have much more data than is useful or necessary. Files made for archival purposes, publication, full-screen web-display, or thumbnails each have different requirements. Likewise, files that will be used for analytic purposes need to preserve the features relevant for that analysis. A file whose data has been averaged may produce compromised results, for instance. Knowing what a file is to be used for will determine decisions about whether a lossy format is acceptable.

Lossy formats use compression techniques to reduce the amount of information needed to produce a usable display, sound, experience, or data set. Lossy format compression algorithms use a range of techniques to eliminate, average, or otherwise reduce the amount of information, thus reducing size. An easy way to think of this is in terms of images, often specified by pixel dimensions (say 200 x 300 pixels). Imagine these are tiles in a mosaic. The value of each of the pixels/tiles (60,000 of them in this example!) must be specified and stored (color, value, and position). If the size is reduced by averaging the values between pixels that are next to each other, the resolution will be less and the image will begin to get fuzzy. In a lossy format, the information cannot be recovered once this change has been made. Lossy compression is irreversible. [See Exercise #1: Format test.]

Compression techniques vary depending on the media. For instance, a sound file can be compressed by eliminating information about amplitude and keeping data on frequency while an image file might be compressed according to criteria about visual perception.[2] The determining factors for compression will depend on what features of the data in the original source need to be represented in the file and preserved. [See Exercise #2: Quality control.]

Digitization

Analog materials will always need remediation into digital formats. Decisions about this process should be made based on the use to which the digital resources will be put. Texts, images, sound, video, and 3-D objects each have different properties. Each will require different formats and processes.

Checklist for digitization

- Analog texts
    - Digitize texts by scanning, photography, or re-keyboarding.
    - Produce OCR readable scans so that the text can be searched (some errors may occur).
    - Produce facsimiles of pages using photography, though these will lack the capacity for search.
    - Re-keyboard to produce a clean, ASCII-based file that can be analyzed and data mined, though this is time-consuming and can introduce errors.
- Images
    - Determine the resolution to be used for scanning as well as the file format.
    - Use 72 dpi for screen resolution, which is quite efficient for web storage and display, but not adequate for print.
    - Consider file format to best serve the purpose of the project: JPEG, TIF, RAW, or other formats preserve different features for research.
    - Create archival scans at 600 dpi or more stored in TIFF format for resources from which other derivatives will be produced (thumbnails, screen display, or print quality of about 300 dpi).
    - Understand the difference between color formats. Many print images are created in CMYK color space while screens display in

  RGB. A translation of these color formats is critical for certain kinds of work.
  - Examine the original format and medium of the image and determine which features are crucial for the research work to determine file format decision.
  - Photograph original works of art or scan them with large format devices. Color correction, lighting, and other elements are crucial.

- Sound recordings
  - Analyze the original recording and its features to determine what should be preserved in the digitization (bandwidth, dynamic range, frequency, noise, etc.).
  - Use a microphone to re-record audio by converting air vibrations to digital information.
  - Use a direct transfer method.
  - Consider whether a WAV file, which is very high resolution, or a lower resolution file like MP3 is more suited to your purposes.

- Video or film
  - Use video and film converters for direct transfer of time-based media into digital files; playback and frame rate are important considerations when transferring media.
  - Consider projecting and re-recording film using a digital camera.
  - Capture analog video through a USB attachment from a tape deck and the correct software.
  - Transfer digital video to copy it directly.

- 3-D objects
  - Scan, video-record, or photograph the object.
  - Provide a 3-D representation of an object that can be viewed from all sides by using photogrammetry.

File naming, folders, and organization of project materials

File naming is an art and requires planning if it is to be useful. Filenames should be readable by humans as well as computers whenever possible. They will be used to sort as well as retrieve information. Once file names and folder structures are established for a project, they will be very difficult to alter without introducing errors into tags and pathways.

To make files human-readable, a naming convention should be established for the entire project at the outset that relates to the conceptual framework of the research. The hierarchy of organization should match the conceptual model of the project. If you are a historian studying maps of battles in a particular region, should the top-level files be "Battles," with "Maps" as an element? Or should the "Maps" be the highest level because a map is used to show multiple battles? Should books be organized by authors or publishers? Dances by choreographers or individual performances? Films by directors or studios? Artifacts to cultures or collections? These questions quickly shift from abstractions to contested territory as part of the conceptual design of a project.

These decisions should be thought through at the beginning, since reworking file structures is expensive, time-consuming, and leads to errors. In general, to be computer readable, file names should not contain any "special" characters (e.g. #, !, or .and other "reserved" signs). They also should not contain spaces. So, My House, Pictures of exterior should be My_House_Pictures_Exterior or MyHousePicturesExterior.

Decisions about the basic organization and structure of files and materials can be governed by professional bibliographical conventions.[3] Archivists, museum curators, and other information professionals have standards for this kind of organizational work, and where these exist for a field, they should be followed. When these do not exist, then conceptualizing a rational framework of organization is crucial, and is also part of the intellectual argument of the research.

Storage and costs

The question of costs is not merely economic. The ecological costs of production and storage of materials in online and server environments should be calculated, as should the cost of production of digital infrastructure. While a book, once printed, can sit on a shelf indefinitely, a digital project is always, in some sense, on life support, dependent on electricity, air conditioning, and other material features of a storage environment. Responsibility for storage should be determined at the outset. Not all cultural institutions have the infrastructure of human or technical resources for long-term support of projects.

In addition, the issues of privacy and security play a part in thinking about storage. Are materials to be stored behind a firewall? Are they protected from spam and bot attacks? And if they were created with public funds, are they accessible and available? Will other researchers be able to use the materials? Particularly when large quantities of primary materials are being digitized, keeping them in formats that conform to professional and/or institutional practices will be essential. If these assets are going to be incorporated into an institutional repository, planning for this from the outset will allow proper metadata (see section ahead) and file naming and format decisions to be made that avoid wasted work. The myth of immateriality is quickly dispelled with the realities of the costs of labor, intellectual input, and institutional resources are taken into account.

Sustainability and forward migration

Issues of sustainability also need to be built into projects from the outset. Will the files still be able to be accessed and used or will they be obsolete, as many programs do not include retrospective updates? Older versions of files are often not readable as programs upgrade and change—or they lose certain features in the process, thus degrading the data. Early versions of animation, movie files, and other digital artifacts which depended on clock time and processing speed are no longer compatible with current platforms.

In addition, files are not always independent of their frameworks or the proprietary constraints. Are the contents of a richly designed research project meaningful without the interface that puts them into relation with each other and a user? If the files are stripped out and stored just as content—images, sound files, or movie files—but all of the interpretative work that provided context or scholarly foundations is gone, then what is saved and what is lost?

All of these things should be taken into account, along with the myth of the "archival" quality of digital files. If anything, digital materials are more vulnerable and subject to decay than analog ones. When files contain sensitive material, they need to be protected by various security and privacy measures. Intellectual property rights for content should be clearly identified and secured. Document all of these aspects of any creative or research work. Finally, the question of forward migration depends upon file format choices. If a format is being maintained, then forward migration to the next iteration is easier than if it has been abandoned. In the short window in which we have produced massive amounts of content in digital form, these issues have often been brushed aside or overlooked.

Takeaway

The importance of making informed decisions about file formats is crucial for the short and long-term success of any digital research project. In addition, the naming conventions and file structures should be established as part of the conceptual work of the project. Consultation with any institutional partners who will have a role in managing or preserving the project should take place in the planning stages.

Exercises

Exercise #1: format test

Using a scanner, your phone, or other device, photograph or scan an analog image. Put it into a TIF file and a JPEG file. What are the differences in size? Look at the file in an enlarged form. What differences are there? Why does it matter?

Exercise #2: quality control

Do a web search for images of the Mona Lisa and specify size. Compare the images. Why are they so different in color? In detail? Even in cropping? What does this tell you about making digital files from analog materials?

Notes

1 The display of fonts is a multi-step process and involves its own set of protocols, rules, libraries, and other procedures. Fonts designed for screens (known as "screen fonts") are designed differently from printer fonts.

2 For instance, human vision makes less use of distinctions among close-toned values in certain color ranges than it does in contrasting black and white. Some information captured mechanically by scanners, cameras, or recording devices may be valuable for human users.

3 One common set of standards is FRBR (Functional Requirements for Bibliographic Records), which organizes information into the categories of work, edition, and object (individual instance, usually what is in front of you).

Recommended readings

Deegan, Marilyn, and Simon Tanner. 2004. "Conversion of Primary Sources." http://digitalhumanities.org:3030/companion/view?docId=blackwell/9781405103213/9781405103213.xml&chunk.id=ss1-5-2.

Manzuch, Zinaida. 2017. "Ethical Issues in Digitization of Cultural Heritage." *Journal of Contemporary Archival Studies* 4. https://elischolar.library.yale.edu/jcas/vol4/iss2/4/.

References cited

Choi, Charles Q. 2020. "World's First Classical Chinese Programming Language—IEEE Spectrum." *IEEE Spectrum: Technology, Engineering, and Science News*. spectrum.ieee.org, https://spectrum.ieee.org/tech-talk/computing/so ware/classical-chinese.

Goldsmith, Jack. 2018. "The Failure of Internet Freedom." In *Knight First Amendment Institute*. New York: Columbia University. https://knightcolumbia.org/content/failure-internet-freedom.

Noble, Safiya. 2018. *Algorithms of Oppression*. New York: New York University Press.

Simpkin, Sarah. 2020. "Getting Started with Markdown." https://programminghistorian.org/en/lessons/getting-started-with-markdown.

Resources

File Format criteria www.ed.ac.uk/information-services/research-support/research-data-service/after/data-repository/choosing-file-formats.
File Formats, Library of Congress guidelines www.loc.gov/preservation/digital/formats/intro/format_eval_rel.shtml.
JPEG standard https://jpeg.org/about.html.
Open Source Formats https://en.wikipedia.org/wiki/List_of_open_formats.
Packet delivery www.sciencedirect.com/topics/engineering/packet-networks.
Sound recording digitization: http://digitalsoundandmusic.com/5-1-2-digitization/.
W3C Consortium Mission Statement www.w3.org/Consortium/mission.
WAVE guidelines https://wave.webaim.org/.

4 Metadata, markup, and data description

4a Metadata and classification

The concept of data might be familiar, but the term *metadata* is likely to be less so. Metadata suggests specialized expertise and a world of professional knowledge—for good reason. But it is also a part of files and documents and is an important aspect of doing research that involves description and classification of digital assets. Think of metadata as the information about a resource or digital asset. When you open the "Get Info" box on any file, it will tell you the date, size, and format of the file. That is metadata. Library records and museum catalogue entries are metadata. Metadata is structured by fields like creator, date, place, medium, format, and other information. For digital resources, two levels of metadata may be required—information about the original source (e.g. a painting or film) and the digital file (who made it, when, in what format, and so on).

Metadata ranges in complexity from very basic (like what is displayed when "Get Info" is clicked for any file) to highly complex (descriptions of where, when, under what circumstances, by whom, for whom, and so on) something was made, acquired, damaged, loaned, or engaged in any process that could be recorded. Every researcher working in digital assets needs familiarity with basics.

General points about metadata

Metadata performs many functions. Most often, as in the example of "Get Info" just given, it is *descriptive*. Metadata can also be *administrative*, helping to organize the data in large sets of records. In addition, it can be *operational*, giving data a role or task, such as the relation of one file to another. The differences among these functions will be discussed later in this section. Metadata has a powerful role in every conceivable discipline that produces information (this is true whether that is in analog or digital form).

Metadata is an essential aspect of any digital scholarship or research. Data have to be described and identified in order to be useful. Without metadata, information in files would be like books without covers or title pages on shelves without labels. Thinking about metadata and designing metadata fields and schemes is heady stuff. And it is where the intellectual and conceptual modeling of research projects takes place.

Metadata is closely related to classification systems and standards. Related concepts include controlled vocabulary, and relations between taxonomies (systems of names) and ontologies (schemes of knowledge organization). These are all terms with enormous history and are also fraught with ethical issues that are the subject of ongoing and essential debates.

Understanding metadata

To reiterate, metadata is information used to describe data, objects, or records. Metadata can be attached to objects or records, but it also stands in as a surrogate. For instance, one common form of metadata is a library record which has fields to describe books and other objects (newspapers, maps, journals, audio-visual materials, etc.). The standard library record has defined fields in which information about the object is specified. The goal of the record is to help patrons locate materials that suit their interests. The library record is also a thing in itself, as well as being a surrogate or stand-in for the object. When surrogates become part of digital systems, their capacity to be analyzed increases as a result of the many benefits of automated processing. But for this to be true, standardization of the organization as well as the substance and format of the information has to occur.

Descriptive metadata is very common. Systems of naming, identifying, and describing objects or entities (including data) are called metadata schemes. Metadata is integral to all systems and activities of knowledge classification. It is essential for organization and access. Metadata is powerful because it frames information in classification systems and terminology. Imagine data as information in any form sitting on shelves, in drawers, or boxes (objects, numbers, or files). Metadata provides the labels for those entities and the organizational system in which they are stored. Think of a vast warehouse for a history museum that has collections from prehistoric settlements to contemporary consumer objects. What system of naming, organizing, and classifying these materials will describe what is what, where is it, and how will you find it? Decisions about how things are described involve challenges of all kinds, since to a great extent, this depends on the anticipated use of those things—and the values attached to them.

Administrative metadata helps to sort data and records according to their use or type. While a catalog record for a book contains certain kinds of information, another set of records might track loans, conservation and repair history, acquisition, provenance, or other features for specialized purposes (that it is part of a particular donor's collection). Administrative metadata might be identified by the type or function it serves within the larger record keeping structure. If descriptive metadata helps to provide information about objects or data, administrative metadata might identify items that have privacy issues attached or should only be shown to authorized individuals. Metadata that is relevant to institutional activity is different in type from metadata describing information or objects.

Operational metadata provides information on the functional requirements—what is needed for its processing or display. It may contain instructions specifying the resolution of an image as a thumbnail, a screen image, or an archival file, or the system needed to make an audio file play. This metadata assists the system in managing and delivering assets as well as describing them.

As already noted, metadata can describe an object or its representation. So, if you have a digital file of a glass plate photograph of a temple in Athens, taken in 1902, does the metadata describe the photograph's creator, time and date, the camera and glass plate, or the temple that is depicted? The photograph is already a surrogate. The digital asset made from the photograph is a surrogate of that photograph. All of this needs to be recorded in the metadata.

Metadata standards

Metadata standards are essential in all disciplines. But they are often highly contested and even controversial because they embody value judgments either implicitly or explicitly. Do all works, for instance, have "creators" or "authors"? Stories and songs from Indigenous communities might not. As concepts of metadata change, older standards come up for debate.

One common metadata standard is MARC (Machine Readable Cataloging) designed in the early years (1960s) of automated library systems' standardized descriptions. MARC was originally used in local automated systems but was integrated into online catalogs as these emerged—thus the benefit of its original design as a machine-readable format. BIBFRAME, a new standard, was launched by the Library of Congress in about 2011, as a proposed replacement for MARC. BIBFRAME contains features deliberately designed for networked environments. These are standards that are used globally, not just in the United States.

Many objects and documents need metadata besides books and bibliographical artifacts. For the fields of cultural heritage materials, CCO (Cataloging Cultural Objects); AAT (Art and Architecture Thesaurus); the Getty Vocabularies (for works of art, but also their surrogates—like photographic documentation—and conservation); UDS (Universal Decimal System), an adaptation of the Dewey system used internationally in many libraries); and CERIF (Common European Research Information Format). Every field you can think of (from astronomy to zoology) has metadata standards associated with its record-keeping practices. Research in many scientific areas is coded into these standards to make the work of individual teams useful across projects. Consider the value of weather data collected and standardized for centuries so it can be used to examine changes in patterns at a global level. Without metadata to identify its source, location, and standards, it will not be useful. Imagine the challenges with gathering weather data when time zones were not linked, measurements were only taken on the ground, and reporting was sparse, intermittent, and distributed. Metadata standards, like data standards, are crucial for aggregation.

Humanities metadata

Many metadata schemes for what is referred to as "resource description" follow the standard known as Dublin Core, originally created in the mid-1990s. This is composed of a minimal set of fields for describing analog or digital resources, but with attention to features like encoding standards relevant to the latter. Learning what is meant by the terms and elements in this standard is a good exercise. [See Exercise #1: Standard metadata.]

Many fields might seem obvious, like "creator," "date," "format," or "language." Others might be less clear, such as "coverage" or "contributor" and "type." Because they are widely used, the Dublin Core metadata standards are a good place to begin a humanities project. Consider which aspects of a specialized research project would not be accommodated in this scheme.

The descriptive fields contain information that stands in for or describes the object. However, more advanced description might be necessary, such as administrative fields to indicate what kind of record this is ("license" or

Table 4.1 Dublin Core fields

Contributor
Coverage
Creator
Date
Description
Format
Identifier
Language
Publisher
Relation
Rights
Source
Subject
Title
Type

"rightsHolder") or point to other aspects of the way an institutional context works. Operational fields might give information about how the object is related to other records or artifacts ("isPartOf" or "isReferencedBy"), or how it is to be used. Here, again, we see the difference between metadata that is descriptive and fields that are operational, defining relations among parts of a collection and/or its records.

In the humanities, many researchers have chosen to customize their metadata to serve particular purposes or to make a point about the materials under examination. The benefits and liabilities of customized metadata have to be weighed against the advantages of standards. Customized metadata structures are also common, particularly in digital humanities projects where the individual researcher or team has a specialized agenda for their work. This same work of art might be part of a study of gendered practices, concepts of artistic identity, or techniques of production. [See Exercise #2: Customized metadata.]

In digital work, the discussion of a "content model" or a "metadata scheme" allows a researcher to consider what features of a work or collection they consider important. If you are putting together materials that are related to each other by a particular theme—an event, site, or topic—thinking through the way they will be described is a significant feature of the intellectual work. In the case of an archive of queer performance, what fields in a metadata scheme allow that identity to be expressed? What types of performance need to be identified and in what vocabulary? Who defines that vocabulary? What are the politics of characterization of queer identity from within the community and from outside? Who speaks in the metadata? Categories that address ethnic and racial identity, sexual orientation, and gender, are particularly fraught since the act of classification can be oppressive.

Keeping metadata consistent is another challenge. Some of this is merely mechanical, such as making sure spelling and vocabulary remain the same so that if a record is being described as containing "colonial" terminology it does not vary into "colonialist" or "imperialist." One way to manage consistency is with "pick lists" that contain all of the vocabulary to be used in the fields of the metadata.

Creating highly customized and detailed metadata can be tempting. Specific expertise and research agendas lend themselves to nuanced and careful descriptive work. But the downside of such specialized activity is that the information may not work well if absorbed into larger systems. (See the discussion of Linked Open Data in Chapter 11 for related issues.) Idiosyncratically named and defined fields may not have a "target" if they are integrated into a system whose fields do not match. This is an old problem and was true for the upload of MARC into other systems as well. The migration of metadata is an ongoing problem.

Keep in mind that while metadata records are often considered a "surrogate" for a thing or object, a stand-in, they are also structured data and can be used for analysis. A study of catalog records, of acquisition records, or any other kind of record can produce a portrait of a field across time. Metadata also provides a profile of institutional practices by tracking the changing descriptions of a collection. At what point, for instance, did the term *artist's book* start to be used to describe a particular kind of publication? Or *'zine*? The fields that are in medical records and census records have changed over time, as have diagnostic vocabularies for mental illness and pathology. *Where* a concept, artifact, or practice appears in a classification scheme can be as important as the terminology. Homosexuality used to be classified as a "pathology" and so books and materials relevant to it were described and positioned accordingly. Where are books about cooking placed (Hoffman 2013)? And what aspects of ethnic or national cuisine are identified? Classification schemes have their own history and though many standards persist, many have been questioned and reworked over time as values change.

Classification

One of the most powerful forms of organizing knowledge is through the use of classification systems—this is true for objects as well as documents. In digital environments (as in analog ones), classification systems are used in several ways—to organize the materials on a site, to organize files within a system, or to identify and name digital objects and/or the analog materials to which they refer. Classification systems impose a secondary order of organization into any field of objects such as texts, physical objects, files, images, recordings, etc. We use classification systems to identify and sort, but also to create models of knowledge. Knowledge models expose and embody cultural differences and values. These are implied in every act of naming or organizing. No classification system is value neutral, objective, or self-evident. All classification systems bear within them the ideological imprint of their production. A system of identifying works of art by their creators might be inappropriate in a community where practices are tied to tradition and repetition, rather than originality and invention.

Classification systems are closely related to metadata. The Dewey Decimal System and the Library of Congress are two different classification systems for published materials. They give each publication a unique identifier within their system and are used for shelving, storage, retrieval, and to position a book within the larger field of knowledge representation. The contrast between them is worth examining. The Library of Congress (LoC) has twenty-six divisions and uses the Roman alphabet as its structuring framework. It uses two of these, E and F, for the history of the Americas and only one, D, for the history of the rest of the world. While naval science and military science each have a dedicated category, caring professions do not appear, nor do activities traditionally associated with women's work, which are all subsumed under larger categories. Like LoC, the Dewey Decimal System begins with philosophy and religion, ends with geography and history as one subsection, and reserves a special place for biography. Looking at a system like Dewey or LoC, one can discern a particular point of view about the world, the knowledge of it, and the values that shape understanding. Many of these systems were shaped by the influence of classical culture on western Renaissance thinkers (like the English scholar Francis Bacon) whose ideas are still legible in these schemes.

Classification systems arise in many fields. Carolus Linnaeus, the 18th century Swedish botanist, created a system for classifying plants according to their reproductive organs. Many of the relationships he identified and named have been contradicted by evidence of the genetic relations among species. Though his system is still used where its principles provide a uniform system, it has been supplemented by approaches that go beyond morphology (physical form). It can be surprising to find out who one's cousins are, genetically speaking. Next time you look in the mirror, see if you see a resemblance with a chicken, fruit fly—or a banana (Breakthrough 2017)! Is admitting to this a problem?

At the most basic level, we need classification systems to name and organize digital files. In addition, we use elaborate systems of naming and classifying that encode information about objects and/or knowledge domains.

Standards

Standardization is essential in classification systems. If you identify something as a "potato" one day and a "spud," or an "Idaho," or "Yukon gold" the next, how is someone to pick the ingredients for a recipe or manage inventory? This is especially true for a computer, which may not know that a "spud" can be turned into French fries. And if you list all your music recordings by artist's name and then list one by title, how will you find the anomalous item? Consistency is everything. When we are dealing with large scale systems used by many institutional repositories to identify and/or describe their objects, such as those mentioned above, then the necessity for standardization increases. If institutional repositories are going to be able to share information, that information has to be structured in a consistent and standardized manner, and it has to make use of standard vocabularies.

Standardization correlates to how information is used. Objects can be organized in an almost infinite number of ways. A collection of music recordings might be ordered by the length of the individual soundtracks, but this would make finding works by a particular artist, composer, or conductor impossible to locate.

Classification systems are used to organize collections, identify characteristics of objects in a system, and to name or identify those objects in a consistent way. They have a significant and substantive overlap with taxonomies and ontologies. Taxonomies are, quite literally, naming systems. They are comprised of selected and controlled vocabulary for naming items or objects. Ontologies are models of knowledge that organize information and concepts into a structured system. There is no need to try to pin these words—classification, taxonomy, or ontology—into hard and fast definitions that are clearly distinct. They are not always distinct, and often resemble each other and are interchangeable with each other. In a general way, taxonomies are lists of terms/names, classification systems describe attributes and relations of objects in a system, and ontologies model knowledge systems. Folksonomies are created by user communities, rather than professionals, and sometimes these groups have specialized expertise, as in fan cultures. Confused? Don't be. Think of taxonomies as sets of names (What should I call it?), and ontologies as models of knowledge (Where does it belong in the scheme of things?).

Person and place names are also subject to standardization. The control of these terms is often linked to Name Authority files managed by professionals. Checking the Library of Congress for standard spellings will make your metadata more useful for exchange. The transliteration of information from foreign languages is styled according to different conventions over time. Being able to link all of these records has a benefit if one is trying to find information on, for instance, the Russian author Fyodor Dostoevsky, which can appear as: Dostoevski, Dostoevskij, Dostoevskii, Dostoyevsky, Dostoyevski, and so on.

Fluid ontologies: the politics of information vs. ideology of information

Before leaving the topic of ontologies, some discussion of the concept of fluid ontologies and politics of information is in order. Local and/or Indigenous knowledge of particular geographies, for instance, such as those of the Sami people who live in the arctic regions of the Northern hemisphere, were embodied in their place names. In some cases, these indicated potential hazards to a geographical feature (e.g. risk of avalanche), but this knowledge was erased in the classification imposed by Europeans. When disasters befell them, the Europeans realized the liabilities. At another extreme, local knowledge of a densely populated urban area and vernacular terminology for a sewer, ditch, or bridge might be essential for rescue and survival, while the managing municipality might have an abstract reference system disconnected from this information. A bulletin warning the population to avoid "Outflow pipe #337 in section A.45" might be meaningless, while an alert about "the lower Tremlow road" would not. The connection between these systems is sometimes referenced through the concept of "fluid" ontologies—the idea that a single naming system may be insufficient without cross-references (Wallack and Srinivasan 2009).

What is at stake in the use of classification and description systems, as well as the naming conventions? Costs (financial, cultural, and human) of mismatches between official and observed approaches to description of catastrophic events can be significant. Ontologies have cultural agency—they both reflect and produce cognitive models of the world. In some cases, including adaptive, flexible tags that reflect local knowledge joined with the official meta-ontologies managed by the State or official cultural heritage institutions could be of value. This raises a question about how folksonomies and taxonomies/ontologies can be merged together. [See Exercise #3: Multiple ontologies.]

This brings the concept of folksonomies into play. Digital systems for tagging—whether attached to images, books, movies, bands, or any other category of cultural material—have proliferated in the web environment. Though great variety might exist in such tags—from the range of judgments to the specific vocabularies—the added value of folksonomies has been recognized by information professionals as well as the broader public. The question of how such information can be incorporated into institutional records is still a matter of discussion, but the fact that readers—expert or amateur—often make observations about materials that, if entered into records, would make these more findable and usable, is clear. Museums and other cultural institutions have been particularly interested in making use of such knowledge, but so are the tourist industry and entertainment realms.

Takeaway

Metadata is the term applied to information that describes information, objects, content, or documents. Metadata is used to classify, describe, organize, and connect records to artifacts and documents and to each other. Standard bibliographic metadata on library records includes title, author, publisher, place of publication, date, and some description of the contents, the physical features, and other attributes of the object. Metadata standards for research data will have other requirements for authenticating information and for making it able to be exchanged and used. Familiarity with metadata in a particular domain is essential for humanities research, whether the project takes place in universities, libraries, museums, and archives, or is produced for individual projects.

Exercises

Exercise #1: standard metadata

Try applying the Dublin Core metadata standard to documents or objects in your research field. Make records for half a dozen of the documents or artifacts. What information that is relevant to your work cannot be fit into this scheme? Which elements of the scheme are confusing or difficult to use consistently?

Exercise #2: customized metadata

Start creating a taxonomy and/or classification system for an area in which you have a high level of knowledge—such as your favorite music, family photographs, memorabilia, or other personal collection. What terms, references, or resources would you want to cross-reference repeatedly? Which should be in a pick list, so you could use them consistently? Is Dublin Core sufficient?

Exercise #3: multiple ontologies

What area of your own experience—health, emotional conditions, knowledge of a neighborhood or travel route, etc.—lends itself to the concept of "fluid" ontologies? Why would different naming conventions be of use?

Recommended readings

Hoffman, Gretchen. 2013. "How are Cookbooks Classified in Libraries?" *NASO* 4 (1). www.researchgate.net/publication/272962458_How_are_Cookbooks_Classified_in_Libraries_An_Examination_of_LCSH_and_LCC.

Pomerantz, Jeffery. 2015. "Introduction." In *Metadata*. Cambridge, MA: MIT Press. www.jstor.org/stable/j.ctt1pv8904.

4b Markup: XML, TEI, KML, JSON, and other standards

Markup languages are sets of codes, embodied in tags, that are used to analyze the contents of textual documents. They are also used to contain metadata about works and artifacts. More recently other formats, particularly JSON (JavaScript Object Notation), have become popular because they are more suited to data description.

HTML was already discussed as a standard for web publishing. HTML identifies the structural parts of documents and allows them to be displayed appropriately and styled. HTML is just one among many markup languages. At the highest level, these are all governed by rules in SGML, Standard Generalized Markup Language, first accepted as a standard in 1986. SGML is an overarching set of rules according to which these markup languages can be defined.[1] Think of SGML as instructions for how to make rules for specifying how to define document types. If this sounds confusing, think about how you would tell someone *how* to specify the rules that distinguish recipes from business letters from census forms. Different elements go into each, but rules about format and contents govern all of these as documents. Rules about how to make rules—the notion may make you dizzy. Perhaps this is a rare moment when a sports analogy is in order: the rules for baseball, basketball, and football are all radically different. But all have rules about scoring, errors, or fouls, and what is and isn't allowed. Imagine making a set of rules to be sure all sets of rules were certain to include those categories (specifying the kinds of rules needed for something to be a "sport"). SGML specifies what rules are needed for something to be a markup language.

The rules of SGML state that if you want to set up rules, the rules themselves have to conform to certain standards (they have be made of tags, tags can carry attributes, and have to be nested). In other words, all markup languages conform to certain guidelines of well-formedness. Individual markup languages are domain specific and will contain relevant components. Like metadata, markup languages are often created within industries or fields as standards so that, for instance, all medical publishing or legal documents can be governed by the same rules. This allows for exchange of information and analysis of large corpora.

A number of markup languages are commonly used in the humanities. These include XML (Extensible Markup Language), used for identifying semantic content; TEI (the standard of the Text Encoding Initiative); and KML (Keyhole Markup Language), used for geographical data. Because XML is easily customized—and human readable—with fields and tags specific to a project, it is used extensively for metadata and thus lends itself to interpretative work. XML schemes are often customized for a project so that description of interpretative features of the research can be formalized.

The most ubiquitous and familiar form of markup is HTML, already discussed. But HTML's purpose was to standardize the *display* of the *structure* of digital publications. HTML did not contain *semantic* tagging. Remember, structural tagging was concerned with the format of documents, not their content. It was focused on elements like headings, paragraphs, and so on. The need for *semantic* markup quickly became evident. If a corpus of six hundred articles was to be styled, HTML could not distinguish an author's name from a title, an article abstract from the body of the text, and a subtitle from a publisher's information when they were identified as "H1" or "H2". Those categories are *semantic* and their tags identify the content, not just the formal identity of the text. These are very fundamental distinctions, and semantic markup goes much further in practice. In fact, as will be seen, it becomes very fine-grained and has many "flavors" that have been developed for different disciplines. The standard format in which semantic mark-up is produced is XML and understanding what it does and how it works is essential for digital publishing and research.

As has already been mentioned, markup languages come in many flavors. Geospatial information uses KML, many text-based projects use TEI, and so on. The use of these standards helps projects communicate with each other and share data. A good exercise is to study a tag set for a domain in your area of interest or expertise and/or make one of your own. For instance, the creation of a specialized tag set allows people working in a shared knowledge domain to create consistency across collections of documents created by different users (e.g. Golf Markup Language, Music Markup Language, Chemical Markup Language, etc.). But a markup language is also a naming system, a way to formalize the elements of a domain of knowledge or expressions (e.g. texts, scores, performances, documents, etc.). [See Exercise #1: XML.]

In spite of the growing power of natural language processing (referred to as NLP), structured data remains the most common way of creating standards, formal systems, and data analysis. Structured data is particularly crucial as collections of documents grow in scale, complexity, or are integrated from a variety of users or repositories. Standards in data formats make it possible for data in files to be searched and analyzed consistently. (If one day you mark up Romeo and Juliet using the <girl> and <boy> tags and the next day someone else uses <man> and <woman> for the same characters, that creates inconsistency. In reality, the implementation of standards is difficult, inconsistency is a fact of life, and data crosswalks (matching values in one set of terms with those in another) only go partway toward fixing this problem (Zhang and Gourley 2009).

The standards for tags in markup languages, and their definition, rules for use, and other guidelines are maintained by the W3C (whom we have already discussed). However, they do not maintain the specifications for individual mark-up languages. All markup languages and structured data are subject to the rules of well-formed-ness. This means the files must be made so that they conform to the rules of markup to display properly, or "parse" in the browser. A file that does not parse is like a play made in a sport to which it does not belong (a home run does not "parse" in football) or a structure that is not correct (a circle that does not close, a square with six sides) because it does not conform to the rules.

TEI: a special subset

One form of XML is termed TEI for Text Encoding Initiative (which refers to the group of scholars who were responsible for creating it as a standard for marking up texts). As in the case of other professional organizations who maintain standards, the TEI is a consortium of nonprofit groups who support and guide its activities. Their guidelines were first released in 1994, and are meant, like other standards, to make digital documents interoperable. That means that the use of standard tags in accord with set rules and protocols allows these materials to be integrated into search, analysis, and research. While the TEI encourages use of standards, they also know that customization is an aspect of humanities research, and their structure allows for and supports this. [See Exercise #2: TEI.]

A quick look at the TEI Guidelines gives a sense of how closely it conforms to the study of bibliographical objects—books and manuscripts in particular. The major divisions of the TEI are Front Matter, Back Matter, and Body. The guidelines are specific to literary and humanistic texts, so there are standard tags for verse that include metrical analysis and rhyme, for instance, or metrical analysis within stanzas. By contrast, tag sets for marking up dictionaries include "entry" and "entry types" with the ability to specific cross-references, abbreviations, and other attributes. The tag sets become very elaborate to indicate every genre and format of text and the many components specific to each one. So, the basic elements in any TEI document are things like quotation, punctuation, unusual language, editorial changes, and so forth, while manuscript description guidelines and performance scripts contain terms specific to these document types.

The first sample, above, shows bibliographical information. The TEI tags define fields for describing an edition. This is standard metadata. In the example below, TEI is used as "markup" to distinguish those parts of the text that are <state> directions from identification of a <speaker> to <l> lines being spoken, alternate readings in variant editions <rdg>, and other elements. The level of detail in the examples is useful for scholarly editions and detailed critical study but goes beyond the basics of metadata used for cataloging objects, books, or records.

TEI Guidelines have been issued in multiple languages in addition to English, including Chinese, Japanese, and Korean, as well as French, German, Italian, and Spanish. This gives a sense of how pervasive they are and why they are of value. But also, they have become widespread in their use and this, in turn, forces the community to take them into consideration and account.

Why would you use TEI? The circumstances in which it makes sense are determined by a few factors. If your project is institutionally based, then adhering to TEI will make the research more useful to others. If you are working on a topic of research that requires cooperation, this is essential. Projects with multiple partners or team members will find conformance a benefit, though interpreting what a particular tag means or requires can still be challenging. If you are working in a specialized area of research, TEI guidelines will structure the way you interpret the documents. For marking up women writers' work, you might want a set of feminist tags and terms. For analyzing documents of colonial politics, you might want others.

Table 4.2 TEI samples of bibliographical information

```
<sourceDesc>
 <biblStruct>
        <monogr>
        <author>Bandol </author>
        <title type="main">Metamorphosis</title>
        <title type="subordinate">Warped Tales</title>
        <edition>Second</edition>
        <imprint>
          <pubPlace>Rome</pubPlace>
          <publisher>Gambolini</publisher>
          <date>1782</date>
  </imprint>
  <extent>"32"</extent>
        </monogr>
 </biblStruct>
</sourceDesc>
```

Table 4.3 TEI markup of dramatic text

```
<stage type="entrance">Enter
          <name>Fairy</name>
          <name>Princess</name>
          and
          <name>Julianna</name>
</stage>


<sp who="prin">
<speaker>Princess</speaker>
          <l>Princess
          <name>Julianna</name>
          and lady
          <name>Jones</name>
          alive
          <app>
          <lem>?</lem>
          <rdg wit="#Q1 #Q2 #Q3 #Q4">,</rdg>
          </app>
          </l>
          <l>Welcome to
          <name>Fairyland:</name>
          the news is most welcome,</l>
          <l>That you are alive.</l>
</sp>
```

TEI is useful for formalizing the interpretation and study of texts. It forces the analysis of a literary work into a formal and explicit framework—is this statement this kind of thing or that? It adds value to a text by virtue of the intellectual labor in the markup that then can be subject to analysis in ways that mere string-searching does not permit. If a tag like "abuser" can be attached to proper names in a large corpus of legal documents, then this category can be searched, analyzed, and addressed. [See Exercise #3: Orlando Project.]

Markup is labor intensive. It cannot be automated very effectively. For many scholars, the activity of doing markup is a form of close reading that allows interpretation to be inserted into the body of the text. This approach has its limitations. Because TEI is based on XML, it is structured in nested hierarchies that cannot overlap. If a literary passage deals with multiple themes and ideas, the markup must be nested. But themes overlap throughout complex literary works, and so do motives or sentiments—which might be assigned to multiple characters across a wide variety of places in the text. For markup purposes, this overlap is not allowed, it will not parse, and the markup will simply have to contain the tags within each chapter. The representation of the text is not identical to its aesthetic structure. [See Exercise #4: TEI and title page elements.]

Other standards are also commonly used in the humanities. Another is Encoded Archival Description, or EAD. It is different from TEI in its attention to the physical features of archival objects and it has its own vocabulary for description. OAI, the Open Archives Initiative is used to "harvest" information, particularly metadata, for integration into specialized, discipline-specific, search engines. Markup is ubiquitous in digital publishing and scholarship.

Another approach: JSON: describing objects rather than inserting markup

Markup is exceptionally well suited to the analysis and interpretation of textual elements, and thus used in literary and humanities work, as well as critical editing in all fields. XML formats are also used to create metadata, and thus to structure and describe the contents of records. But collections of documents lend themselves to other kinds of structured data description in file formats designed specifically for information exchange of data. The most popular of these is JSON format.

Not all data formats are text, and many files created in JavaScript contain information that cannot be readily transferred between a server and a browser and that won't fit easily into XML. JSON was developed to address this problem. It is text-based but can describe many data formats. It is thus a very useful standard with which to be familiar in order to facilitate exchange. JSON is used for storage as well as exchange and has the advantage that it is relatively simple to learn and is highly customizable.

JSON's notation scheme was designed so that it could describe data objects effectively. That means that its syntax contains ways to identify data types so they are not confused with each other. Also, JSON's syntax is very similar to that of Python and other languages, making it easy for those familiar with programming to learn and use it. Metadata, classification, and markup schemes have certain features in common. They are all ways of disambiguating data types, formats, and structures so that they can be processed and either analyzed or displayed properly—or exchanged and integrated into new projects. The crucial principle is that code of any kind conforms to formal rules that disambiguate data, content, and information in order to make their statements computable.

JSON is a simple but powerful way to take existing data formats and files and extract their information for the purpose of exchange or integration. Where XML and TEI are used to markup parts of texts—either thematically (an XML schema on genre might insert the term <mystery> or <thriller> as part of its analysis) or formally (a TEI scheme might contain the term <roleName> to provide highly specific information about an individual)—JSON syntax identifies types of structured data. It builds on JavaScript, but is a notation system (hence its name) for describing or representing what is in a data file. XML and JSON serve different purposes, but both are components of digital research projects. If you are working with already structured content that contains complex data structures, files, or a range of formats, JSON is a useful way to describe it for transmission. JSON has a large user base and is likely to be supported as a format for the foreseeable future. These are also important considerations. [See Exercise #5: Contrast JSON and XML formats.]

Takeaway

Structured data comes in many forms. The choice to use markup languages or other formal methods of either analyzing or describing the contents of documents or files will depend upon the nature of the project, tasks to be performed, and use to which the information will be put. XML and JSON are both highly flexible and allow for considerable customization while also being of great value in storing and transmitting information. Subsets of XML are often discipline specific and provide standards for individual fields of expertise. The advantage of formal languages is that they disambiguate among components of text or data. Paradoxically, this is also their disadvantage—since so many humanistic documents or artifacts are filled with ambiguity that human readers have no difficulty processing. Computers, however, cannot tolerate ambiguity. This fundamental difference is worth keeping in mind. Is there an ethical issue in taking something that is fundamentally "both/and"—a metaphor and a literal statement, a fact and a project, a dream and a reality—and having to choose between representing it as one or the other? Absolutely.

Exercises

Exercise #1: XML

XML schema exist in many fields and disciplines. Look at this list, pick one, and begin to see how it identifies elements of documents for this field. While you are looking at the list, compare it to the Library of Congress and to the Dewey Decimal System. Why is it so different? https://en.wikipedia.org/wiki/List_of_types_of_XML_schemas

Exercise #2: TEI

TEI is a highly specialized XML standard for marking up literary and textual documents. It is divided by genre and its tags must be used in particular orders, hierarchies, and are highly defined. Compare the elements for 7. Performance Scripts, and 10. Manuscripts.

https://tei-c.org/release/doc/tei-p5-doc/en/html/index.html

Exercise #3: Orlando Project

Look at the documentation for the XML scheme and think about the customization of its tags and features. www.artsrn.ualberta.ca/orlando/

Exercise #4: TEI title page elements

Look at the elements for TitlePage in TEI www.tei-c.org/release/doc/tei-p5-doc/en/html/DS.html#DSTITL and think about how using these terms limits the kinds of materials that can be marked up. Are there publications that would not follow this form? Elements that might need to appear for it to work? What about artists' books? Or zines?

Exercise #5: contrast JSON and XML formats

Examine the contrasts in the JSON and XML formats of the same information. The main difference is the syntax and the way that the values are specified. Here are two excellent examples www.w3schools.com/js/js_json_xml.asp and https://json.org/example.html

Note

1 For those with an interest in rule-based systems and the highest level of document type specification, understanding the syntax of SGML boils down to a way to "declare" the contents of and the ways they can be used.

Recommended readings

"JSON vs XML." 2020. *W3schools*. www.w3schools.com/js/js_json_xml.asp.

Schwartz, Michelle, and Constance Crompton. 2018. "Remaking History: Lesbian Feminist Historical Methods in the Digital Humanities." In *Bodies of Information: Intersectional Feminism and the Digital Humanities*, edited by Elizabeth Losh and Jacqueline Wernimont, 131–56. Minneapolis, MN: University of Minnesota Press. Muse.jhu.edu/book/63017.

References cited

Breakthrough Staff. 2017. "How Genetically Related Are We to Bananas?" *Breakthroughs*. www.breakthroughs.com/foundations-science/how-genetically-related-are-we-bananas.

Wallack, Jessica, and Ramesh Srinivasan. 2009. "The Local and the Global: Reconciling Mismatched Ontologies in Development Information Systems." HICSS Hawaii International Conference on Systems Sciences. 1–10.

Zhang Allison B., and Don Gourley. 2009. "Creating Metadata: Metadata Crosswalk." In *Creating Digital Collections*. Oxford: Chandos Publishing. www.sciencedirect.com/topics/computer-science/crosswalk.

Resources

DUBLIN Core https://dublincore.org/.
JSON (vs. XML) www.w3schools.com/js/js_json_xml.asp.
KML https://developers.google.com/kml/documentation/kml_tut.
Library of Congress Classification www.loc.gov/catdir/cpso/lcco/.
MARC Records www.loc.gov/marc/bibliographic/.
Mark-Up Languages (Wikipedia) https://en.wikipedia.org/wiki/List_of_XML_markup_languages.
Metadata Standards, European Union www.dcc.ac.uk/guidance/standards/metadata/list.
SGML www.w3.org/TR/WD-html40-970708/intro/sgmltut.html.
www.w3.org/MarkUp/SGML/.
TEI https://tei-c.org/.
www.tei-c.org/release/doc/tei-p5-doc/en/html/index.html.
Weather data and metadata standards 19th and 21st century versions https://mrcc.illinois.edu/data_serv/cdmp/cdmp.jsp.
www.almanac.com/weather/history/CA/Los%20Angeles/2018-07-02.
XML https://tei-c.org/release/doc/tei-p5-doc/en/html/SG.html.

5 Database design

5a Database basics

We have already seen how structured data can be made and managed in a variety of formats: spread sheets, XML files, JSON, and so on. But as data becomes more complex and relations among elements of data more elaborate, neither flat (spread sheet) nor hierarchical (XML or JSON) structures are efficient for managing or processing. The shift from a flat database to a relational one is conceptual as well as technical. Understanding when and why such a shift should take place, as well as how to implement it, is crucial to making a relational database. Very simply, a relational database is composed of multiple tables that separate different types of information to make it more efficient to manage and easier to control. This is true at any scale, but becomes more pressing in larger projects.

The phrase "big data" is bandied about constantly, and it conjures images of nearly infinite amounts of information codified in discrete units that make it available for analysis and research in realms of commerce, medicine, surveillance, population research, epidemiology, and political opinion, to name just a few domains. To reiterate what has been stated earlier, all data starts with decisions about how it is made. Data does not exist in the world. It is not a form of atomistic information waiting to be counted and sorted like microorganisms in a water sample or cars on a highway. Instead, data is made by defining parameters for its creation—even the category of "cars" would need to be defined, as would microorganisms (count only living ones or also dead?). What about words on a page? Are all words to be counted (including "the" or "and") or only some? What is significant? Nothing is as simple as it appears to be at first.

Data can be big without being complex: a massive number of entries in a very simple spread sheet might list all 300 million people in America by age, or, by first name, or by height and weight. Data can be deep without being big: a spreadsheet might contain highly detailed information about a small number of entries—a hundred books and their authors, characters, plots, sentiments, vocabulary, sentence length, editions, page numbers, annotations by multiple readers, materials of production, reception histories, and many other details. In both of these instances, the data could be accommodated readily in a spreadsheet. Each entry is linked to a single unique identifier that does not change, but in the second instance, a great deal of redundancy might appear, and in the first, age will change each year on a particular date. How should these matters be managed?

Keeping information consistent and error-free is a challenge for updates and other management tasks. The key to understanding relational databases is to think through the connection of one kind of information to another. Age changes by date, but birthdays are attached to individuals. An address for an individual might change multiple times and also be used by others. A work address might change without affecting a residential one. These might vary independent of age. Some might be in a unique relation to an individual (we share our birthdays with others, but each of us has only one). While these are unfamiliar concepts at first, examples should make this clearer.

In a designing a database, distinguishing "dependent" and "independent" relations is essential. In statistics, an independent variable is considered a cause and a dependent variable an effect: change the number of chickens in a room (independent) and see how many eggs they produce (dependent). For the purpose of structuring humanities databases, this insight helps determine what items should be in which table. Information that varies "dependently" (birthdays and individuals) should be grouped. Information that varies "independently" (residential addresses or car registration) should be in separate tables. The database construction described here is focused on consistency and efficiency for entering, managing, and querying data.

From flat to relational: an example

A spreadsheet is a single table. A relational database is a collection of tables connected to each other. One of the main reasons to break information out into multiple tables is to make it easier to manage—and to keep consistent. If I have many authors and the authors have many books, keeping the spelling and other biographical information in an "Author" table and the "Book" information in another allows them to be linked. The author information can be changed or updated in one place and therefore be less at risk of error introduction. This approach also keeps the database smaller and more efficient for queries, particularly in very large data sets. The programs that manage relational databases are called, believe it or not, RDBMS (Relational Database Management Systems). These systems manage the functions and operations of the database. They are programmed applications that build in the most common functions needed by users.

Here is an example of data in a spreadsheet format:

Table 5.1 Spreadsheet and tables example

(a) SPREADSHEET: A flat structure (every entry is one row with values in column).

Artist	*Birthdate*	*Title*	*Medium*	*Date*	*Owner*
Picasso, Pablo	1881	Portrait	Oil	1914	MoMA, NY
Matisse, Henri	1869	Dance	Collage	1922	MoMA, Paris
Carrington, Leonara	1917	I dream of you	Oil	1946	SFAI
Carrington, L.	1917?	The mask	Gouache	1951	Chicago Art Inst.
Matisse, Henri	1869	Red room	Oil	1907	Sotheby's
Tanguy, Yves	1900	Landscape	Oil	1932	SF MoMA
Walker, Kara	1969	Their house	Acrylic	1992	Whitney
Mitchell, Joan	1925	Abstract #2	Oil	1963	Private owner
Kandinsky, Wassily	1866	Composition	Oil	1917	SFAI
Tanguy, Yves	1900	Landscape	Oil	1937	High Musuem
Carrington, Leonora	1917	Dreamscape	Oil	1949	MoMA, Paris
Matisse, Henry	1869	Still Life	Oil	1923	Picasso Museum
Carrington, L.M.	1917	Interior	Collage	1951	MoMA (on loan)
Picasso, Pablo	Self-Portrait	Oil	1954	Met, NY	
Kandinsky, Vassili	1866	Landscape	Oil	1924	Tate, London

(b) TABLES: What information belongs with what and what are the connections?

ARTIST	*WORKS*	*MUSEUMS*
Last name	Title	Name
First name	Medium	Location
Other names		
Year of birth		

Note that in the spreadsheet, variant spellings of the artists' names appear. A report generated on work by "Carrington, Leonora" would not return all of the entries relevant to this artist. In the table below, all the information about the artist is specified and associated with a unique Artist ID. Because the information is specified in the Artist table, the ID is considered a *primary key*. But it can be cited by any table as a *foreign key* and used consistently throughout. Any changes made to the information about the artist are made once and only once but become part of the entire database.

Other changes or modifications might be necessary in the tables above. Works can be listed by title—but how will similar titles by the same artist and owned by the same institution be distinguished? And is Museums really

Figure 5.1 Table structure (NS)

the right definition for owners? Should museums and owners be separated? A painting on loan from a private collection might be on display in the Museum of Modern Art, but it is not owned by the Museum. For purposes of permissions, insurance, and other logistics, this distinction is significant.

When these tables are translated into database tables, each artist entry will have a unique ID, probably a number, as will the works, museums, and owners. These IDs will be cited as the foreign keys in order to keep the information completely unambiguous, as in the tables shown. So, a citation for a painting will have an Artist ID, a Work ID, and an Owner ID. Should Museums be kept separate since they might be the site of display for a work even though they do not own it? If so, then the Work table would need a field for the Museum foreign key, as here, so it could point to the institution.

The value of the primary key is defined in the table to which the information belongs. One could make an entire table of years and point to them as the year of birth with a key and also use the same date table to reference the date of a work. But then we are conflating two kinds of dates—birth year and the year of a work. A query searching for birth year would not be able to distinguish the dates in a table. The concept is simple: primary keys define values that can be cited in any other table. This keeps the information consistent and allows it to be managed in one place. This concept is crucial to the function of a relational database, just as figuring out what belongs in what table is crucial to the design of the database. Relational databases can have dozens of tables, even more, depending on the complexity of data being managed. One feature of most RDBMS is a view that shows the tables and their relations in graphical form.

More advanced topics in database design build on these fundamentals. An "association table," for instance, can be used simply to link keys to each other. When a database has hundreds of tables and millions of entries, these structures are essential. But databases, like any file, are vulnerable to hacking, corruption, and obsolescence. Databases containing personal or sensitive information need to be secured behind firewalls and with passwords and other security measures. User roles can be assigned, so that only certain entries or tables can be accessed—allowing someone to look at names, for instance, but not financial information. But the preservation of data for research purposes also needs protection. The records of oppressive regimes, data collected about stolen and appropriated intellectual or artistic property, records of disappeared or disenfranchised persons, etc.—all of this information is part of the history of human culture whether it is in analog or digital formats.

Database design process

Whether you build a database in a software program like Access, Filemaker, MySQL, or any other DBMS, the principles just demonstrated are essentially the same for all relational databases. A relational database consists of tables of information related to each other.

Workflow for designing a database:

1) Design the content model (defining the information in the database and its organization), define the fields for data entry, and design the relationships.
2) Next, build a form-based entry for putting data into the database. This might be organized very differently from the database in order to make it more useful or coherent.
3) Manipulate and use the data through searches/queries, reports, and other methods, including visualizations, reports, and analyses.

Other forms of database structures exist, such as object-oriented databases. In a relational database, the data is stored separately from operations or functions. In object-oriented databases these might be combined.[1] The contents and functions of databases are all computational; data are and must be machine readable at the basic level where they are stored. RDBMS do this behind the scenes where, for instance, datatype is specified (character data, integers, Boolean operators (or in other systems URLs), binary strings, and shape files or other data formats). With databases, as with other systems and components, the decisions about which format and what design to use will depend on the research agenda.

The basic principles of database management and design are modularity, content type definition or data modeling, and relations, and then the combinatoric use of data through selection and display. Databases are powerful rhetorical instruments. A database is a logical structure and it is configured in the computer. Configuring the database is an intellectual task and has to be done to suit the needs of the project to which it is being put. Databases exist for years, even decades, and may have multiple contributors and innumerable users.

Particularly in institutional contexts, considerations of security and authentication are factors in database design. Most beginning digital researchers are not going to build a database from scratch, but instead, will use a program like Filemaker Pro, Microsoft Access, or an open source or non-proprietary version. To reiterate, all follow the same procedures: modeling the tables (fields and content type) and relations among them, creating forms for data entry, and performing queries and creating reports. [See Exercise #1: Modeling a database.]

Collections management and content management

Content management systems and collections management systems are both common in the management of cultural heritage materials. Collections management is just what it sounds like—a way to describe and manage collections. The tasks for collections management include everything related to tracking objects or artifacts, making records (metadata again!), and keeping updates for acquisitions, conservation treatments, loans, use, and so on. By contrast, a content management system is designed to create and present content, often in a web-environment. Both of these systems have database back ends, and common content management systems include Omeka (created by humanists), WordPress, and Scalar (also designed for humanities and media work). These will be discussed in greater detail in the Web Presentation section. The point is that in both cases, the back-end organization of data is managed in a database.

Table 5.2 SQL Query Note that the SQL query is the information that follows "SELECT" in the lines below.

```
// Let's see what's in the Artists table.
SELECT * FROM Artists;
// Let's say you want to know all artists in the database that are from a particular
  location.
SELECT * FROM Artists WHERE Location='California';
// Numerical data can be filtered or calculated (SUM, AVG, COUNT)
SELECT * FROM Works WHERE Price > 10;
// Dates on the other hand need to be treated as strings, denoted with quotations,
  as long as the data is consistent.
SELECT * FROM Works WHERE Date BETWEEN'1978–01–01' AND'1996–
  01–01';
// Note the similarity in structure between this and and Location query.
SELECT * FROM Works WHERE Medium='Ceramic';
// Join connects two tables based on the primary and secondary key between two
  tables. For example, this query provides the artist first and last name from the
  Artist table and joins it with the work title from the Work table. The two tables
  join on the Artist ID, which is the primary key in the Artist table and foreign
  key in the Work table. Note also that SQL queries can span multiple lines; only
  semicolons indicate the end of a SQL command.
SELECT Artist.ArtistID, Artists.FirstName, Artists.LastName, Work.Title FROM
  Artists
INNER JOIN Work ON Artist.ArtistID=Works.ArtistID;
```

Whatever platform or application is used to create a database and manage it, the crucial intellectual issues are expressed in the data model. The conceptual feature of relational databases that differentiates them from flat spreadsheets and hierarchical XML structures is that they consist of linked tables. The information in these tables is referenced by other tables and can be called on in queries and in making reports. The conceptual structure and identity of the data to be stored in the tables is crucial.

Tables, forms, reports

The basic components of a relational database are somewhat more complicated than those of a spreadsheet, but they are conceptually similar. A **table** structured to store information. A **form** is a screen designed to enter information into the database. It is the front end of the tables. Multiple **forms** can be built on top of the same tables. A database of bibliographical information might have a front end in which readers put comments, or rankings, or add keywords or tags. But another form might be reserved for researchers who are establishing the biographical details of the same authors in a consistent manner and linking them to various authoritative biographical databases and what are known as "name authority files" that help disambiguate one author from another. **Reports** are the output of queries to the database. A user might ask what an author published in a particular year, or with a particular publisher. If a user is going to be able to query across a span of years, then the database has to be set up to accommodate this or the user will have to query each individual year. A database management system allows the database to be used for generating queries and reports, visualizations and displays, export functions, and other operations, including being accessed live on the Web. The most common database language is SQL, which stands for Structured Query Language.

Database and database management systems are intellectual instruments that pass as technical ones. Is there such a thing as a "feminist" table? Or a "racist" form for data entry? Can format embody bias, or only content? The structure of data is always fraught with values and the very act of defining categories can create exclusionary results. Data collection is often shaped by biases and data can be constructed to support almost any position on the ideological and political spectrum. Lack of differentiation or nuance can be equally damaging. Issues like national identity are problematic since countries, boundaries, and their names change over time, in some regions more often than in others. The break-up of the former Yugoslavia, for instance, created new independent states. Recognizing the historicity of categories and considering ways in which these details can be incorporated into the data structure is important for ethical reasons as well as for research purposes.

The power of relational databases resides in the ability to control information carefully for consistency, but also, for analysis across fine-grained features of the data. Attention in the design phase to what pieces of information are dependent on which should be carefully tested against scenarios for future query and use. This can be done on paper without ever building anything digital, and should be. Once the database construction is underway, tools within the applications, such as visualization of tables and relations, will be extremely helpful in seeing the shape of the conceptual model and the argument it contains. Tools for building databases with visual means exist as well, for those whose logical faculties work better in graphical form.

Takeaway

The construction of a database for a humanities research project requires analytic rigor and sorting out what belongs with what, and what relationships these entities—and information about them—have with each other. Keep in mind the basic advantages of relational databases are to reduce redundancy, increase efficiency, and decrease errors. Analyzing your project to understand what can be put into a field or a table, and how these relate to each other is the fundamental challenge. Then, defining identities that can be referenced logically will make the relations logical as well. In spite of all of this formal structure, however, a database should be understood as an act of interpretation that makes a rhetorical argument.

Exercises

Exercise #1: modeling a database

Analyze your research to create tables of information that can be managed effectively. What data belongs in which table? What benefits are there to this organization and structure?

Recommended readings

Geeks for Geeks. 2019. "Difference between RDBMS and OODBMS." www.geeksforgeeks.org/difference-between-rdbms-and-oodbms/.

Microsoft (written for Access, but the principles are applicable to any database). https://support.microsoft.com/en-us/office/database-design-basics-eb2159cf-1e30–401a-8084-bd4f9c9ca1f5.

Ramsay, Stephen. 2004. "Databases." In *The Companion to Digital Humanities*, edited by Susan Schreibman, Ray Seimens, and John Unsworth, Ch. 15. Oxford: Blackwell's. www.digitalhumanities.org//companion/.

5b Database issues: legacy data, ethics, use

Database design, as outlined above, involves decisions that are conceptual as much as technical. Every step of implementation involves choices that structure values and arguments into the relations in the database. These decisions may incorporate biases within the very infrastructure of the technology and its implementation—but they are also opportunities for transformation of knowledge and its representation (Masters 2015).

Other issues also arise with humanistic use of data. Some involve high-level questions about what kind of rhetorical and/or intellectual structure a database embodies. Is it linear? Narrative? Combinatoric? Why does this matter in humanistic fields where arguments have tended to follow certain conventions? The question of whether databases offer *new* forms of argument, are only being used to support traditional arguments, or are not arguments at all is much debated.

Other concerns come from the use of what is called "legacy data." This is data that was created by someone else (individual or institution) and may come with little documentation or rationale. The decision about how it was made (gathered, cleaned, and edited) and what this process left out or changed may not be recoverable. We are left with what may be a consistent data set, but may also be a highly flawed and biased one.

The re-use of data raises ethical as well as intellectual questions. Whose data was this, what permissions were required for its production, whose intellectual property is it, and what privacy concerns or intellectual property issues might its use raise? How is it to be standardized to make it FAIR: "Findable, Accessible, Interoperable, and Repurposable," the four principles articulated by one European scholarly organization?[2]

Data that has been created through a specific research project that is particularly dense and rich may not be usable if it does not provide access points for query. The design of the database and the implementation of user, front-end, methods of search and retrieval are separate processes. Structuring an interface to a database creates a secondary argument—also shaped by assumptions about who the user might be and to what tasks or purposes the project might be put. A simple example of making a database more useful might be replacing a search box that is simply a free text field with one that is linked to controlled vocabulary in a "pick list" that orients the user to terms in the data fields. Particularly in areas where the data has been carefully structured according to specialized expertise, this will offer a way into the contents.

Finally, no single database design fits all projects and even a single project might need multiple modes of access for different communities. Levels of permission, decisions about display, questions of who has what role in an ongoing project, how to secure the project from malicious attack or spam—these are other issues for projects that have a public face and invite participation.

A note on the history of databases

While spreadsheets and tabular records have been part of human culture for thousands of years, the relational database is a surprisingly new innovation

(Computing History Organization's History of Database n.d.). Computer scientist Edgar Codd is given credit for the idea of the "relational database." His work in 1970–72 defined the underlying structure of relations—that instead of flat or hierarchical structures, efficiencies and benefits could be implemented through relational organization (Brown 2002). Codd's insight was fundamental—why not cross-reference tables that contained different parts or types of information instead of having everything stored in a single set of rows and columns? This insight was revolutionary (Codd 1970). Codd worked at IBM, as did his fellow researchers, Raymond Boyce and Donald Chamberlain, who invented the programming language for queries, originally named SEQUEL.

The breakthrough for industry applications came around 1979, however, when Dan Bricklin and Bob Frankson invented VISICALC (a contraction of the words "visible calculator"). Known as the "killer app," it transformed personal computers from things used for hobbies to essential tools for commercial purposes. The idea of a program that could calculate spread sheets automatically by altering the value of variables gave every business from insurance to manufacturing ways to project financial scenarios instantly. As a labor-saving application, it was an instant success for its capacity to recalculate spreadsheets on an Apple computer. One major addition to these technologies has been object-oriented databases (mentioned earlier) which combine operations and entities in their design. In addition, various databases that do not rely on SQL to query and retrieve information, such as graph databases (which underlie networks and support their visualizations), have joined their predecessors (Panwar 2020). What is remarkable is how few new database structures have been added, and how robust (long-lived) and viable these forms of data structure have been.

Debates about databases

Debates in the digital humanities in the 2000s addressed fundamental definitions of database forms in relation to traditional scholarly formats, such as essays and narratives. More recently, discussions of race and power, exclusionary practices, and politics of the academic world and knowledge work have also made critical contributions, but few have focused on database structures, only design and implementation.

The idea that databases were the new, current, and future form of knowledge and that they would replace narrative in the study of history, the creation of literature, or the development of artistic expression was asserted by several digital humanists in the 1990s and early 2000s. In the North American context, this argument received considerable attention when the publication of the Modern Language Association, the main scholarly organization for humanists in literary studies, dedicated a special issue of its publication to the topic. This 2007 issue of the PMLA (*Publications of the*

Modern Library Association), pitted the two formats—traditional narrative arguments and database structures—against each other. The approach generated much controversy.

Among the assertions was that databases were non-linear while narratives were linear, that processes of selection resulted in fixed narrative modes while processes of combination are at the heart of database "logic." The potential for multiple readings of information, even of interpretative data in structured fields, seemed to suggest a radical shift in methods of working with humanities materials. The arguments had a strong techno-deterministic tone, suggesting that changes in ways of thinking are the direct result of changes in the technology we design and use. Counter arguments suggested that combinatoric work and content models are integral elements of human expression and have been since the beginnings of the written record, which can be dated to five or six thousand years ago in Mesopotamia.

The distinction between database structures and narrative forms is real, but are they in opposition to each other or merely useful for different purposes and circumstances? Why make such strong arguments on either side? At stake seems to be the definition of what constitutes discourse, human expression, and the rules and conventions according to which it can create the record of lived and imaginative experience. But also at stake is an investment in the ways we value and assess new media and their impact, understand digital media and its specificity but also its effects.

The PMLA discussion led off with a statement by a scholar named Ed Folsom, who was co-Director of an important project, the Walt Whitman Archive. Folsom asserted that databases were a "genre" that promoted access to materials. Prior to the implementation of the Web, archival materials like original manuscripts, letters, photographs, and other primary documents were kept in institutional collections that could never be aggregated. Scholars had to visit these collections in person, and even copies or facsimiles of original materials were difficult and expensive to maintain. The transformation of scholarship in a project like the Whitman Archive was that these materials could be accessed through a single project where the database structure pointed to resources in other institutions (or, more rarely, stored digital copies as assets on a single institutional server). The database had become a familiar humanities tool, and the intellectual work of building and creating this framework provided a novel experience for humanists used to close reading, note taking, and prose arguments.

Folsom's opposition between database and narrative was accompanied by multiple responses. Some scholars appreciated the constrained and organized nature of databases as an interpretative and critical act but stopped short of seeing them as narratives. Others stressed the linear character of narratives, even in scholarship, and put them into opposition with the spatial structure of databases. Scholars compared databases to the traditional index cards and notes that track the research but disappear from view in a final article or book. In the database, the materials remain segmented, structured, and also defined and described by the very processes described earlier.

Massive databases that provide access to scanned and marked-up materials now exist but using them without any narrative framework can prove challenging. A visit to the Digital Sanskrit Buddhist Canon online demonstrates this point quite dramatically, as does a look through digitized medieval manuscripts in the British Library. Without an interpretative frame, the materials appear in their original language, sometimes with metadata, often not, and are difficult to use for anyone without expertise. Data—whether in the form of original documents or their description—is an addition to and not a replacement for other forms of scholarship. The same is true for metadata—it adds whole dimensions to the scholarly endeavor that add value as well as producing controversy because of the legacy of classification.

Legacy data and its challenges

While many humanistic records of great antiquity can be considered "data," they have to be remediated to become digital data and computationally tractable. Examples of such "legacy" data sets are the Roman census records, inventories of monastic libraries, and the lists of settlement records in Iceland. (See the Coda for a brief discussion.) These can be—and many have been—put into digital form for study and analysis. Another type of legacy data would be of the sort made digitally for an unrelated purpose or project that is being used for research. This will be dealt with in the "repurposing" section.

King's College London, which has long been involved in digital humanities research, took on the challenge of assessing the data inherited from early three decades of projects. While this does not sound like a long time, the period has witnessed considerable changes in practices of digital methods (Smithies et al. 2019). The group identified about a hundred "legacy projects" that spanned "a wide spectrum from text analysis and annotation tools, digital corpora of texts, images and musical scores to digital editions, historical databases and layered maps" (Ciulla 2020). The team decided to collect considerable information about the projects—team members, funding, period of time in which the project took place, standards used, and other details. Among the difficulties addressed were the security breaches that had occurred on "unmaintained applications" (Smithies et al. 2019). Another issue was managing expectations of various team members, particularly in situations where partners from different countries and institutions were stakeholders. Preserving data and metadata in a variety of formats is expensive, but without the original interface, it may be illegible or unusable. Some of these concerns will come into focus again in the discussion of sustainability.

For the researcher, using legacy data has other concerns. Data made for specific research projects is often idiosyncratic and may not be documented. The quality control on data production may have been uneven (Wuttke 2019). Legacy data issues are particularly complex in medical humanities and social sciences, fields where the possibilities of violating original agreements about collection of information might be at risk of being broken in new projects. Any identifying information that can be "re-engineered" could put human subjects at risk or violate their privacy. In addition, monetizing any data in a use for which it was not originally intended poses ethical issues. Finally, legacy data often do not reveal the process by which they were modelled. What was eliminated in the process and what was conflated? Data have great potency and appear to have an authority as statements of facts, and so knowing their source and history is crucial.

Many cultural institutions produce elaborate datasets from which interesting research projects can be built. For instance, the New York Public Library, the Library of Congress, most museums, and the data.gov sites are rich resources. These can be made use of for humanities research by posing certain kinds of questions. The advantage of proceeding from data to humanities questions, rather than trying to make data to address a research problem, is that the data already exist. [See Exercise #1: Asking humanist questions.]

Metrics and standards

Metric standards have their own strange histories. We know that inches and centimeters are human-created standards for measure of space and dimension. But a year has a relation to a natural cycle of motion around the sun, as the day is determined by the turning earth. But what is the means by which a "minute" is determined, or a day broken into hours? Are all hours the same? Medieval monks had a system for dividing the day into twelve hours of daylight and twelve of darkness throughout the year. In summer the daylight "hours" were longer than in winter, and vice versa, but the division of units served their purposes. If we are transcribing the record of activities from a monastery in this period, how do we reconcile these differences with the standard measures of time we are accustomed to using?

Temperature data seems to be empirically derived, based on the thermal condition of phenomena under investigation. But the Fahrenheit and Celsius scales have very different units. The Fahrenheit scale is an idiosyncratic scale, rooted in the experience of the man who designed it. He defined the low end as the coldest temperature taken in the town where he lived and the midpoint as his body temperature and the high point as that at which water boils. This was later refined and made in a more precise system, but that a standard metric was created with a human reference point—he had a slight fever when defining the precise body temperature—is remarkable.

In an important sense, all metrics share this characteristic—they are created in reference to human experience—but they function as if they are value-neutral and universal.

Among the considerations that need to be brought to bear on repurposing data are the many ways it can be assessed. The need to support data-driven research has become a major topic of discussion in the library community (Padilla 2016). In their role as information professionals, librarians have been attentive to ways in which standards for use and assessment can aid researchers in both creating and sharing digital assets. Their contributions to this conversation are essential. Similarly, data professionals in areas of scientific and humanistic research are well aware of the ways in which data can be tampered with and misused. The larger challenges of missing data, partial data, and inaccuracies can never be fully managed since, by definition, the human record is constructed only from what remains.

Restricting access

The assumption that all data should be available, and that complete transparency is optimal, may not apply in all cases. (See Chapter 10 for discussion of access.) When the web presentation platform Mukurtu was being developed for use in digital projects that contain Indigenous knowledge, the rationale for the platform was that not all communities wish their cultural heritage information to be fully available to all viewers. Within many cultures, what can be accessed depends upon the role, class, position, age, or gender of individuals—or the caste or kinship group to which they belong. Taking such considerations into account with regard to data means shifting one's assumptions away from a single approach and recognizing the degrees of granularity that might need to be built into control of data retrieval, access, or use.

Further constraints on data access arise from other ethical considerations. Students should not have access to other students' records and confidential information should not be shared in personnel and health matters. Personal information should not be shared without consent. And individuals' data should not be monetized without their being informed. But other forms of data may be sensitive as well, and researchers dealing with controversial materials should be attentive to the harm these can do, or the risks of their being misappropriated.

Debates about digitization include its capacity to increase disparity and to level it. Does access to information promote inclusion? Does control over the creation of online resources replicate patterns of exclusion long in place? The tensions between Global North and South, for instance, around preservation of cultural heritage, have been a regular concern for UNESCO (Kulesz 2016). Their discussion of these matters takes into account that fundamental differences in attitudes about cultural production need to be recognized, rather than simply applying a single approach across communities. Questions of rights for intellectual property are a matter of negotiation and cannot be ignored. Data structures that build different levels of permission into their design recognize the need for decisions to be made with informed understanding of the ways cultural assets might be appropriated once they are digitized.

Takeaway

In the day to day creation of data sets and databases, theoretical questions are not generally asked. Instead, they are implemented using standard metrics, categories, classification systems, and spreadsheets to make databases. Databases come in several forms, flat, hierarchical, relational, object-oriented, graph, and so on. Databases can be described by their contents, their function, their structure, or other characteristics. But questions of ethics and use arise around legacy data and its repurposing, as well as around access and retrieval by asking if these should be assumed as universal.

Exercise

Exercise #1: asking humanist questions

Go to data.gov and look at the data sets under Agriculture. What humanities questions can you ask of this data? Why would a data set like Farm-Plenty be useful for humanistic research? What other information would you want to link to this dataset once you have formulated your project?

Notes

1 In object-oriented databases, a set of behaviors is merged with the data into a single object.
2 For a complete discussion of issues and recommendations by ALLEA (All European Academies), see: www.ria.ie/sites/default/files/allea_sustainable_and_fair_data_sharing_in_the_humanities_2020_0.pdf

Recommended readings

Christie, Michael. n.d. "Computer Databases and Aboriginal Knowledge." www.cdu.edu.au/centres/ik/pdf/CompDatAbKnow.pdf.

Nodegoat. 2017. "Formulating Ambiguity in a Database." *Nodegoat.net*. https://nodegoat.net/blog.s/21/formulating-ambiguity-in-a-database.

References cited

ALLEA (All European Academies). 2020. www.ria.ie/sites/default/files/allea_sustainable_and_fair_data_sharing_in_the_humanities_2020_0.pdf.

Brown, Farmer. 2002. "A Brief History of Modern Relational Database Management Systems." www.mountainman.com.au/software/history/it1.html.

Ciulla, Arianna. 2020. "Exposing Legacy Data." *King's Digital Library Blog*. www.kdl.kcl.ac.uk/blog/legacy-project-datasets/.

Codd, Edgar. 1970. "A Relational Model of Data for Large Data Banks." *Communications of the ACM* 13 (6). https://history.computer.org/pioneers/codd.html.

Computing History Organization's History of Database. n.d. www.comphist.org/computing_history/new_page_9.htm.

Kulesz, Octavio. 2016. "Intergovernmental Committee for the Protection and Promotion of Diversity of Cultural Expressions." *UNESCO*. https://en.unesco.org/creativity/sites/creativity/files/sessions/10igc_inf4_the_impact_of_digital_technologies_octavio_kulesz_en_0.pdf.

Masters, Christine L. 2015. "Women's Ways of Structuring Data." *Ada: A Journal of Gender, New Media, and Technology*. Issue No. 8

Padilla, Thomas H. 2016. "Umanities Data in the Library: Integrity, Form, Access." *D-Lib Magazine* 22 (4). www.dlib.org/dlib/march16/padilla/03padilla.html.

Panwar, Arjun. 2020. "Types of Database Management Systems." www.c-sharpcorner.com/UploadFile/65fc13/types-of-database-management-systems/.

Smithies, James, Carina Westling, Anna-Maria Sichani, Pam Mellen, and Arianna Ciula. 2019. "Managing 100 Digital Humanities Projects: Digital Scholarship & Archiving in King's Digital Lab." *Digital Humanities Quarterly* 13 (1). www.digitalhumanities.org/dhq/vol/13/1/000411/000411.html.

Wuttke, Ulrike. 2019. "Here there be Dragons: Open Access to Research Data in the Humanities." *OpenMethods Metablog*. https://dhmethods.hypotheses.org/262.

Resources

British Library www.bl.uk/manuscripts/BriefDisplay.aspx.
Digital Sanskrit Buddhist Canon www.dsbcproject.org/gallery.
Mukurtu https://mukurtu.org/.
Noun project https://thenounprojects.com.

6 Information visualization

6a Basics of visualization

Information visualizations are a part of everyday communications and scholarship. These graphics have powerful rhetorical force. The visualizations are often more easily consumed than the complex research data on which they depend. Understanding the process by which visualizations are made helps bring into focus what they show and what they conceal.

All information visualizations are metrics expressed as graphics. The implications of this simple statement are far ranging. Data can be very difficult to interpret in tabular form. Very few individuals are skilled at reading spread sheets, let alone relational databases, to make sense of information. A query might produce thousands of data points. Information visualizations are used to make this quantitative data legible. They are particularly useful for seeing patterns in large amounts of information, making these apparent in a condensed form.

Anything that can be quantified (given a numerical value) can be turned into a graph, chart, diagram, or other visualization.

Points, lines, and areas can be plotted using analog tools—paper and colored pencils—and many of the formats used in digitally produced visualizations are centuries old. The process of making graphs by hand is slow and deliberate. Each point has to be marked, each line created by connecting dots or using mathematical formulae, and each area calculated. At each step of hand-drawing a graph or chart, we reflect on how it is made.

But the ease of production afforded by computational means makes it possible to create polished and sophisticated graphics without critical reflection. We can easily overlook the fact that all parts of the process—from creating quantified information to producing visualizations—are acts of interpretation. In addition, the ability to *read* a visualization requires understanding the *semantics* of graphic formats. Visual forms create meaning, they don't just display it. A bar chart makes a different statement than a pie chart, for instance, and such insights are crucial to the critical engagement with information visualization (Lengler and Eppler 2007).

Benefits and liabilities

To begin, consider the two components of a visualization separately—the metrics and the graphics. Here are two versions of the same information, a table and a bar chart:

	A	B	C
1	1969	4	
2	1970	11	
3	1970	24	
4	1971	8	
5	1971	54	
6	1971	25	
7	1972	20	
8	1972	20	
9	1972	20	
10	1972	54	
11	1972	52	
12	1972	48	
13	1972	1	
14	1973	30	
15	1973	5	
16	1973	15	
17	1973	16	
18	1973	6	
19	1973	6	
20	1973	21	
21	1973	37	
22	1973	1	
23	1973	30	

Figure 6.1a Segment of a table and *6.1b* Bar chart generated from the same information (JD)

The table is not very complicated, it puts dates in one column and number of pages output by an author into a second one. All of the information in it makes good sense but trying to read columns of numbers to see a pattern in them is difficult. The chart makes clear that a steady output of pages occurred in 1972, matched by one spike in 1971, and followed by

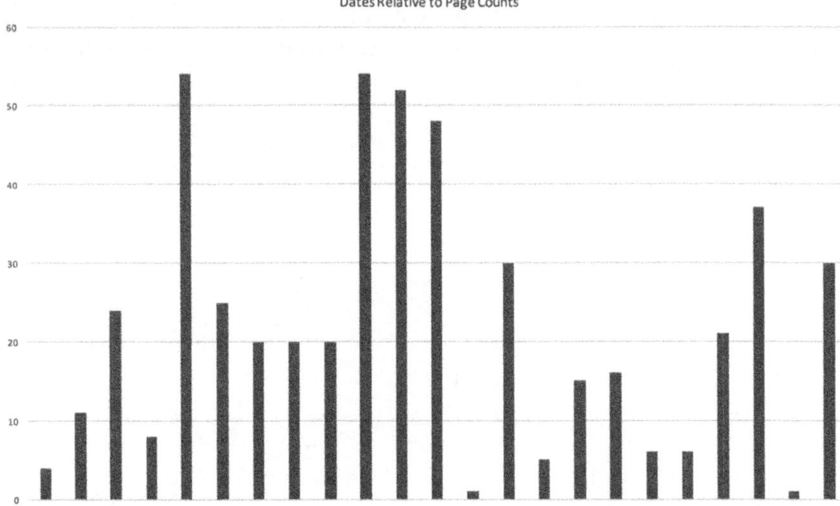

Figure 6.1a Continued

low output in 1973. The comparison of values is easily done in the visual format, and if we imagine extending the table to include hundreds or thousands of data points, this fact would be even more dramatically clear.

What is the relationship of the data to the visualization? In this situation, a line of dates is charted on the x-axis and a set of values is indicated by the y-axis. The conventions of charts make this easy to read and even intuitive in layout. But is there an inherent visual form in the data? One interesting exercise is to put the same data into other graphical formats to see what happens. Here are two examples of the same data but in a line chart and a pie chart.

We are immediately confronted with the question of what features of the graphical display are meaningful. For instance, the *continuous* line on the left graphing the dates suggests that the *rate of change* in the data about pages is a significant factor. But the "number of pages" data is actually a *discrete* value. While the bar chart *compares the values* of each segment to each other, the line chart makes these part of a continuous process, though this is not the case. By contrast, the pie chart suggests that each entry is *part of a whole*—that the sum total of pages is significant, not the difference in their value. The values are hard to compare, the dates are lost entirely, and the concept of the "whole" of the author's output has no meaning. Neither of these charts makes the correlation of date and page output as clear as the initial bar chart. These are both "bad" graphics (and possibly bad data as well).

The point is that nothing in the data dictates the form of the visualization. These and a host of other charts can be generated from the same data.

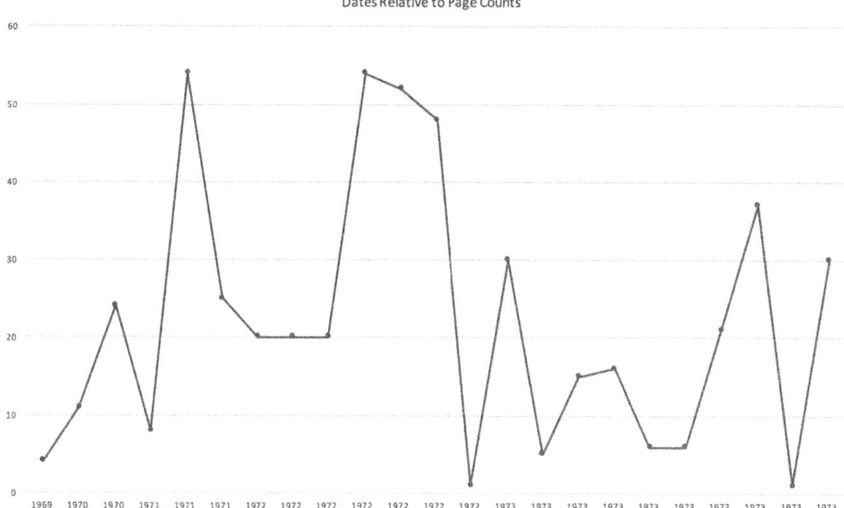

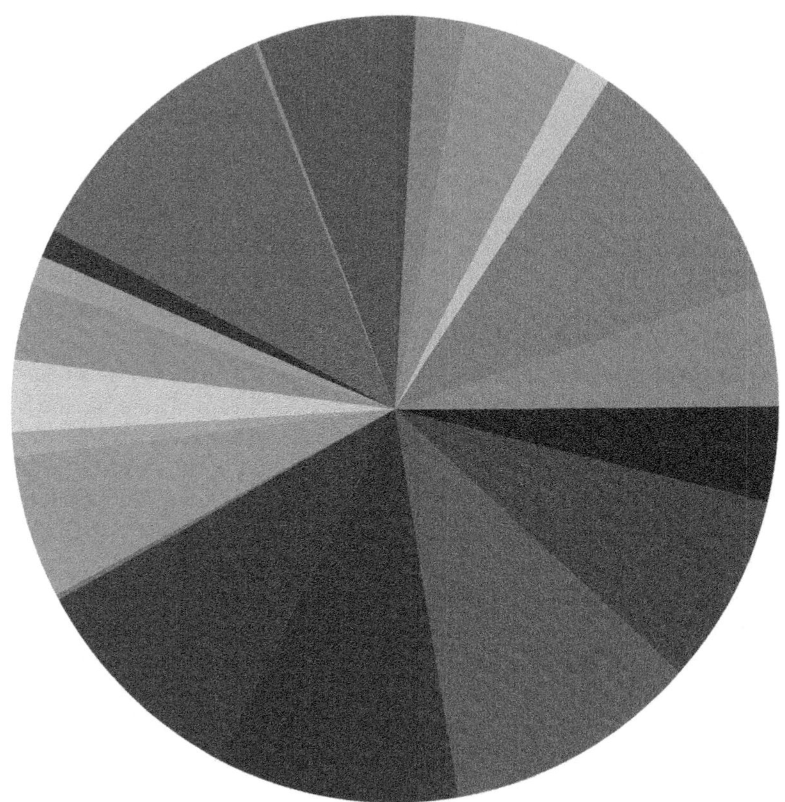

Figures 6.2 and 6.3 Other visualizations of the same data in Figure 6.1 (JD)

Any data set can be put into a pie chart, a continuous graph, a scatter plot, a tree map, and so on. The challenge is to understand how the information visualization creates an argument and then make use of the graphical format whose features serve your purpose. Any sense that data have an *inherent* visual form is an illusion. [See Exercise #1: A range of graphs.]

Data creation, as we noted in earlier (see Sections 2a and 2b), depends on parameterization. As stated before, this means that anything that can be measured, counted, or given a metric or numerical value can be turned into data. The concept of parameterization is crucial to visualization because the ways in which we assign value to the data will have a direct impact on the ways it can be displayed. Visualizations are convincing by virtue of their graphic qualities and can easily distort the data. While all visualizations are interpretations, some are more suited to the structure of a given data set than others.

Visualization basics

In many cases, the graphic image is an artifact of the way the decisions about the design were made, not about the data. Understanding some basics of the relation between graphics and metrics is essential.

Here are some fundamental guidelines for thinking about which chart to use:

- The distinction between discrete and continuous data is one of the most significant decisions in choosing a design. Example: in visualizing the height of students in a class, making a continuous graph that connects the dots makes no sense at all. There is no continuity between the height of one student and another. Individual height is a discrete value.
- If you are showing change over time or any other variable, then a continuous graph is the right choice. Example: Change in height for individual students over a five-year period.
- If a graph shows quantities with area, use it for percentages of a whole, like a pie chart, not comparative value. If you increase the area of a circle by length of the radius, or a square from the length of the side, you are introducing distortion into the relation of the elements. This is a common error. Example: The population in the town doubled from ten thousand to twenty thousand in five years. The data is visualized with two squares on a map, with the second having its sides twice the length of the first (10,000 to 20,000). But the area of the second square four times that of the first, not double.
- The way in which you label and order the elements in a chart will make some arguments more immediately evident. If you want to compare quantities, be sure they are displayed in proximity. Example: when comparing the population size of states should you put the states in

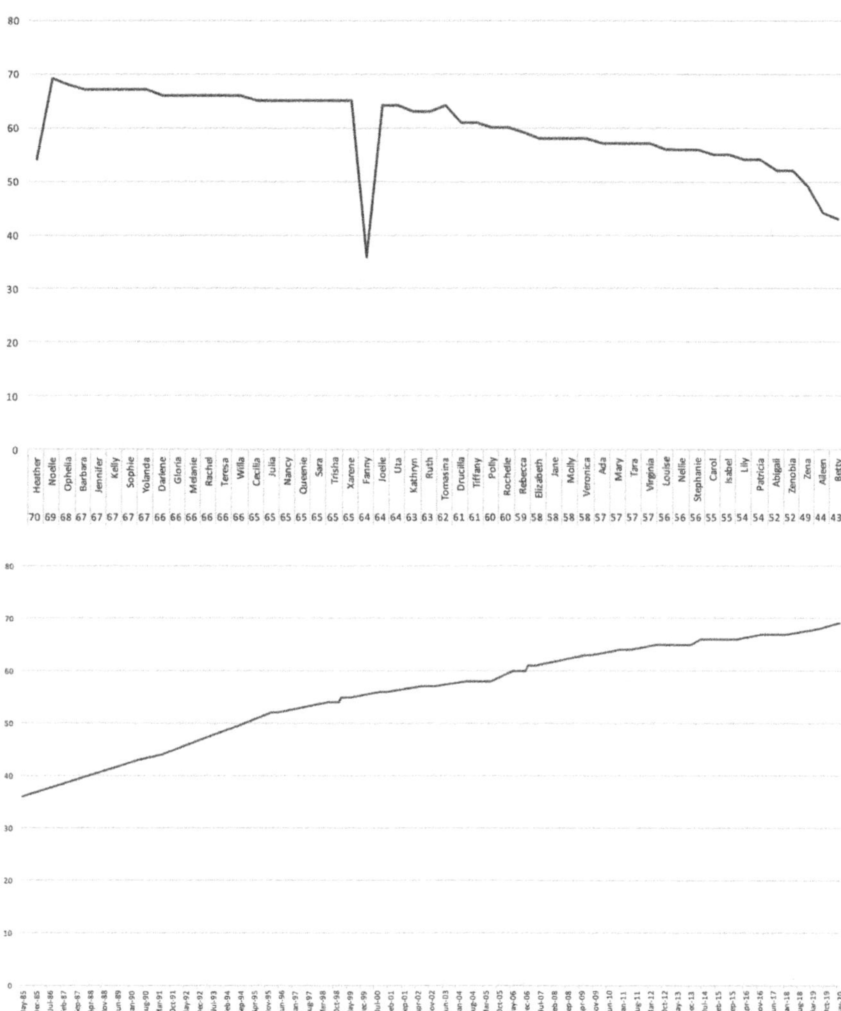

Figure 6.4a Meaningless graph of height among a group of girls graphed continuously and *6.4b* Graph of the change of one girl's height changing over time (JD)

alphabetical order or put the data in size order? Which is going to make the information more legible?

- The use of labels is crucial and their design can either aid or hinder legibility. Where are the labels? How much work are you adding to your reader's experience?
- Another consideration and challenge is the choice of a scale. When values are relatively close, the scale of the chart can be kept consistent.

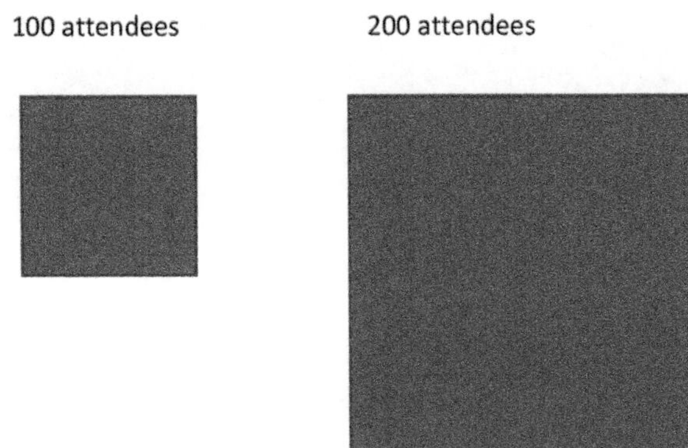

Figure 6.5 Classic error in which a value increases numerically but the area increases geometrically. The quantity on the right is twice that on the left, but the area is four times as large (JD)

But imagine the charts of date and page outputs in the example above if in one year the author produced 2000 pages. To show this value, the scale would need to extend to forty times its current height. The result would be that the difference between 20 pages and 50 pages would barely register. The legibility of the graph and patterns would be altered. To deal with such anomalies, charts are drawn with "broken" or modified scales, leaving a gap between lower and upper values. These gaps need to be noted and taken into account in some kind of legend, labeling, or documentation. [See Exercise #2: Reverse engineering a visualization.]

The rhetoric of graphics

Every visualization has a history to its format (Friendly 2007). The earliest forms of visual records seem to have been observations of the planets and other natural cycles. Early accounting systems for tracking inventory and also for taking census information used tabular forms. These allow easy correlation across values. The notion of continuous graphs, line charts, and other visual representations of information from natural or social phenomena did not appear until modern times. These emphasize continuous change. William Playfair, the 18th century statistician, is credited with the invention of many forms of bar chart and continuous graph still in use today. Playfair was working with what he called "Political Arithmetik," or the tracking of information relevant for guiding politics and policy in economic arenas (Norman 2004–2020). Playfair's visual solutions were very elegant as well as highly legible. Keep in mind that the science of statistics is also relatively modern, originating chiefly in the 17th century with techniques developed

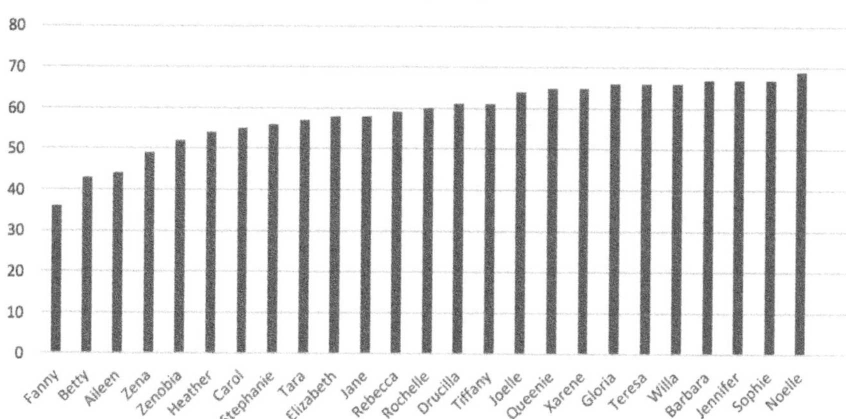

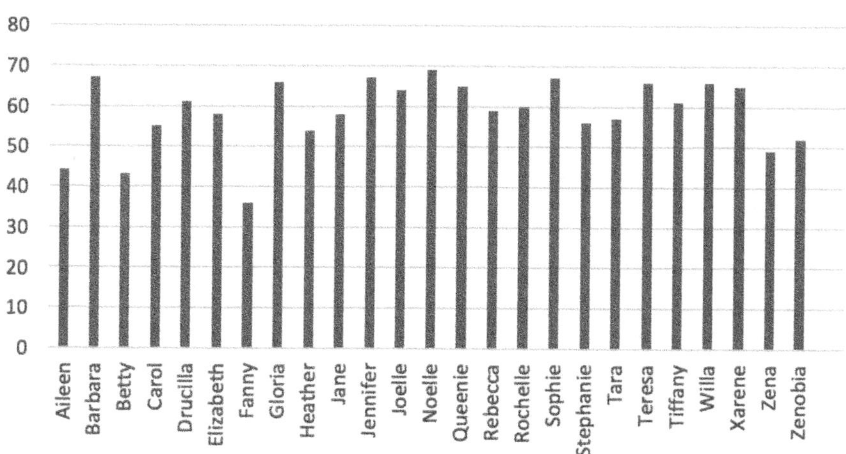

Figure 6.6a and 6.6b Charts showing ordering and labels: The first chart makes it easy to find individuals by name, the second makes it easy to compare heights and correlate with names (JD)

by the French mathematicians, Blaise Pascal and Pierre de Fermat, to gauge the risks of gambling (Apostol 1969).

The power of visualizations has been understood for a long time. In the 19th century, the nurse and activist Florence Nightingale created a specific format—known as the cockscomb because of its resemblance to the rooster's crown—to make her point about the fact that more deaths occurred among the wounded in field hospitals than on the battlefield. She deliberately chose

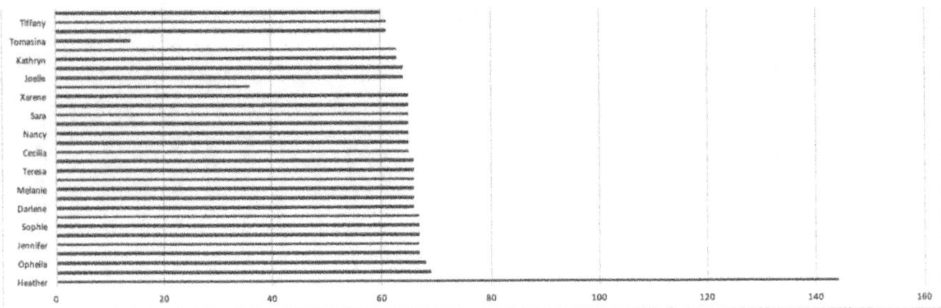

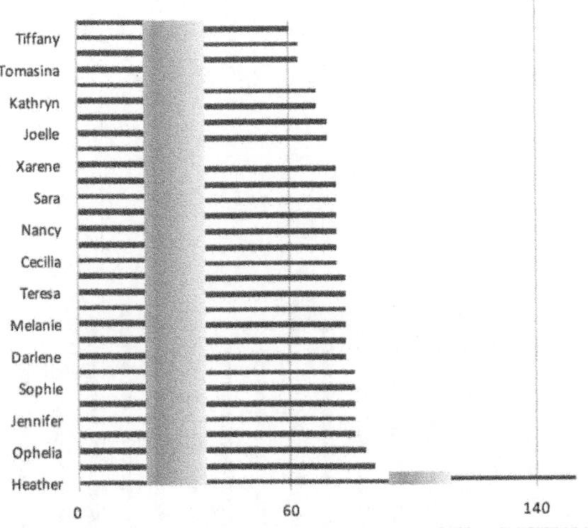

Figure 6.7 The scale has to stretch to include the height of the outlier and makes it difficult to compare the differences among the close values in the middle range. Making a "break" in the scale could allow focus on the area in which the meaningful information is present (JD)

a format that exaggerated this information. She used the difference in her data values to set the length of a radius in a circular form, also known as a polar area diagram, thus distorting the area. (This is similar to the example of the square, above, but here the area is calculated by the standard formula $A = \pi r^2$ (area = pi x square of the radius r). The contrast was dramatic, and she won her argument.

This kind of exaggeration can be very misleading in any chart that uses area as a feature of its graphical form. As already noted, when using graphics that are based on area, such exaggerations are built in. This distortion is a regular feature of information display on maps, as will be seen ahead.

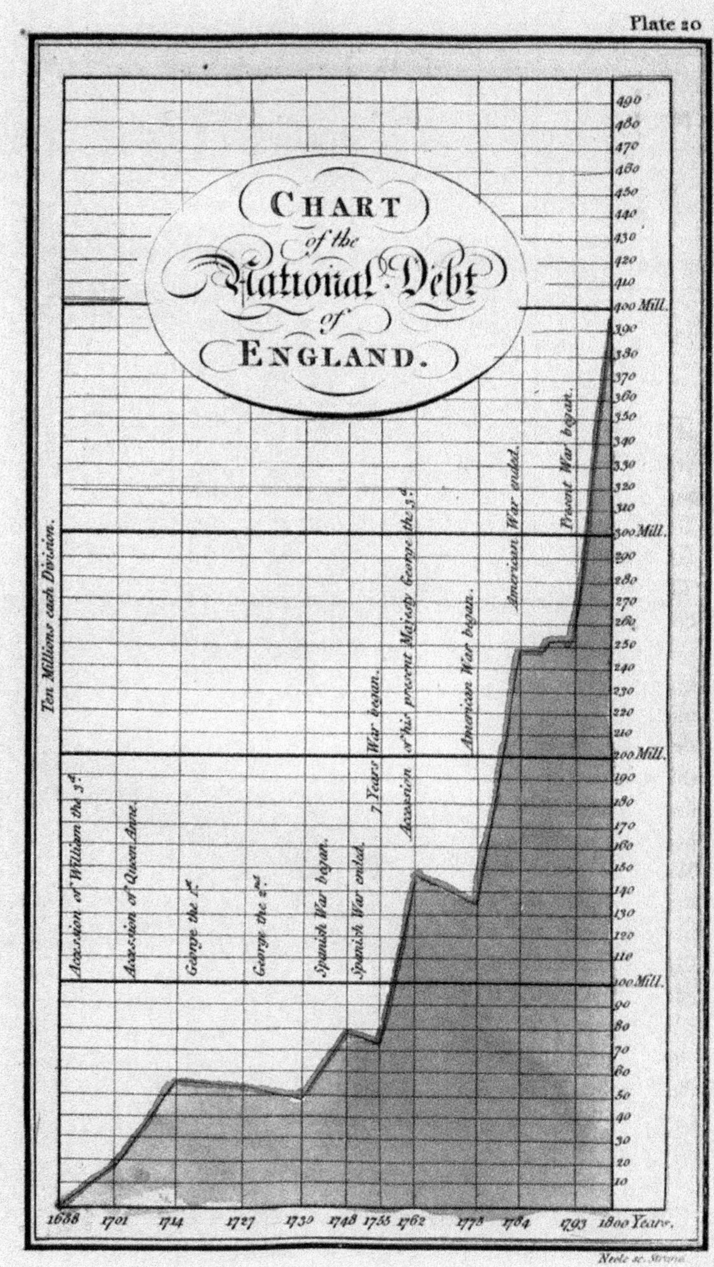

Figure 6.8 William Playfair Chart of the National Debt, *The Commercial and Political Atlas*, 1786 (Public domain)

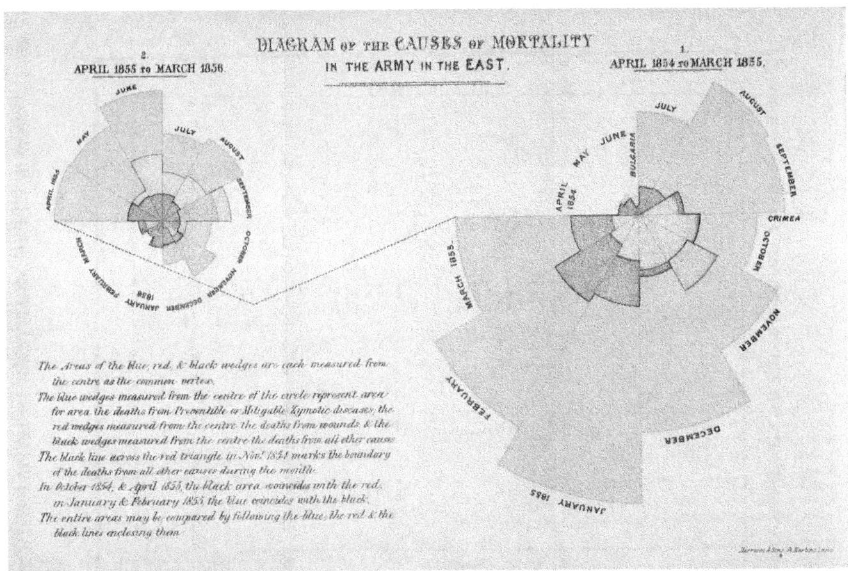

Figure 6.9 Florence Nightingale, cockscomb diagrams, 1854–55 (Public domain)

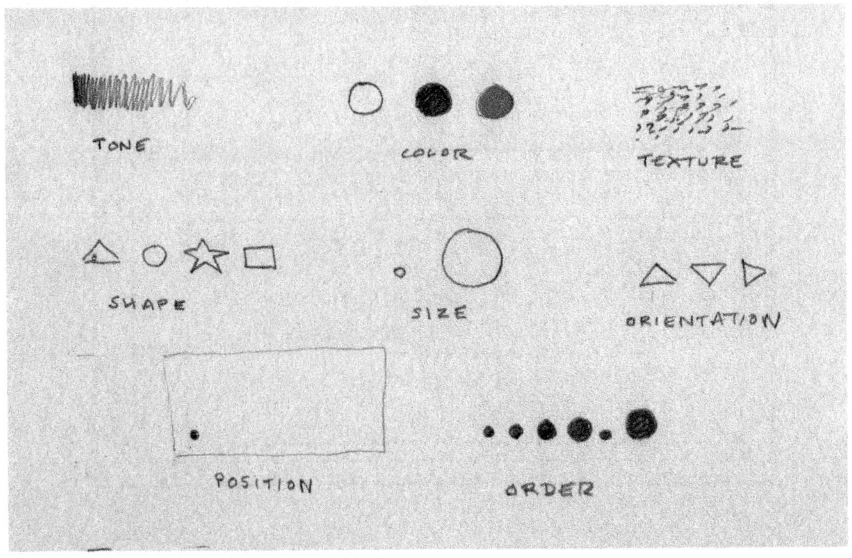

Figure 6.10 Graphic variables (JD)

Components of visualizations

When considering visualizations, a few fundamentals besides the type of chart and the rhetoric of its impact can be useful in guiding design decisions. The components of visualizations include *axes, elements, scales, order/ sequence, values of coordinates*, and the *graphic variables*.

Axes establish the basis for mapping values. Typically, the x-axis (left to right) is used to graph a value that changes over time (dates) while the y-axis is used to chart a specific value (cost of living, sea levels, etc.) against it. These are sometimes, but rarely, augmented with a z-axis that gives depth to the chart. However, mapping a third variable is trickier than it sounds, and it is often easier to simply have this information displayed as a second set of points or lines (earnings might change, for instance, as page outputs increased in our reference example). The basic coordinate x-y system was invented by René Descartes and is sometimes referred to as a Cartesian grid. (The apocryphal version of the story is that he was trying to figure out how to pinpoint the location of a fly on his ceiling (Wild Maths n.d.).) The grid uses standard metrics that remain the same across the full extent of the chart. One question to ask is whether you can imagine situations in which a metric might need to change? What conditions might require an alteration in one area of a neutral grid. Is every square the same—even if a spider is lurking in one?

Elements are the bars, lines, points, symbols, or other features that express value. They are always read against the axes. Even in a pie chart, the percentage is read in relation to an axis—this is the circumference, which forms the 100% boundary of the whole.

Scales set the specific metric to be used—inches, feet, number of units, dates, and so on. Scales have a start and endpoint. If I am measuring the difference in height among a group of giant statues, all of which are over twenty feet high but less than twenty-one feet high. Should I measure them in light years? Millimeters? Some scales are too large or too small to be useful. If I am measuring the occupancy of an airport, a scale of years might be too large, but a scale of seconds will be too small.

Order and sequence are generally determined by data and given as logical an expression as possible. Putting the work of an author into size order might be trivial and putting all of the paintings in the world into a single date sequence might be meaningless. The order and sequence should be meaningful to the research—and for communicating information in a visualization.

Values of coordinates are generated by the axes. But a major difference exists between the value of crossing points—where one axis intersects another—and continuous values within the lines, grid, or tick marks. Are discrete or continuous values being gauged and presented?

Finally, graphic variables are the features of visual language: color, tonal value, size, shape, orientation, position, and texture. These will be revisited in the discussion of mapping but designating a variable for a specific purpose makes good sense. Shape is very legible, so distinguishing different data types with stars, circles, squares, triangles, and other icons in a chart makes for legibility—provided there are not too many types of data. Tonal value is useful for showing changes of intensity, as in heat maps. Size generally indicates quantity, but can signal importance, particularly with typography. Color, like shape, is very legible and makes distinctions highly visible, as does texture. Use color to distinguish themes or topics (the height of freshmen relative to the height of seniors). Dotted lines are easily distinguished from solid ones. These allow information to be carried by the visual elements, not just their labels. Orientation should be used when a feature of the data correlates to it—like wind direction. Position is generally determined by coordinates but can also be part of the overall design—what is near what and why when proximity is significant.

Using graphic variables systematically increases the communicative legibility of your visualization. [See Exercise #3: Analyze the data-graphic connection.]

Checklist for visualizations

- Assess your data: Is it composed of discrete or continuous information?
- Choose the appropriate scale: too small a scale may make the important differences in value hard to spot and too large may exaggerate it. If outliers stretch the scale for a few data points, consider a gap in the scale and an explanation.
- Is the labeling efficient for use? What order should the information take to be meaningful and usable (alphabetical order of country names makes them easy to find but might separate values and make them hard to compare visually)?
- Use graphic variables carefully: shapes carry information readily, tonal values should be used for data that has a gradient, texture has little "meaning" in itself, and color can carry symbolic value or simply be used for differentiation.
- Proximity of labels to values is optimal for reducing cognitive load; make it easy for the viewer to correlate information.
- Never use changes in area to show a simple arithmetic increase in value.
- Review the graphic to see if it contains elements that are "incidental" artifacts of production rather than semantically meaningful ones.
- While illustrations, images, or exaggerated forms may be considered "junk," they can also help set a theme or tone when used effectively.

A few last thoughts

Visualizations do not usually show the lifecycle of the data. Decisions about parameterization, even the way samples were taken and what elements of the data were "cleaned" up and removed are all missing from the final visualization. Similarly, the history of the data within its institutional or research context may not be documented. Finding the source for the information can be difficult once the visualization exists. Thus, the question of whose authority—whose voice and point of view—is represented in the visualization can be very difficult to answer. A process of reduction, simplification, and what is known as *reification*—making a concept appear to be a *thing* (solid, tractable, and understandable)—takes place in the production of visualizations. The statement, "Information visualizations are reifications of misinformation," suggests that the apparent straightforward communication in a visualization should be treated with skepticism, rather than simply accepted, in spite of the value of these images for data presentation (Fenton 2015). In data journalism, these concepts are referred to as "the lie factor," and ethical practitioners work conscientiously to avoid misleading graphics. [See Exercise #4: Misleading graphics.]

Recent scholarship draws attention to critical concerns in this area of digital research. The work of feminist scholars questions some of the assumptions about who controls the technology of production and whose values are embodied in the information design process (D'Ignazio and Klein 2016). A cache of hand-drawn works by the African-American activist, W.E.B. Du Bois, sheds light on this formerly little-known aspect of his work and the way he made use of data visualization for advancing critical discussions of race (Mansky 2018). Their hand-drawn quality inflects their presentation, raising questions of equitable access to resources. A very different approach to hand-drawn visualizations appeared in a "Dear Data" project of letters exchanges between Georgia Lupi and Stephanie Posavec, both sophisticated information designers who used the experiment as a way to explore the possibilities of analog presentation (Lupi 2017). Many artists have been intrigued by data flows and visualizations as opportunities for aesthetic investigation, some of which will be touched on ahead in the discussion of complexity.

Takeaway

Information visualizations are metrics expressed as graphics. Information visualizations allow large amounts of (often complex) data to be depicted visually in ways that reveal patterns, anomalies, and other features of the data. No data has an inherent visual form. Any data set can be expressed in any number of standard formats, but only some of these are appropriate for the features of the data. Certain common errors include misuse of area, continuity, and other graphical qualities. The rhetorical force of visualization is often misleading. All visualizations are interpretations, not presentations of fact. Some graphic features of visualizations are artifacts of the display, not of the data, and can contribute to the reification of misinformation. Understanding the language of graphics is an art that combines conceptual insight with design acuity. Still, even a novice can produce useful graphics with current platforms and tools. The challenge is to produce graphics that are appropriate to the research task and communication of arguments.

Exercises

Exercise #1: arange of graphs

Try various visualizations for suitability. Take one of these data sets through a series of Microsoft Excel visualizations. Which make the data more legible? Less?

- United States AKC Registrations http://images.akc.org/pdf/archives/AKCregstats_1885-1945.pdf
- Sugar Content in Popular Halloween Treats www.popsugar.com/fitness/Calories-Halloween-Candy-Fun-Size-Treats-5452936

Exercise #2: reverse engineering a visualization

Look at Google's Public Data directory and the visualizations generated from the files. Can you locate the basic components (axes etc.) and evaluate them for common errors? Consider where the data comes from and what may be missing from its visualization.

www.google.com/publicdata/directory

Exercise #3: analyze the data-graphic connection

Imagine you are collecting data from the classroom on 1) classroom use, 2) attention span of students, 3) snack preferences, 4) age, height, and weight comparisons in a group? For what kind of data gathered in the classroom would you use a column chart? Browse this D3 gallery of visualizations for other formats: https://observablehq.com/collection/@observablehq/visualization

Exercise #4: misleading graphics

What is the concept of the "lie factor" and how is it visible at the following link?

www.datavis.ca/gallery/lie-factor.php

In each case consider legibility, accuracy, or the argument made by the form. What is meant by a graphic argument?

Recommended readings

D'Ignazio and Lauren Klein. 2016. "Feminist Data Visualization." *IEEE*. www.academia.edu/28173807/Feminist_Data_Visualization.

Drucker, Johanna. 2011. "Humanities Approaches to Graphical Display." *Digital Humanities Quarterly*. www.digitalhumanities.org/dhq/vol/5/1/000091/000091.html.

Lupi, Giorgia. 2017. "Data Humanism: The Revolutionary Future of Data Visualization." *PRINT*. www.printmag.com, www.printmag.com/post/data-humanism-future-of-data-visualization.

6b Networks and complex systems

The concept of a network has become ubiquitous in current culture (Zer-Aviv 2016). Almost any connection to anything else can be called a network, but properly speaking, a network has to be a system of elements or entities that are connected by explicit relations. The term network is frequently used to describe the infrastructure that connects computers to each other and to peripherals, devices, or systems in a linked environment. While that is an accurate description, the networks we are concerned with in digital humanities are created by relationships in an information system. This might be the connection of books to authors, paintings to collections, people in communication with each other, or objects and ideas in circulation.

Unlike other data structures we have looked at—databases, markup systems, classification systems, and so on—networks are defined by the specific *relations* among elements in the system rather than simply by the content types or components. The elements of networks are *nodes* (points or entities) and *edges* (links or relations that connect the nodes).

Good examples of networks are social networks, traffic networks, communication networks, and networks of markets and/or influence. Many of the same diagrams are used to show or map these networks, and yet, the content of the relations and of the entities might be very different in each case. Standardization of graphic methods can create a problem when the same techniques are used across disciplines and/or knowledge domains, so a critical approach to network diagrams is useful.

Technically, networks are graphs, not visualizations. The distinction is important because graphs can include the feature of *directed* or *undirected* connections. These indicate a one-way (or two-way) movement in the connection. For example, money may flow from a parent to a child, but more rarely flows back in the other direction. Influence may move from a predecessor in a field to a new development, but might not flow both ways, particularly if the author of the earlier work is deceased.

The computational process by which graphs are produced requires that data be structured in a specific way: source > relationship > target. The vocabulary of nodes and edges is used to differentiate entities (source and target) from their relationships (edges). Particular features of networks are used to process the data in relation to notions of *centrality, closeness*, and *between-ness*. Centrality is the measure of how important any particular node is, measured by the number of connections and type (to or from other nodes) (Bhasin 2019). In graph theory, which governs the description and production of networks, other factors are gauged to assess the factors of between-ness and closeness based on the pathways established among and through nodes. The important principle here is that while some features of the display can be read literally (numbers of connections and directions), the literal distance of nodes from each other in a visualization can only be read logically. This is because the display algorithms try to preserve the statistical features of the data but are often optimizing legibility at the same time. As with all visualizations, it is important to be careful about reading the visual display literally. A node pulled out to a great distance might simply be far from the center so that its label can be seen.

Sketching network concepts

You can sketch a network on paper quite easily. Imagine yourself as a node and then draw lines to everyone you know in your immediate circles (family, friends, clubs, and groups) around you. Draw their links to each other. Think about degrees of proximity and also connections among the individuals in different parts of your network. How many of them are linked to each other as well as to you? If you can code the lines that connect persons to indicate something about the relationship, how does that change the drawing? What attributes of a relationship are readily indicated? Which are not? Think about the difference between how *often* you exchange communications with someone and how *central* they are to the exchanges among others. A parent might be someone to whom everyone is connected, but your own communications might be more frequent with your siblings. When a network algorithm processes data, it tries to calculate these properties.

Social networks are familiar and the use of social media has intensified our awareness of the ways social structures emerge from interconnections among individuals. A network may or may not have emergent properties, may or may not be dynamic, and may have varying levels of complexity. Simple networks, like the connection of your computer to various peripheral devices through a wireless router in your home environment, may exhibit very little change over time, at least little observable change. But a network of traffic flow is more like a living organism than it is like a set of static connections. Though nodes may stay in place, as in airline hubs and transfer points, the properties of the network have capacity to vary considerably. This is certainly true with social networks, most of which are highly dynamic, even volatile.

Properties of networks

Networks exhibit varying degrees of closed-ness and open-ness. Researchers interested in complex or emergent systems are attentive to the ways boundary conditions are maintained under different circumstances, helping to define the limits of a system. Social networks are almost never closed, and like kinship relations or communications, they can quickly escalate to a very high volume of connections. Epidemiologists trying to track the spread of a disease are aware of how rapidly the connections among individuals grow exponentially in a very short period of time. Network analysis is an essential feature of textual studies, particularly of citations and influences. Network analysis plays a large role in policy and resource allocation as well as in other kinds of research work.

To reiterate what was already stated, the basic elements of any network are nodes and edges. The degree of agency or activity assigned to any node and the different attributes that can be assigned to any relation or edge will be structured into the data model. The data for linked "nodes" are understood as "source" and "target" (even though these can be reciprocal, and also, unrelated). Edges are the connections specified between the nodes.

For an example of this in action, look at the project, Kindred Britain, which studies connections of about 30,000 British individuals. The project is meant to show the many ways in which connections form through social networks, family ties, business, and political circumstances.

Another interesting example looks at the genre of "exchange poems" that were part of medieval Chinese culture. These had traditionally been characterized by schools and styles. But new research positioned them in social networks. To paraphrase the work of the project director, Tom Mazanec, it turns out that the Buddhist monks in the 7th to 10th centuries of the Tang dynasty were central "nodes" in the network of literary production (Mazanec 2017). Graphing these has changed the way this form of Chinese poetry is understood and its place in cultural and social life. Relations between literary forms and social activity that were not noted before were revealed through the analysis.

Art historians Pamela Fletcher and Anne Helmreich used network analysis to study the London art market, and found surprising insights from sales records and auction catalogs (Fletcher and Helmreich 2012). Artists and styles that have not necessarily been seen as important by later art historians turned out to play a significant role in the markets of the time, even if they have largely vanished from the canon. [See Exercise #1: Kindred Britain, a social network project.]

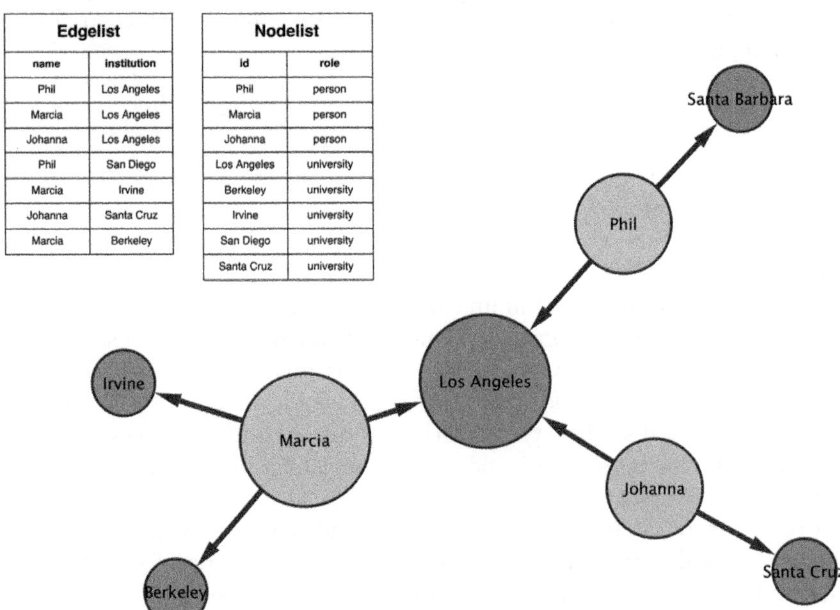

Edgelist	
name	**institution**
Phil	Los Angeles
Marcia	Los Angeles
Johanna	Los Angeles
Phil	San Diego
Marcia	Irvine
Johanna	Santa Cruz
Marcia	Berkeley

Nodelist	
id	**role**
Phil	person
Marcia	person
Johanna	person
Los Angeles	university
Berkeley	university
Irvine	university
San Diego	university
Santa Cruz	university

Figure 6.11 Network graph, edgelist, and nodelist (Image courtesy of Nick Schwieterman) (NS)

Tools and tutorials

As is the case with most digital methods, the fundamental principles of networks are well-established but the tools and platforms change over time. The principles that need to be understood are those of the data structure just mentioned (source > relation > target). The relations among entities, known as edges, can carry weight and also annotations. Network graphs are generated using statistical processes. In a network, the graph is generated by statistical assessment of frequency and weight of relations. With a massive data set—think of a day of Twitter feeds—these calculations become highly complex. Though a simple network can be sketched by hand (you know who is in your immediate social circles), generating a graph of a complex data set would be almost impossible without computation since it involves calculation of relative values across a number of variables (frequency, weight, directionality, etc.).

One tool frequently used in digital scholarship for generating network diagrams is Cytoscape, an open-source platform that can be downloaded directly from the Web and installed on a laptop or desktop. Gephi is another. Learning to use such a tool takes some time but has the advantage that it is a professional level program designed to handle data at every scale from small to large. Understanding the data model before you begin—what is connected to what and how are you characterizing the links or relations—is essential if the digital tools are to be used effectively. Conceptualizing the network before it is visualized automatically helps keep a critical view of what the program produces. [See Exercise #2: Comparing network diagrams.]

Cytoscape and Gephi make use of data in a number of structured formats, among them, some specifically designed for graphs (Rana 2018). These include GraphML, or Graph Markup Language, standards for networks. They readily store information about labels and attributes of the nodes and edges. CSV, Comma Separated Values, a common format in all spreadsheets, can be used to define nodes and edges in weighted to/from pairs (or in linked pathways). GEXF, or Graph Exchange XML Format, was designed by the developers of Gephi, another free, open-source tool for network production and analysis. Networked data formats have specific requirements and a strict syntactic structure. Creating a small data set to work through the tutorials with your own examples is the best way to see what is happening at each step. [See Exercise #3: Cytoscape tutorial.]

Though the data structure is critical in network diagrams, learning to read the graphical output generated is also important. In an initial visualization, especially of large datasets, networks tend to look like "hairballs." They are tangles of lines connecting points, often very densely packed into a small image. Working to open up the nodes and stretch the edges allows insight into the ways the network is branching and where the main areas of connection lie. As has been mentioned above, keep in mind that a network diagram display conforms to protocols that optimize screen space for legibility. While the relationships in a network display are generally accurate, the literal distances on the screen are not. Attaching semantic value—meaning—to the spatial placement of the nodes, can be misleading.

A final challenge is visualizing dynamic systems in static form. Very few social networks are static, though the analysis of historical materials, connections, and activities may be. Information in the data set needs to be carefully scrutinized to be sure that events from different time periods or unrelated events are not conflated into a single graph.

Complex systems

Systems that follow non-linear processes of development are called complex. This does not mean complicated. A complex system can be as simple as a relationship between two people, a person and an environment, or an environment and changing conditions (Clemens 2019). What makes it complex is that the development of the system cannot be predicted—because the processes are non-linear and/or non-deterministic from a statistical standpoint.

The conditions in which they emerge continue to change and elements in the system interact in unpredictable ways. Weather systems are a paradigmatic example of complex systems, but so are stock markets, political processes, social relations of all kinds, and cultural activities. Who could have predicted that a conceptual artist named Marcel Duchamp would confound the conventions of the Western art world in 1917 by displaying a urinal upside down in an exhibit? Or that Mao Tse Tung would come to power in the Chinese Revolution? Or that the presence of the Missions in Australia would create an opportunity for art practices that were 20,000 years old to become codified in the medium of paint on oil and board? (Artlandish n.d.). These are examples of complexity at work. Many—even most—cultural processes are complex but modeling these requires more than creation of a data set. This work involves modeling behaviors of agents and conditions in a system.

Information designers—and artists—have been intrigued with visualizing complexity. Art exhibitions featuring data aesthetics have become common (Remondino, Stabellini, and Tamborrini 2018). The result has been a rich vocabulary of vivid and dynamic information visualizations—as well as some "eye candy" that may be more seductive than meaningful (Lima 2013). The process of constructing data and formulae for visualizing complexity is more complicated than it is for other visualizations (Yau 2007–2020). [See Exercise #4: Complexity.]

Advanced network theory pays attention to emergent properties of systems. The capacity of networks to "self-organize" using very simple procedures that produce increasingly complex results makes them useful models for looking at many kinds of behaviors in human and non-human systems. Networks do not have to be dynamic, but complex systems almost always are. The study of systems theory and of networks is relatively recent and only emerged as a distinct field of research in the last few decades. We might argue, however, that novelists and playwrights have been observing social networks for much longer, as have observers of animal behavior, weather and climate, and the movements of heavenly bodies held in relation to each other by magnetism, gravity, and other forces. Most dynamic phenomena are complex systems governed by non-linear processes.

Takeaway

Networks consist of nodes (entities) and edges (relations). The data model for a network is a simple three-part formula of entity-relation-entity. This can be structured in a spreadsheet and exported to create a network visualization. Networks emphasize relations and connections of exchange and influence. Refining the relations among nodes beyond the concept of a single relation is important and so is the change of relations over time. Social networks change constantly, as do communication networks, and the relations among the technology that supports a network and the psychological, social, or affective bonds can alter independently.

Exercises

Exercise #1: Kindred Britain, a social network project

Explore the site and then discuss the selection of individuals, the character and quality of relations, explicit assumptions and implicit ones, and the diagrams and their rhetorical power.

http://kindred.stanford.edu/#

Exercise #2: comparing network diagrams

Go to: https://linkedjazz.org/network/ Determine what information you can reasonably extract from this graph. Now toggle between modes. Does this change your understanding? Or go to: www.databasic.io/en/connectthedots/ Network visualization with interactive sample data sets created by Rahul Bhargava and Catherine D'Ignazio.

Exercise #3: Cytoscape tutorial

This manual can be accessed without downloading and goes step by step through the basics of network graph construction. It is provided free of charge by the people who designed and maintain the standard platform for this work. Read through the table of contents and introduction to get oriented. http://manual.cytoscape.org/en/stable/Introduction.html

Exercise #4: complexity

Look at half a dozen examples on Nathan Yau's site: https://flowingdata.com/about/

What are the dimensions added in complex systems that are different from those of static visualizations? What is the correlation between graphic expression and information?

What role does aesthetics play in these projects?

Recommended readings

Grandjean, Martin, and Aaron Mauro. 2015. "A Social Network Analysis of Twitter: Mapping the Digital Humanities Community." *Cogent: Arts and Humanities* 3 (1). www.tandfonline.com/doi/full/10.1080/23311983.2016.1171458.

Weingart, Scott. 2011. "Demystifying Networks, Parts I & II Journal of Digital Humanities." *Journal of Digital Humanities* 1 (1). http://journalofdigitalhumanities.

References cited

Apostol, Tom. 1969. "A Short History of Probability." In *Calculus*, Vol. II. John Wiley & Sons. http://homepages.wmich.edu/~mackey/Teaching/145/probHist.html.

Artlandish. n.d. "Australian Aboriginal Art." www.aboriginal-art-australia.com/aboriginal-art-library/the-story-of-aboriginal-art/.

Bhasin, Jasin. 2019. "Graph Analytics—Introduction and Concepts of Centrality." *Towards Data Science*. https://towardsdatascience.com/graph-analytics-introduction-and-concepts-of-centrality-8f5543b55de3.

Clemens, Marshall. 2019. "Visualizing Complex Systems." *New England Complex Systems Institute*. https://necsi.edu/visualizing-complex-systems-science.

Fenton, William. 2015. "Humanizing Maps: An Interview with Johanna Drucker." *PC*. www.pcmag.com/news/humanizing-maps-an-interview-with-johanna-drucker.

Fletcher, Pamela, and Anne Helmreich. 2012. "Local/Global: Mapping Nineteenth-Century London's Art Market." *Nineteenth Century Art Worldwide* 11 (3). www.19thc-artworldwide.org/autumn12/fletcher-helmreich-mapping-the-london-art-market.

Friendly, Michael. 2007. "DataVis." www.datavis.ca/index.php.

Lengler, Ralph, and Martin J. Eppler. 2007. www.visual-literacy.org/periodic_table/periodic_table.html.

Lima, Manuel. 2013. *Visual Complexity: Mapping Patterns of Information*. New York, NY: Princeton Architectural Press. https://medium.com/@mslima/visualcomplexity-com-ad9a12fa2c1a.

Lupi, Georgia. 2017. "Dear Data, the Project." http://giorgialupi.com/dear-data.

Mansky, Jackie. 2018. "W.E.B. Du Bois's Visionary Infographics Come Together for the First Time in Color." *Smithsonian Magazine*. www.smithsonianmag.com/history/first-time-together-and-color-book-displays-web-du-bois-visionary-infographics-180970826/.

Mazanec, Tom. 2016–17. "Chinese Exchange Poems." https://cdh.princeton.edu/projects/chinese-exchange-poems/.

Norman, Jeremy. 2004–2020. "The History of Information." www.historyofinformation.com/detail.php?entryid=2929.

Rana, Ashish. 2018. "Getting Started with Network Data Sets." *Towards Data Science*. https://towardsdatascience.com/getting-started-with-network-datasets-92ec54958c07.

Remondino, Chiara L., Barbara Stabellini, and Paolo Tamborrini. 2018. "Exhibition: Visualizing Complex Systems." https://systemic-design.net/wp-content/uploads/2019/05/RSD7Exhibition_VisualizingComplexSystems.pdf.

Wild Maths. n.d. https://wild.maths.org/rené-descartes-and-fly-ceiling.

Yau, Nathan. 2007–2020. "Flowing Data Site." https://flowingdata.com.

Zer-Aviv, Mushon. 2016. "If Everything Is a Network, Nothing Is a Network." Visualising Information for Advocacy, visualisingadvocacy.org. https://visualisingadvocacy.org/node/739.html.

Resources

Cytoscape https://cytoscape.org/.
Gephi ttps://gephi.org/.
Kindred Britain http://kindred.stanford.edu/#.
Network Graphs (Flourish Studio) https://app.flourish.studio/@flourish/network-graph.
Social Network Graphs https://gwu-libraries.github.io/sfm-ui/posts/2017-09-08-sna.

7 Data mining and analysis

7a Data mining and text analysis

The idea of data mining seems far removed from the humanities and its use for analysis of literary and aesthetic objects has prompted many immediate and strong responses, such as the claim that "literature is *not* data" (Lamarche 2012). Made as part of a larger diatribe against the digital humanities, the defensive posture suggests that data mining was meant to replace methods of reading that have a long history in cultural practice. More reasoned and informed discussions from within the practice of digital humanities have argued for the value of these techniques, particularly given the unprecedented scale of cultural materials available in digital formats (Kirschenbaum n.d.). What can data mining offer to the humanities that augments traditional methods without replacing them?

Data mining is an automated analysis that looks for patterns and extracts meaningful information in digital files (Underwood 2017). While it is not limited to analysis of so-called "big" data, it is particularly useful at large scales. Data mining has long been incorporated into the natural and social sciences. It has become a part of research methods in text, music, sound recording, images, and multimodal communications studies with tools customized for these purposes. Text analysis is a specialized subset of data mining that focuses on analysis of language (Schmidt 2013). Keep in mind that data mining always processes digital files, which means that for analog originals, these are surrogates, representations whose properties might be quite different from those of their source. For instance, a scan of a sculpture that reduces it to two dimensions only preserves some of the original information about form. Data mining only takes place on the information literally in the file, so clarification about the process is essential.

One advantage to data mining is the analysis of cultural materials in their native format—as texts, images, and media. But much processing has to occur before text or image analysis can proceed. Concepts like "distant reading" and the more pejorative "not reading" have arisen to describe some of these approaches. As with any method or technique, the question of value is best posed by seeing what these methods add to existing and/or traditional approaches, rather than dismissing them out of hand—or embracing them with uncritical enthusiasm. One easy to use example of text analysis applied to the corpus of Google Books is the Ngram Viewer, which displays all of the many problems and some of the benefits of these approaches. [See: Exercise #1 Google Ngram Viewer.]

Beginnings of automated textual scholarship

A milestone frequently cited in early digital humanities projects is the work of Father Roberto Busa. He was engaged with text analysis in the form of a concordance—a list of all words in a work or body of work. This was a form of analysis with a long history within religious and classical scholarship, but Father Busa's project was ambitious intellectually as well as logistically. He was focused on the concept of "presence" in the Latin texts of the 13th century scholar Thomas Aquinas. This was a metaphysical concept, and thus had no simple literal meaning.

Busa had tracked the instances of the words *praesens* and *praesentia* to address their contexts in the 1940s (Busa 1980). He created thousands of index cards for individual instances and the phrases in which they were found. When he realized that the full corpus exceeded ten million words, he began to consider mechanical aids. This led him to a collaboration with IBM, thanks to the support of its CEO Thomas Watson. Many of the approaches Busa designed for his project, such as identifying text types (for example, the use of citations) have become part of standard markup and statistical analysis. Working with punch cards and a list of typological codes, Busa established a systematic approach to the analysis of natural language, including linking all forms and versions of a word to its root (Terras and Nyhan 2016). Busa was working in analog materials but developing formal methods compatible with automated processes.

A second area of early automated text analysis was in the area of stylometrics or stylometry (Hai-Jew 2015). Longstanding debates about whether or not William Shakespeare was the author of all of his plays, or whether some were actually composed by Christopher Marlowe, remained pressing matters through the 20th century (Fox, Ehmodea, and Charniak 2012). The idea that statistical approaches could be brought to bear on the problem motivated formal analysis of style. Sentence length, grammatical structure, vocabulary choices, and other features of the texts were used to make comparisons. Many of the features on which style was formally addressed had a history in analog scholarship. The task of making formal parameters on which to analyze style is a useful intellectual exercise, as is any other attempt to make explicit parameters on which to formalize traditional humanistic approaches for computational purposes.

Methods for statistical processing are now far more complex than the counting and sorting of words into lists that were central to Busa's early project or the techniques developed for analysis of style (Sculley and

Pasanek 2008). Current tools and platforms combine counting and sorting techniques with statistically driven capacities. The differences between these will be a recurring theme.

Fundamentals of data mining and text analysis

Data mining is not limited to texts. Many applications for extracting meaningful statistical information from humanities materials operate on quantitative data, by which is meant information that originates in numerical form. Quantitative research is central to the social sciences, and not surprisingly, historians frequently adopt such methods for analysis of numerical data from economic records (taxes, census records, demographic analyses of social groups, and so forth). Quantitative history is generally considered to have originated in the 1960s, in a shift to studies of broader populations and trends, and away from the conventional focus on political history and events among leaders and elites (Guldi 2018). This continues to be a motivation within digital humanities where patterns of events, not just individual accomplishments, are examined. Increased scope in collections allows once marginal figures and works to come into view and to be accessed. The availability of computational tools, desktop and then laptop computers, to create and process data made quantitative methods integral to the history field. More than half a century later, these methods have been codified into a set of highly flexible and useful tools that can be readily acquired and used across the humanities.

At the heart of data mining and text analysis are several processes that should be understood critically. These are the same processes noted earlier: parameterization and tokenization. These identify what can be counted and how the counting is done. Additional considerations come into play with data mining, which are the statistical analyses of frequency, proximity, and value of individual data points within the larger sets. Principles like *collocation* of words are judged relative to other usage—and in contrast to the sum of all other words in a sample. In other words, multiple factors go into determining how any individual word is valued, not just the number of times it appears. The difference between counting and statistical analysis is brought into focus by this contrast.

In text analysis, questions of proximity and frequency are gauged against the statistical probability of occurrence in relation to all of the words or instances in a work or corpus (depending on the boundaries set for the analysis). Thus, the frequency of occurrence of a word is not simply counted but calculated in relation to the frequency of other words—and to the likelihood or probability of its being used. These are considerations that are rarely part of humanities reading practices. Understanding the workings of automated processes is essential for engaging seriously with this work.

Sample size and testing procedures are central issues in statistics, and they are brought directly into humanities work in data mining and textual analysis (Delice 2010). Questions of generalizability and reliability determine the extent to which the results of an analysis can be applied outside the single sample (Sandelowski 1995). For example, in analyzing the relationship between class position and letter-writing in a particular period, are the records of a historical society in New England and another in the pre-Civil War South comparable? How many of the letters need to be analyzed? What if there are two hundred by one author and only two by another—do they carry the same weight? On what terms should the contrasts between the language of these authors be assessed? How representative are these letters—and representative of *what?* They can only give an idea of what has been preserved, but can the analysis be extrapolated to discuss education, literacy, and gendered language across a small segment of the population?

As we know, data in the cultural record is notoriously incomplete. The estimate is that of the 30,000 novels that were published in English in the 19th century, only 6,000 of these have survived, of which less than 300 are considered canonical. How are traits or features of these works to be assessed in relation to the wider reading experience of a past century?

Text analysis and distant reading

The term distant reading was invented in about 2000 by Franco Moretti, the scholar who was central to its development for literary study. (Serlen 2010) Distant reading is the idea of processing content—subjects, themes, persons, or places—or information about publication date, place, author, or title in a large number of textual items without engaging in the reading of the actual text. Could texts be "read" at a scale that exceeded human capacity? The "reading" is a form of data mining that allows information in the text or about the text to be processed and analyzed.

Debates about distant reading range from the suggestion that it is a misnomer to call it reading, since it is really statistical processing and/or data mining, to arguments that the analysis of the corpus of literary or historical (or other) works has a role to play in the humanities (Underwood 2017). Proponents of the method argue that text processing exposes aspects of texts at a scale that is not possible for human readers and which provides new points of departure for research. Patterns of changes in vocabulary, nomenclature, terminology, moods, themes, and a nearly inexhaustible number of other topics can be detected using distant reading techniques, and larger social and cultural questions can be asked about what has been included in and left out of traditional studies of literary and historical materials.

Moretti's earliest automated work was focused on questions of genre—the type of text produced in literary publications. The initial decisions about how to characterize genre—distinguishing mysteries from romance, didactic works from sentimental ones, and so on—had to be done with close reading techniques and conventional methods. Certain vocabulary words and terms, phrases, and other textual features were selected as markers of genre. This was done by human judgment, and these decisions play a major role in the way the automated processes unfold. Then a large corpus of digitized materials was analyzed using these terms in order to sort them by genre. Moretti described the process as one of reduction "to a few elements" that could be abstracted "from the narrative flow" (Serlen 2010). As in all such work, the outcome is only as good as the model on which the data are abstracted. Terminology shifts and changes. Usage also transforms the meaning of individual words over time. And characterization of vocabulary terms always involves some judgment.

One of the positive claims for distant reading was that it might shift focus away from the established canon, allowing for a broader insight into cultural patterns of reading. The recovery of a wide swath of ignored titles from the oblivion into which habits of teaching and critical writing had cast them promised to address class issues, and to some extent, those of race. But the works that are digitized in Hathi Trust, Google Books, and other major repositories cannot recover fully lost texts, only make available a wider array than the narrow canon that had formed a core of literary study. Problems in the relationship between distant reading and critical race studies have been brought up by Richard Jean So and Edwin Roland (So and Roland 2020). Distant reading requires explicit quantification, and the terms of racial identity, only sometimes explicit in authors, characters, and texts, have to be defined to expose the limits of the ways computational approaches have been formulated as well as to expand the possibilities for writing the histories of people of color as cultural figures.

In a large-scale project, for instance, to characterize sentimentality and its relation to bestsellers, Andrew Piper and Richard Jean So made use of a library of terms put together by a scholar, Bing Liu, who had produced lexicons of terms characterized according to their "positive" or "negative" sentimental value. They processed their corpus of digitized literature by looking for these words (negative terms were *abominable* or *shady* and positive ones were *admirable*, *courageous*, or *rapturous*, etc.) to see where different genres and also prize-winning works were situated relative to each other. Another example was a study of "mood words" in 20th century fiction by decade, to see if any correlation existed between large scale events like economic downturns, wars, or periods of prosperity and the tone of novels (Acerbi et al. 2013). The results are fascinating, but not altogether surprising. The "sadness" score was greatest during the years of the Second World War but, oddly, "joy" was highest during the period of the First World War.

Research results are generally shown in graphs that aggregate information. This raises questions about how outliers and anomalous individual works are treated. If a single highly popular work had a particular sentiment attached to it that was out of sync with the mainstream, it would be lost in the smoothing and averaging processes of data analysis. Also, something as basic as a publication date for a work can be complicated. Leo Tolstoy's mid-19th century novel, *War and Peace*, is still in print, the works of

William Shakespeare were widely read in English throughout the 20th century, and so were *The Holy Bible* and the first Harry Potter book. Are these 20th century works? Are they part of the corpus because they were read? How is the volume of consumption measured? School texts commonly supplied the Shakespeare plays. Tolstoy's novel may well have been borrowed from a public library. The Bible texts were likely to have been available in the home, perhaps even in a family heirloom handed from generation to generation. What are the dates of publication for such works? How is their reading registered in relation to that of market records for commercial publishers of Harry Potter titles?

A critical framework for discussion of results of any data mining and text analysis is required to keep it from standing on its own, decontextualized. While patterns emerge, and large trends can be discerned, the question of what these are indicative of remains. Do they only show trends in the *data*? Or can they reveal trends in *phenomena* of the actual and lived world (Lee 2019)? What is the relation between these two? Abstraction, extraction, reduction, and simplification are frequently used terms in discussing large data sets. The value of the research needs to be measured against these considerations. As in so many aspects of digital work, the value is in the dialogue with traditional methods. Distant reading often points out areas where close reading will be of value.

Tools for text analysis

One platform for exploration of text analysis, Voyant, was developed by humanists, Geoffrey Rockwell and Stéfan Sinclair. Voyant is meant to be useful without technical expertise and is freely available for use online (no downloads and no learning curve). More advanced researchers will use Mallet and the Natural Language Toolkit, both built in the programming language Python. These are tools that can be trained on a text, with results modified by the user by eliminating some results and strengthening others, until the outcome conforms to the research goals. Advanced tools used for text analysis often connect with the language R, which is designed for statistical analysis and is also readily connected to libraries of visualizations. Any researcher serious about data mining and text analysis will need to commit to learning these programs, but to experience text analysis without the programming skills, Voyant is extremely helpful. [See Exercise #2: Voyant and Mallet.]

Voyant is a dashboard-based platform. This means its various functions and tools can be accessed simply by going to the site and entering text or URLs directly without any pre-processing or specialized knowledge. The tools automatically output the results into a set of screens. Voyant, as per its tagline, "Sees through your texts," and offers an array of visualizations through which to get results. The processing happens out of sight, and the various panels display a range of visualizations, such as WordClouds,

TermsBerries (a cute name for a cloud of circles bouncing around next to each other), Bubblelines, columns, bar charts, area charts, and so on. The tools are particularly useful for comparisons, and filtering terms within works, narrowing the segments, and focusing on individual terms produces correlated visualizations. So, clicking on a single circle in a "berry cloud" changes what is shown in the trends window next to it. Correlation is one of the crucial features of data analysis, and Voyant is designed to facilitate these connections.

Voyant also offers an introduction to topic modeling in one of its panes. This feature clusters terms according to their connection (frequency and proximity) in the document(s) as a whole and exposes themes within a work or corpus. Keywords in context, or KWIC, provide another useful comparison tool for "reading" a corpus through crucial themes. Keywords that repeat are often clues to themes or topics in a body of work and seeing how the terms are resituated is a useful tool for seeing the facets of an argument to which the term is central. Using Voyant, and other text analysis tools, is most successful when applied to a text with which the researcher is familiar. Then the results can be gauged against prior understanding and assumptions.

Topic modeling and advanced text analysis

Topic modeling is what it sounds like—a model of a topic that appears in a text. In more advanced work that uses machine learning tools, the program

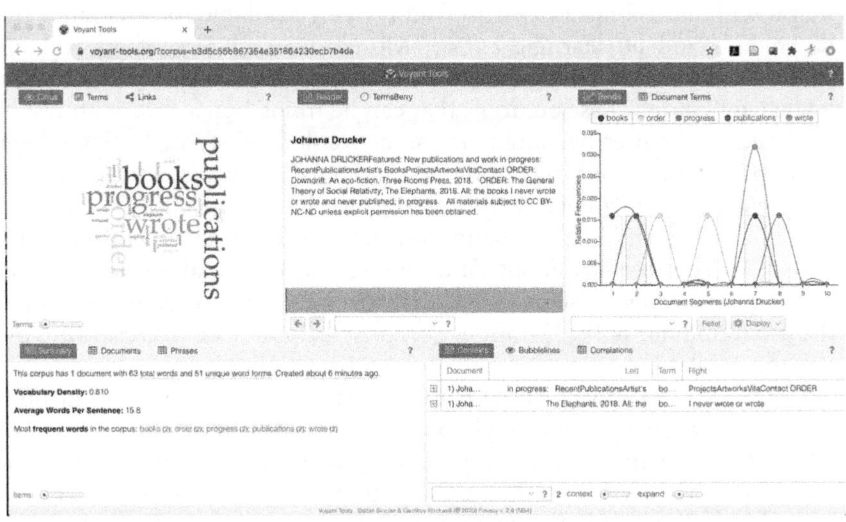

Figure 7.1 Voyant screen (Voyant Tools, Stéfan Sinclair and Geoffrey Rockwell, CC BY 4.0.) (CC License)

can be trained to produce more refined and precise topic models by eliminating certain terms and privileging others. The standard description of a topic modeling activity is that it "extracts" topics from the analysis of texts. This makes it seem as though topics are already present in a text, rather than being produced as an act of reading or interpretation. Like other computational techniques, topic modeling is often defined in opposition to human reading practices. This characterization mistakenly represents the processes as value free and neutral.

Topic modeling depends upon machine learning and natural language processing. Sophisticated tools for the analysis of parts of speech, and what are referred to as "named entities"—proper nouns with specific (but sometimes ambiguous) references, and other features of natural language have been developed by Stanford's Natural Language Processing Group. This means that it is "trained" on texts and then develops "knowledge" of how to analyze them. The training involves human interaction and reinforcement but is rooted in neural net processes (a machine learning technique that works from a "bottom up" approach) that depend on reinforcement. Because they work with natural language, which does not have the formal constraints that computational languages possess, these analyses also make use of dictionaries compiled to help disambiguate word usage.[1]

Text analysis brings the contrast between natural and formal languages into sharp relief. In formal languages, any expression has to be explicit and unambiguous. In natural language, the context and syntactic structure in which the word appears are crucial. So are definitions and probabilities of occurrence. What, for instance, tells a program to read the word "compound" as an adjective, a noun, or a verb? How is slang and dialect—frequently present in literary work—to be interpreted? What about words that might have widely variant meanings? For instance, a term like "sure" uttered in a response might mean anything from "yes," to "no," to anything in between. The other crucial category of words generally left out of topic modeling is what are termed "stop words." The term simply means they are not factored into the analysis, and tend to include the conjunctions (and, but, etc.) and articles (the, a, an). But think of the distinction between "the savior" and "a savior," "the god" and "a god." The definite and indefinite articles are crucial for meaning production, so leaving them out of an analysis can introduce distortions.

Like all computational activity that depends upon models, the processes can be criticized. Does text analysis find what it is trained to find, or engage in a discovery that is neutral? One area where this issue has been addressed directly is in the analysis of gendered identities and texts. In a critical text focused on this issue, Laura Mandell posed the question of whether particular approaches to cultural analytics "find" or "make" their stereotypes (Mandell 2019). The fundamental recognition is that gender is not a simple Male/Female binary equated with biological categories. Mandell's distinctions reinforce an approach in which gender is constructed—in literary work, language, lived experience, roles, and characterizations. But her critical eye focused on work that assumed gendered identity as a given and then tracked it in literary texts. She noted that this resulted in the reaffirmation of gender stereotypes, since the model on which the text analysis was carried out took gender difference as an a priori category.

Mandell's critical insights arose from work on gender, but they are also relevant to other topics or themes. Modeling is a powerful instrument, and it asserts its values in seeking confirmation of what it details. Numerous scholars thought distant reading would avoid the biases of close reading. But "macro-analysis," to use a term identified with Matt Jockers, has often replicated the very value judgments it was believed computation would avoid.

This section has dealt with methods of data and text analysis. In addition, it is useful to address ways of extracting data from online sites. For this purpose, a combination of features is useful: one part, known as APIs, provides access to data on a site. The other consists of tools for "scraping" data from online resources. Both are powerful assets for research.

APIs: application programming interfaces and web-scraping

One crucial source of data for digital research is in projects and sites that offer a well-structured option for export and re-use of their files. The main method by which this is accomplished is in the use of APIs, applied programming interfaces, which are designed to package data to make it portable and usable. APIs are built. They are not automatically present. Scholars who see their work as useful for others will add this feature to their online repositories or sites. Other methods of data mining can be used to extract information from such a site if an API is not present, in a process known as "web-scraping," which consists of tools used to capture data from social media sites and other platforms.

The ethics of data capture and re-use from online sites are subject to the same considerations as repurposing of any data. Attention to intellectual property and privacy concerns forms one set of ethical issues, and authentication and verification of data form another. Here, as in other practices, documentation is essential to preserve the trail of scholarship, even if the data themselves are no longer recoverable from an original source.

An API is actually a program designed to let another program access or manipulate data through an interface. We usually think of interface as a human-to-computer function, but programs can also have this capacity. Of course, it will be a human user who takes advantage of the protocols built into the API—to query the data on a site and search and extract information from its repositories. But the code is designed to make it easy for human users to get one machine to talk to another for purposes of information exchange and export.

When a site is enormous—like a national library—then it can be a rich resource for many kinds of research. The Australian National Library, for instance, has a platform called "Trove" that supports use of its API through "query syntax" and a collection of case studies that demonstrate what can be done with its tools. The Australian National Library uses a console format to guide users in constructing searches that can be incredibly broad (everything) or highly focused (newspaper weather reports in a particular place on a particular day). You will find that many APIs return their results in JSON, which we discussed earlier as a popular data exchange format.[2] [See Exercise #3: Trove: Reading an API.]

Web-scraping tools are designed to acquire data from existing sites without the use of APIs or custom coding. These are also frequently built in the already frequently mentioned language, Python. Off-the-shelf tools exist, most of which were developed to serve marketing and commercial purposes, but they can be used for humanities research as well. They extract data in real time and many allow for anonymous data collection, the ethics of which you will need to consider not just as a user of these tools, but as someone whose work and information might be scraped and put to purposes you did not envision or authorize.[3] A look at the description of these tools will acquaint you with vocabulary relevant to the automated operation of web-scrapers and their ability to bypass bots, to crawl sites automatically, to convert data to a usable format, and to collect and store cookies from other sites.

Some of the simplest scrapers can be installed as browser extensions, and in fact, Zotero, a bibliographical tool designed by humanists, can be used to "scrape" data and store it for research purposes. Zotero stores metadata from sites and is particularly focused on the information relevant to scholarly bibliographical formats. It works at a very small scale and only when initiated by a user, while many web-scraping tools used commercially operate automatically to generate massive data sets in all sectors of private and public activity.

Takeaway

Fundamental issues of digital humanities are present in distant reading: the basic decisions about what can be measured (parameterized), counted, sorted, and displayed are interpretative acts that shape the outcomes of the research projects. Distant reading is a combination of text analysis and other data mining performed on metadata or other available information. Natural language processing applications can summarize the contents of a large corpus of texts. Data mining techniques can show other patterns at a scale that is beyond the capacity of human processing (e.g. How many times does the word "prejudice" appear in 200,000 hours of newscasts?).

The term distant reading is created in opposition to the notion of "close reading," the careful attention to the composition and meaning of texts, images, musical works, or other cultural artifacts that is at the heart of humanistic interpretation. Automated web scraping and data export through APIs allow data to be captured and repurposed at multiple scales for research purposes.

Exercises

Exercise #1: Google Ngram Viewer

Open the Google Ngram Viewer and select a date range. Enter several terms or names and see what has changed over time. How much can you trust your results? What are they based on?

Exercise #2: Voyant and Mallet

Go to https://voyant-tools.org/ and enter a block of text with which you are familiar. Look at the first display and figure out what each pane is showing. Play with the other tools and display modes. Do they match? Why is there a range of results in the displays? Then, see if you can understand the workings of Mallet: https://programminghistorian.org/en/lessons/topic-modeling-and-mallet

Exercise #3: Trove: reading an api

Look at the Australian National Library Trove API console. What can you learn from reading the documentation? Construct a query and assess the results. What ideas does this give you for designing an API? Compare the results of a search in the library's catalog and the format of its results, with the XML output generated by Trove which is useful for data analysis. http://troveconsole.herokuapp.com/#otherzones Also useful: https://studentwork.prattsi.org/dh/2019/05/13/getting-data-for-digital-humanities-with-apis/ tutorial for DH data extraction with APIs.

Recommended readings

Janicke, S., G. Franzini, M. F. Cheema, and G. Scheuermann. 2015. "On Close and Distant Reading in Digital Humanities: A Survey and Future Challenges." EuroGraphics Conferenceon Visualization. https://pdfs.semanticscholar.org/20cd/40f3f17dc7d8f49d368c2efbc2e27b0f2b33.pdf.

Piper, Andrew and Richard Jean So. 2015. "Quantifying the Weepy Bestseller." *The New Republic.* https://newrepublic.com/article/126123/quantifying-weepy-bestseller.

Schulz, Kathryn. 2011. "What is Distant Reading?" *New York Times Book Review.* www.nytimes.com/2011/06/26/books/review/the-mechanic-muse-what-is-distant-reading.html.

7b Cultural analytics, multi-modal communication, media, and audio mining

Text analysis, topic modeling, and other computationally enabled processes of producing meaning from language-based documents play a significant role in digital humanities. So does the analysis of quantitative data. Texts and numbers are readily remediated into computationally tractable forms. Numbers have a discrete identity and texts can be processed at the level of the word, or phrase, with relative efficiency, even if their meanings may be ambiguous or complex. Though it sounds reductive and mechanistic, numbers and texts can both be correlated to keystrokes and this gives them a structure within digital file formats. They are essentially alphanumeric code which translates easily into machine code and binary files.

But what about other forms of cultural expression—images, audio recordings, video and film, and the many representations in photographs and other documents? Every medium poses its own set of challenges for extracting information in a meaningful way. But each process has in common the same set of requirements—to translate analog or digital materials into a form in which a feature set can be identified, parameterized, tokenized, and processed computationally. This generally involves making discrete features from continuous phenomena. As in all such processes, the conceptual work and the technological developments have to coordinate. The ways we think about music or images will structure some of the ways digital representations are created—and the purposes to which they are put. In whose interest is it to do data mining of images or social media? Art historians, or police surveillance units? And music? Artists looking for inspiration, scholars studying historical materials, or industry sleuths tracking piracy—or those indulging in it (Kennedy and Moss 2015)?

Cultural analytics

Images pose particular challenges for data mining. They are not expressed in a structured notation (like letters, punctuation, and spaces) in the same way as language. In spite of these apparent impediments, experts in image recognition and analysis have developed useful tools and platforms in the humanities (alongside other developments in science and applied research). One of these is the Cultural Analytics, a term coined by Lev Manovich to describe work that uses digital capacities to analyze, organize, sort, and computationally process large numbers of images. Images have different properties than texts. As we noted in the section on digitization, the act of remediating an image into a digital file involves choices that determine what kind of information it contains. If the human visual apparatus can glean more from visual information in certain areas of the spectrum or even color wheel, then what is the point of digital files that contain other visual content? Machine processing may not correspond to human perception, and in many advanced imaging technologies, this is an advantage to discovery and exploration (Jofre et al. 2020).

Manovich's project, however, pioneered the processing of visual image data and its analysis in visualizations. Manovich's research was motivated by the question of how to analyze images at scale, just as Moretti's was prompted by "reading" massive amounts of text. What features of digital surrogates could be quantified and used for comparison? Metadata on images also plays an important role in data mining, particularly for those features like size, medium, artist, collection, provenance, date, and other information that is not visible. But cultural analytics focuses on those features of a visual surrogate that can be extracted automatically. If an image is stored as a pixel-based file, then color values supply crucial information. If it is stored as a vector-based-graphic, then shape and proportion lead. If the image is black and white, then tonal range, values, and contrast are particularly conspicuous. Image recognition at the level of iconography relies on combinations of object and scene recognition, and links to image libraries that are working with deep learning algorithms.

Nuance is still lacking. At what point is an image of a mother holding a young child actually a Madonna? Can the Mona Lisa be distinguished from other portraits by Leonardo da Vinci—and can her emotional state be discerned automatically (Dunne 2015)? Can a religious allegory of a sheep be differentiated from a literal painting of animals in a pasture? All discussions of automated learning and processing come up against these limits with regard to issues of context and learned conventions within human experience. Many machine learning projects use human labor, such as Mechanical Turk, to provide sample data sets to train the algorithms (Anderson 2017). [See Exercise #1: Cultural Analytics.]

Multi-modal analysis

Recent work in digital humanities and computer vision have developed a "Distant Viewing" approach to moving image analysis (Tilton et al. 2018). These focus on color and lighting, time codes for shots and breaks, means of establishing boundaries for identifying faces and other objects, sound analysis, automatic voice to text transcripts for speech, and so on. Each of these dimensions requires its own computational processes and functions with different degrees of accuracy. However, consider that an archive of oral histories might contain a hundred thousand hours of recordings. For an individual to watch all of these, working ten hours a day, would take ten thousand days . . . about thirty years. Automated techniques for searching and sorting clearly have a purpose. The development of parsers—programs that can automatically detect features and structural elements to a degree that starts to resemble detecting the content of images—has been rapid and has produced workable results. These combine the "generative" or "top

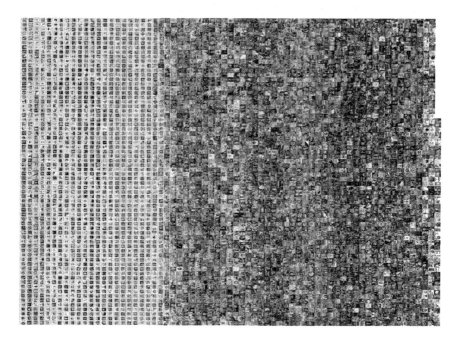

Figure 7.2 Cultural Analytics analysis of features of *Time* magazine covers

Source: (Image courtesy of Lev Manovich and Jeremy Douglass, Cultural Analytics Lab.)

down" analysis (using classification systems and categories) with "discriminative" or "bottom up" processes (Kuhn 2018).

Biases are built in. Multiple studies confirm that facial recognition and emotion detection work differently on images of people of color. Voices with accents or unusual timbre will not translate to text. Experimental and avant-garde films, even independent and documentary footage, will be processed differently than commercial ones. Above all, the multiple layers of meaning production identified by art historians like Erwin Panofsky, that require situating an image within a field of others to understand how it communicates in a particular cultural moment, are not likely to be grasped by an algorithm. Nor, sad to say, is humor. Jokes, references, parodies—all of the features of communication in which images play a role, are difficult to codify. A dog in glasses? A cat in a dress? A drunk frog on a cocktail napkin? We read these easily as commentary on human activities—but can a computer?

Automated processing of sound and audio-visual media

The issues of feature recognition and segmentation in file formats plague data mining, as does the quality of digital surrogates. Only some features of an analog experience are represented in a sound recording. Formats matter in the analog world as well as in the digital. Analog sounds are continuous waves so translating them into discrete units of binary information involves translation. At a small enough granularity, human ears will not detect this, any more than we see the "pixels" on a screen image. But since sound is a time-based medium, sampling rates, the number of channels, and the bits-per-sample have to be taken into account. Audio analysis research and applications exist in a generative tension between machine capabilities and the simulation of human perceptual experience. In many ways, the advantages of digital processing are best appreciated for doing what humans cannot do rather than for trying to emulate our capacities (Giannakopoulos and Pikrakis 2014).

Audio classifications of acoustic data, environmental sound, and musical classification have been applied to historical materials as well as contemporary ones. Sentiment analysis in voice, as in texts and facial recognition, depends on classification of sound, but also, assessment of value across a range and at a rate of change. Voice recognition has profound gender and race biases, as do the facial recognition processes already mentioned. But tools for editing, for "pumping up" signals, and for recovering lost or damaged sound information has many benefits in the work of historical preservation.

Attempts to classify massive numbers of musical recordings that are not identified, but are accessible in online environments, have prompted development of musical data mining techniques (Patchet, Westermann, and Laigre n.d.). Industry applications have led professional groups, like the IEEE (Institute of Electronic and Electrical Engineers) to turn their attention to multimedia analysis (Ogihara and Tzanetakis 2014). Cross-mediation, or the rendering sound data in visual format for analytic purposes has become a common feature of audio editing. Images are easier to work with on a screen, and rendering audio files as visualizations has become common practice (Hartquist 2018).

Sound analysis has also been applied to the study of poetry performance and other voice recordings. Humanities scholars, such as Charles Bernstein and Al Filreis, who have been the directors of Penn Sound, an archive of recordings of poetry readings, offer challenges for research. How does inflection, or variation in the oral production of a work, vary over time—and how is the significance of this to be identified and analyzed. As sound studies have grown, so have digital techniques for engaging with a wide range of ambient, human, musical, industrial, and natural sounds. Historical archives of sound recordings, digitized and made available, provide another important research corpus for humanists (Clement 2012). [See Exercise #2: Sound files.]

Time-based media pose their own specific problems for both digitization and analysis. Recording times and running times may not be the same, and time-stamped files may play at different rates on different platforms. Emulation stations for recovering the correct display of audio-visual materials (and other file formats) are designed to wrestle with these technical issues. Emulation has been particularly important for preservation of games but is relevant across genres and formats.

Multi-modal communication, the phrase used to describe the ways human cognition processes image, sound, inflection, body language, and other features in a dimensionally rich experience, has also been an object of research in digital analysis and processing. Multiple features need to be identified for such work—and translated into computable elements. In a 1998 paper, Tsuhan Chen listed these: lip reading, facial animation, speaker verification, joint audio-visual coding, and so on. But when these many facets of expression are at odds with each other—when a speaker's tone deliberately contradicts a message, or when gestures undermine a statement—how are these coded and processed? What can be learned from the attempts to train automated systems in these matters? Defining the research questions from which humanists can benefit requires strategic thinking. [See Exercise #3: Media processing.]

What is clear is that most computational processes produce benefits at scale—making it possible to search, query, and make use of large corpora for specific purposes. But some valuable results have come from automated processing of small data sets, not just large ones. The imaging work of the Western Semitic Epigraphy project has pioneered techniques that make use of aggregated image data. The photographic and imaging techniques they combine to extract information from ancient inscriptions combine digitization and computation. One of these is Reflectance Transformation Imaging. This depends on making multiple photographs from different directions and with different lighting angles. In combination with multispectral imaging, which makes use of different wavelengths of light, it reveals information that is simply not visible to the human eye under any circumstances. Ultraviolet or infrared light can reveal traces of chemicals that have vanished. By aggregating the features that each imaging technique can record, the researchers are able to create a "picture" of an artifact that is legible in digital formats. This is work that focuses intensely on a very small corpus of materials but extends its value in ways that would not be possible without computational processing.

Takeaway

Computational tools to analyze big data have to balance the production of patterns, summaries at a large scale, with the capacity to drill down into the data at a small scale. Automated analysis of materials in all media—images, sound, video, and even material objects—has produced new insights into the dialogue between digital tools and humanistic research goals like recovery of historical materials, study of vast corpora, and trends in current cultural practices. Challenges for the claims to objectivity and scientific method remain—and one of the crucial questions is that of repeatable results. In many instances the repeated applications of tools of data mining and cultural analytics return shifted and changed outcomes. The corpus is unstable, for one thing, but the probabilistic character of processing contributes to this as well. Perhaps that is the most human aspect of what is otherwise a technological operation.

Exercises

Exercise #1: cultural analytics

Look at Lev Manovich's http://lab.softwarestudies.com/2008/09/cultural-analytics.html and design a project for which cultural analytics would be useful. Think in terms of the large scale of comparison and stay within humanities disciplines.

Exercise #2: sound files

Examine the project by Tanya Clement, Hipstas "John A. Lomax and Folklore Data." What are the ways in which these folklore files from the early 20th century become more useful as a result of the digital interventions? What other kinds of materials do you think would benefit from such research? https://hipstas.org/2015/05/11/john-a-lomax-and-folklore-data/

Exercise #3: media processing

If you were given the task of teaching an automated system to distinguish between news stories and advertisements in a television broadcast, what features would you identify for digital processing? Keep in mind that the task is to identify features that can be distinguished on the basis of their formal properties.

Notes

1 A look at the work of the Stanford Natural Processing Group, including analysis of their topics and tools, provides useful insight into this aspect of computational work.
2 See the Programming Historian for lessons on developing an API with Python. The lessons include information on downloading and installing Python and Flask to do this work.
3 A few useful tools for getting data from online sites include: Conifer, Beautiful Soup, and Webscraper.io.

Recommended readings

Bajorek, Joan Palmiter. 2019. "Voice Recognition Still Has Considerable Race and Gender Biases." *Harvard Business Review*. https://hbr.org/2019/05/voice-recognition-still-has-significant-race-and-gender-biases.

Manovich, Lev. 2011. "How to Compare One Million Images." *Cultural Analytics*. http://softwarestudies.com/cultural_analytics/2011.How_To_Compare_One_Million_Images.pdf.

Hartquist, John. 2018. "Audio Classification Using FastAI and On-the-Fly Frequency Transforms." *Towards Data Science*. https://towardsdatascience.com/audio-classification-using-fastai-and-on-the-fly-frequency-transforms-4dbe1b540f89.

Harwell, Drew. 2019. "Federal Study Confirms Racial Bias of Many Facial Recognition Systems." *Washington Post*. www.washingtonpost.com/technology/2019/12/19/federal-study-confirms-racial-bias-many-facial-recognition-systems-casts-doubt-their-expanding-use/.

References cited

Acerbi, Alberto, Vasileios Lampos, Philip Garnett, and R. Alexander Bentley. 2013. "The Expression of Emotions in 20th Century Books." *PLoS One* 8 (3). www.ncbi.nlm.nih.gov/pmc/articles/PMC3604170/.

Anderson, Steve. 2017. *Technologies of Vision*. Cambridge, MA: MIT Press.

Busa, Robert. 1980. "The Annals of Humanities Computing: The Index Thomisticus." www.alice.id.tue.nl/references/busa-1980.pdf.

Clement, Tanya. 2012. "Announcing High Performance Sound Technologies for Access." http://tanyaclement.org/2012/08/09/hipstas/ and https://hipstas.org/2015/05/11/john-a-lomax-and-folklore-data/.

Delice, Ali. 2010. "The Sampling Issues in Quantitative Research." *Educational Sciences: Theory and Practice* 10 (4). https://files.eric.ed.gov/fulltext/EJ919871.pdf.

Dunne, Carey. 2015. "Microsoft's New Emotion-Detecting App Deems the Mona Lisa 43% Happy." *Hyperallergic*. https://hyperallergic.com/261508/microsofts-new-emotion-detecting-app-deems-the-mona-lisa-43-happy/.

Fox, Neal, Omran Ehmodea, and Eugene Charniak. 2012. "Statistical Stylometrics and the Marlowe-Shakespeare Authorship Debate." https://cs.brown.edu/research/pubs/theses/masters/2012/ehmoda.pdf.

Giannakopoulos, Theodoros, and Aggelos Pikrakis. 2014. *Introduction to Audio Analysis*. Academic Press. www.sciencedirect.com/book/9780080993881/introduction-to-audio-analysis.

Guldi, Jo. 2018. "Critical Search: A Procedure for Guided Reading in Large-Scale Textual Corpora." *Journal of Cultural Analytics*. https://culturalanalytics.org/article/11028.

Hai-Jew, Shalin. 2015. "A Light Stroll through Computational Stylometry and its Early Potential." *C2C Digital Magazine*. https://scalar.usc.edu/works/c2c-digital-magazine-fall-winter-2016/a-light-stroll-through-computational-stylometry-and-its-early-potential.

Jofre, Ana, Josh Cole, Vincent Berardi, Carl Bennett, and Michael Reale. 2020. "What in a Face? Gender Representations of Faces in Time, 1940s-1990s." *Journal of Cultural Analytics*. https://doi.org/10.22148/oo1c.12266.

Kennedy, Helen, and Giles Moss.2015. "Known or Knowing Publics? Social Media Data Mining and the Question of Public Agency." *Big Data & Society* 2 (2), SAGE Publications Ltd. DOI: 10.1177/2053951715611145.

Kirschenbaum, Matthew G. n.d. "The Remaking of Reading: Data Mining and the Digital Humanities." www.academia.edu/35646247/The_remaking_of_reading_Data_mining_and_the_digital_humanities.

Kuhn, Virginia. 2018. "Images on the Move." In *The Routledge Companion to Media Studies and Digital Humanities Routledge*. New York: Routledge.

Lamarche, Stephen. 2012. *LARB*. Los Angeles, October. https://lareviewofbooks.org/article/literature-is-not-data-against-digital-humanities/.

Lee, Changsoo. 2019. "How Are 'Immigrant Workers' Represented in Korean News Reporting?—A Text Mining Approach to Critical Discourse Analysis." *Digital Scholarship in the Humanities* 34 (1): 82–99. DOI.org: 10.1093/llc/fqy017.

Mandell, Laura. 2019. "Gender and Cultural Analytics: Finding or Making Stereotypes?" In *Debates in Digital Humanities*. Minneapolis, MN: University of Minnesota Press. https://dhdebates.gc.cuny.edu/projects/debates-in-the-digital-humanities-2019.

Ogihara, Mitsunori, and George Tzanetakis. 2014. "Special Section on Music Data Mining." *IEEE Transactions on Multimedia* 16 (5): 1185–187. https://ieeexplore.ieee.org/document/6856270.

Patchet, François, Gert Westermann, and Damien Laigre. n.d. "Musical Data Mining for Electronic Music Distribution." www.music.mcgill.ca/~ich/classes/mumt621_09/Query%20Retrieval/Pachetwedelmusic.pdf.

Sandelowski, Margarete. 1995. "Sample Size in Qualitative Research." *Research in Nursing and Health*. https://onlinelibrary.wiley.com/doi/abs/10.1002/nur.4770180211.

Schmidt, Benjamin M. 2013. "Words Alone: Dismantling Topic Models in the Humanities." *Journal of Digital Humanities*. http://journalofdigitalhumanities.org/2-1/words-alone-by-benjamin-m-schmidt/.

Serlen, Rachel. 2010. "The Distant Future? Reading Franco Moretti." *Literature Compass* 7. https://warwick.ac.uk/fac/arts/english/currentstudents/undergraduate/modules/fulllist/special/en264/serlen_reading_franco_moretti.pdf.

So, Richard Jean, and Edwin Roland. 2020. "Race and Distant Reading." *PMLA* 135 (1): 59–73. www.mlajournals.org/doi/abs/10.1632/pmla.2020.135.1.59?journalCode=pmla.

Sculley, D., and B. M. Pasanek. 2008. "Meaning and Mining: The Impact of Implicit Assumptions in Data Mining for the Humanities." *Literary and Linguistic Computing* 23 (4): 409–24. DOI: 10.1093/llc/fqn019.

Terras, Melissa, and Julianne Nyhan. 2016. "Father Busa's Female Punch Card Operatives." In *Debates in the Digital Humanities*. Minneapolis, MN: University of Minnesota Press. http://dhdebates.gc.cuny.edu/debates/text/57.

Tilton, Lauren, Taylor Arnold, Thomas Smits, Mark Williams, Lorenzo Torresani, Maksim Bolonkin, John Bell, and Dimitrios Latsis. 2018. "Computer Vision in DH." In *Digital Humanities 2018*. Mexico City. https://dh2018.adho.org/computer-vision-in-dh/.

Underwood, Ted. 2017. "A Genealogy of Distant Reading." *Digital Humanities Quarterly* 11 (2). http://digitalhumanities.org:8081/dhq/vol/11/2/000317/000317.html.

Resources

API data creation https://programminghistorian.org/en/lessons/introduction-to-populating-a-website-with-api-data. and https://programminghistorian.org/en/lessons/creating-apis-with-python-and-flask.
Computer Vision (Heidelberg University) https://hci.iwr.uni-heidelberg.de/compvis/projects/digihum.
Cultural Analytics http://lab.culturalanalytics.info/p/projects.html.
Emulation https://libguides.bodleian.ox.ac.uk/digitalpreservation/emulation.
Image-Net www.image-net.org/.
Inscriptifact. www.inscriptifact.com/aboutus/index.shtml.
Natural Language Processing https://nlp.stanford.edu/software/.
Python (an introduction) https://wiki.python.org/moin/SimplePrograms.
Quantitative history http://historymatters.gmu.edu/mse/numbers/what.html.
R (an introduction) www.r-project.org/about.html.
Voyant. https://voyant-tools.org/.
Zotero www.zotero.org/.

8 Mapping and GIS

8a Getting started

To use maps effectively a few practical and critical considerations are essential. From a practical point of view, clarifying the relationship between maps and research is essential—is your project about the effect of *space* or is the map merely a convenient way to show *where* something happened? Is yours a historical project or a contemporary one? What kind of data is available for your project and to what extent does it lend itself to spatial presentation?

This section addresses practical issues and fundamentals for implementation. Critical issues in the representation of spatial experience will be the focus of the section that follows.

Getting started

The first step is to clarify what the maps are being used for and why in a project and what form the data will take, since this will inform the choice of tools and platforms for research (Sack 2017). As with all digital tools, those for mapping have matured considerably. They also range from quite simple platforms that can be used to make a map within a few minutes to extraordinarily complex programs that serve professional geographers working with spatial analysis of data.

Mapping tools are an integral part of political and social work with statistical information. They address demographics, resource management, infrastructure development, security concerns, and other issues. All of these have a human dimension, of course, but they tend to be far from the study of cultural artifacts and events that are central to the humanities. However, mapping tools clearly have a role to play in the study of history, culture, literature, and community activism, as will be clear from the examples discussed later. (White 2010)

While mapping platforms vary in complexity, all make use of a base-map, data points, and labels. Many use layers, legends (those keys to symbols that indicate landmarks and other features), and customizable graphic elements. Most basic mapping tools have excellent tutorials. One place to begin is with

Leaflet—though even using this relatively easy platform will likely require assistance at the outset. In addition well-designed lessons from within the digital humanities community provide an introduction to the vocabulary and range of practices in this area. Keep in mind that many mapping tools are not designed for web presentation, but for analysis and publication. Other platforms are entirely web-based and allow data to be uploaded and used on their sites (these are rarely private or secure, so that should be kept in mind). [See Exercise #1: QGIS and Leaflet applications.]

Start by looking at the documentation of a platform like Leaflet or QGIS. The contrast between them is educational. QGIS begins with data. Its features are designed with attention to the analytic functionality of its platform, leading with data types and formats specific to geospatial information work. Leaflet focuses on the graphical components and research behaviors they support: maps, layers, controls, and graphical features and utilities. Leaflet assumes you want to make a map and show things on it. Either can be used to show information that is specific to geographical data.

No matter what platform or tool is used, a few elements will be common to all: selection of a base map, the possibility of layers to selectively contain information, a way to create or use symbols and define them in a legend, and methods of displaying and working with data in an appropriate format. All mapping tools will require that data contain geographical coordinates (Gregory, Donaldson, and Hardie 2018). The only exception to this is if a map is simply being used as a picture (in which case, geospatial information tools are not needed; symbols, annotation, and other elements can simply be added as they would be to any other image).

Conceptualizing a mapping project

The conceptual work of a project drives the decisions about tools. Having an understanding of the specific capacities of spatial analysis will expand the possibilities of the research. But the platforms just mentioned, and other GIS tools, were developed to support spatial data and its analysis and display. Grasping what this means will set the intellectual framework for a project. A map can be made in minutes in Google Maps without prior experience, but the challenge is to understand *why* a map is useful. What *kind* of map should it be? What aspects of the *research* are *geographical*, *spatial*, or *related to the maps themselves*? Is information in the map essential to the research, or just a presentation format, or is the map itself an object of study? Are you trying to answer a research question based on what the map shows or geospatial data you can generate from its features? If you were analyzing how a particular railroad route was planned, the height of mountains, width of rivers, or presence of lakes would be relevant. You may simply be showing *where* something happened: Napoleon was defeated in battle at Waterloo. Or you may be asking how various features of the spatial experience contributed to that defeat. How will it be used—in static or dynamic form? Online or in print? What kind of data is available to populate the map?

The list below describes ways in which maps are used in humanities research. It is not exhaustive, but it provides a starting point for thinking through different aspects of the use of maps. The purpose of using a map in the project might be to:

- *Show* something on a map.

To show something on a map consider what will be shown and what map is appropriate. The ease of using Google Maps makes the web application attractive. But even in the most basic mapping project, questions about the kind of map are significant. Does it show roads and transportation networks or physical features of the landscape? Are administrative borders and boundaries marked, cities and towns, or elevation and other topographical details? Is it a historical map or a recent one? Many more such questions can be asked since maps are often designed for particular purposes and needs.

- *Analyze* an aspect of spatial experience.

Questions about how far things are from each other, how long it takes to move between them, what natural and social features exist to define a region or locale, and how space factors into patterns of culture all raise issues specific to spatial experience. These intersect with matters such as accessibility, transportation, isolation, communication, and development patterns, as well as the values of land and location in relation to status, class, value, and symbolic issues (myth and ritual). Separating those features of research that are actually *spatial* from those that are *incidentally* related to space by location is crucial. *Where something is* might not be a spatial issue—but *how long it takes to get there* might be.

- *Narrate* an event using a map or maps to present the argument.

Many historical events take place in space or in locations—battles, conquests, and struggles over territory, but also disease, development, and transformations of infrastructure. These can be shown and narrated using maps. Again the question is whether the map merely provides a reference frame (*this* is *where* something took place) or whether the location had an active role in the events (the spatial features of the location *played a part* in what occurred: think of the scholar scenario in Chapter 1 focused on the Caribbean island slave rebellion). If the location played a role, then is a flat map adequate to show how the physical features of the place factored into the event?

- *Interpret* a map as a historical and critical form.

A map can be an object of research in its own right. How does it present an understanding of a territory? Through what means was it constructed?

It might contain vivid graphical features in iconographic form, showing houses, streets, churches, graveyards, and roads that no longer exist. It may contain mythical and symbolic images—sea monsters, dragons, or outsized renderings of other flora and fauna. For humanities scholars, these features are important aspects of the map's identity and information. Place names also contain historical information, and the extraction of this information from a historical map might be crucial for studying language, cultural issues, and other matters in addition to the geographical details of a place.

- *Create* a map from place-based references.

Many literary works and primary documents contain references to places. These may or may not correspond to actual or once existing places, but culling these from a work to create a map of the narrative can create an image of a place from references. Rather than using a map as a pre-existing structure in which to place events, this process allows a location to emerge from geographical references. Finding ways to express knowledge embodied in a text allows literary and literal aspects of geography to complement each other.

- *Employ* coordinate data or use the map as a picture.

Many historical maps are pictures. They are images that depict knowledge of a territory or symbolic and metaphoric representations. But whether they have fanciful or mythic details, all maps used in connection with geographical coordinates or geographically coded information have to have this information attached to them. Another crucial consideration is the size, scope, and scale (relation of the size of the map to the actual space it represents). The map needs to show the geographical context—region, nation, continent, and hemisphere—in a manner that is adequate for the argument.

All digital mapping projects that use spatial data rely on GIS (Geographic Information Systems) platforms to create their argument, analysis, and/or presentations. [See Exercise #2: Storymaps.]

Using GIS

As noted above, the acronym GIS stands for Geographic Information Systems. These systems are designed to integrate maps with data for analysis and presentation. GIS systems were not developed for the humanities, but to map natural and social phenomena. GIS systems embody certain positivist assumptions that privilege physical reality over social and cultural experience (Pickles n.d.). Humanists have adopted these tools and platforms for research about places and spatial experience. [See Exercise #3: Spatial scholarship.]

Humanists also study maps as cultural artifacts, interpreting their representation of spatial and geographical phenomena. Early maps of exploration, for instance, tend to favor detail about coastline features, rather than knowledge of a landmass's interior, while Indigenous mapping may have very little information about coasts and borders and focus instead on pathways and ritual sites. GIS systems were not made to accommodate the rhetorical specifics of many of these maps or the spatial experience they record.

Georectification and georeferencing

Since many historical and non-standard maps were not made according to a specific standard system, they must be assigned spatial coordinates to be useful. This process is called *georectification*. Take the example of a hand-drawn map given to you by a friend to guide your driving route to their house. Now consider putting it into digital form so it can also be matched to a map application on your phone. Similar issues arise with maps of early explorers finding the New World that need to be matched to modern latitude and longitude coordinates. Problems will arise that require decisions about how to proceed with fitting one system to another.

Even maps that have coordinate systems need to be "referenced" to a particular standard so that the coordinates are legible within the digital environment. This process is called *georeferencing*. Other adjustments to maps allow shapes and distortions to be "corrected" and aligned with different coordinate systems. While georectification and georeferencing might treat the file of a map as a picture with two axes, other forms of correction need to treat the map as a set of shapes described in a data format.

Geocoding information

Another common task in translating textual material to maps is that of finding coordinates for named locations. Suppose you have a long list of place names, perhaps the homes of authors, or sites on a pilgrimage, or locations in a novel, or a collection of letters. The most common way of placing these on a map using a digital application is to assign them longitude and latitude values. This can be done automatically using geocoding web services that assign coordinates. Such automated work (Google Maps has one such service) always needs to be checked. In spite of the sophistication of the libraries that check place names and assess the probability of their occurrence, locations can end up in odd places. If something looks odd, it may well be wrong. (Did Santa really go to the *South* Pole at the end of his flight? Probably not on the same night as he was in all those other places. Dancer and Prancer might have gotten their coordinates confused.)

Visual formats and data types

Shape files and pixel images are two ways of creating and storing information for mapping. (These distinctions hold true in other visualizations as well, as per Section 6a.) Shape files carry geospatial vector data. That allows the specific descriptions of geographical area to be mapped and also transferred from one GIS platform to another. These are vector-based files, which can be readily scaled and resized without losing their shape. Pixel based images are like tapestries, they record color and value, but they do not identify shapes. They may be given coordinate data, but that requires georeferencing. Each has advantages. Pixel-based images work well for maps that are being used as images, as historical references, or for presentation of information layered onto a base map. These do not require the areas of the map be analyzed as shapes since they will not be manipulated independently. For work that requires analysis or modeling, vector-based graphics are essential. The graphical format will play a role in how it can be altered. For changing shape and area, shape files are the best. For merely attaching coordinates to the map as an image, the pixel-based or "raster" format is fine. These two formats will be discussed again below.

The data used in mapping generally defines points, lines, or areas. Again, a pixel-based image can readily position a point or line within the axes of its implied grid, just as if it were putting a marker on a tic-tac-toe board. But the calculation of area—particularly features of boundaries and edges—might be better achieved with a vector graphic. A pixel-image can work like a jigsaw puzzle piece and be as complex in form as it needs to be, but it cannot be manipulated as a shape, just copied, pasted, and moved.

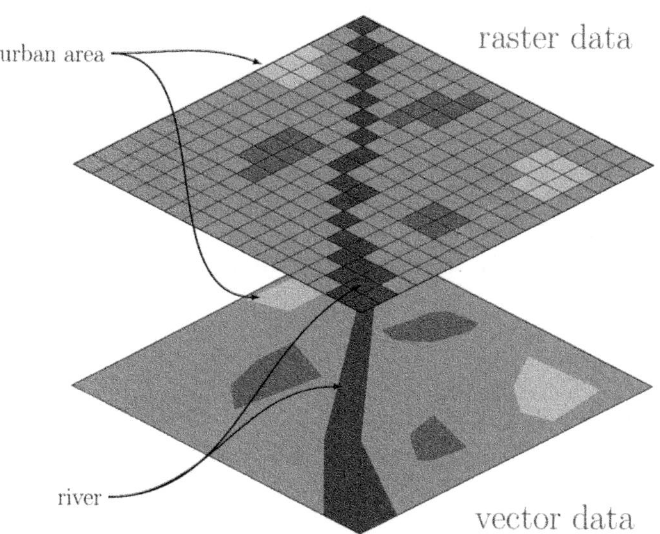

Figure 8.1 Note that rasters are pixel maps with individual values for each spot while vectors are point-to-point lines that describe shapes (CC license).

Source: (Image courtesy of GNU license N—CC BY-SA 3.0.)

Maps have their own graphic logic and conventions. For instance, administrative boundaries are often used to display demographic information linked to populations. But when the results of opinion polls are mapped, should they be displayed by coloring the entire area inside the boundaries of the counties or nations, by points showing distribution, or in a shape proportional to the percentages? The term *chloropleth* refers to those maps in which entire areas are given a color value (counties, states, countries) to show thematic information aggregated by region. In some cases, this may make sense, as when a candidate wins an election and wins a state. But in mapping consumer preferences, perhaps more precise counts and locations are significant. If you are trying to track an epidemic, then transportation networks as well as population centers and points of contact are important. Natural phenomena (insect invasions, weather, migratory patterns, etc.) do not regard national boundaries, but are regularly presented on maps that mark these strongly—sometimes even cutting countries out from continents. Because area is a feature of geography, its connection to data should be correlated closely. When area is made to represent quantity (size of population in a city) as well as geography (the size of a region), this becomes confusing since the graphical value is being used in two different ways.

Datatypes: CSV, GeoJSON, and KML

The easiest, simplest way to store geographical *coordinate* information is in a spread sheet, exported as. csv. Place name, latitude, and longitude are the basics of geospatial data. A standard format for geospatial information is KML, Keyhole Markup Language. As a markup language, and a flavor of XML, it has the advantage of being highly descriptive, domain specific, and being a broadly adopted standard. However, given the popularity of JSON for storing data, the development of GeoJSON comes as no surprise. Like KML, GeoJSON is relatively user-friendly, which is to say, human readable, in its formal syntax and expressions.

Here are examples of the same information in KML and GeoJSON:

KML:

```
<?xml version=“1.0” encoding=“UTF-8”?><kml xmlns=“www.opengis.
net/kml/2.2”>
<Document><Placemark><ExtendedData><Data name=“LOCATION”
><value>Bridgeport</value></Data>
<Data name=“DAY”><value>Saturday</value></Data><Data
name=“Map”><value>(41.83081542, -87.64123528)</value>
</Data></ExtendedData><Point><coordinates>-87.64123528,41.83081
542</coordinates></Point>
</Placemark><Placemark><ExtendedData><Data
name=“LOCATION”><value>Seaway Bank Farmer’s Market</value></
Data>
```

<Data name="DAY"><value>Wednesday</value></Data><Data name="Map"><value>(41.73649711, -87.60784689)</value></Data>
</ExtendedData>

Same file in GeoJSON:

{
"type": "FeatureCollection",
"name": "farmers_markets",
"crs": {"type": "name", "properties": {"name": "urn:ogc:def:crs:OGC:1.3:CRS84"}},
"features": [
{"type": "Feature", "properties": {"Name": null, "description": null, "LOCATION": "Bridgeport", "DAY": "Saturday", "Map": "(41.83081542, -87.64123528)"}, "geometry": {"type": "Point", "coordinates": [-87.64123528, 41.83081542]}},
{"type": "Feature", "properties": {"Name": null, "description": null, "LOCATION": "Seaway Bank Farmer's Market", "DAY": "Wednesday", "Map": "(41.73649711, -87.60784689)"}, "geometry": {"type": "Point", "coordinates": [-87.60784689, 41.73649711]}},

Look at the differences between the data structures here. The tags in the KML sample are easy to read, as are their attributes. The GeoJSON structure is slightly more specialized in its elements. Both are nested hierarchies with terms used to disambiguate information stored in their formats.

Maps as rhetoric

Many digital humanities projects use mapping. Looking at a few will provide some evidence of the ways they function as arguments. [See Exercise #4: Gallery of projects.]

One straightforward demonstration of the use of GIS is the *Chinese Civilization in Time and Space* project (Fan n.d.). Its historical information is distinctly geographical and map-related. For instance, one of its maps shows "Changes of the Administrative Boundaries," within China between 210 BCE and 1996. Another shows the changing meander of the Yellow River, different locations of the capital, and changing place names. This information is fundamentally geographic. Mapping it required sequencing the data for an animated display.

By contrast, *Torn Apart/Separados* uses a map to connect the actions of the United States ICE (Immigration and Customs Enforcement) and elected officials, business interests, and displaced populations (Xpmethod Group 2018). The project uses maps to pinpoint the location of elected officials and compare them with the sites of deportation and removal in the United States. The project tracks money channeled into various businesses (small, minority owned and large corporate enterprises). The issues of their locations are more complex than that of the site of the capital of China at any given moment in time. The interpretation of the ICE information addresses government practices, such as the difficulty of seeing how quickly the situation was changing. The project faced challenges with privacy issues (difficulty in using data without de-anonymizing it). Other obstacles were conceptual, such as identifying who in the media was discussing the issue and understanding the relationship of media personalities to spatial information.

In another contrast, *Troubled Geographies: A Spatial History of Religion and Society in Ireland* is a multi-faceted study of distinctly spatial information about the country (Gregory et al. 2013). The maps show the impact of various events—famine, war, and partition—on the population of Ireland before it was divided and after. The maps begin with the first census in 1821. The most recent data was from 2001. The maps are driven by demographic data—percentages of the population by religion, degrees of literacy, patterns of farming, and so on. The data is collected at the county level, and location is a factor in the cultural patterns from which the information is abstracted.

Offering a further contrast, the Frankenstein Atlas project is literary, rather than historical (Kelly 2018). The study links place names in a novel to a 19th-century "Gazeteer," or list of places. The project contains maps produced *from* the textual analysis—such as a polar voyage described in the final sections of the book—as well as historical materials contemporary with the novel's composition. The project contains thorough documentation of the approach and method. This includes the markup scheme (see Section 4b) and detailed discussions of the source materials for geographical study that would have been available to author Mary Shelley in her lifetime. The project begins to address—and attempt to visualize—conceptions of space and geography that informed the literary project, not merely to put pins on a map.

As GIS tools and platforms have penetrated the humanities community, many activists and researchers concerned with social justice issues have made use of these methods (Bond 2017). The systematic character of inequity becomes vividly clear when mapped. The "Anti-Eviction Mapping Project" demonstrates this forcefully (McElroy 2018). So does the mapping of the disproportionate exposure of people of color to toxic pollution by Samantha Teixara and Anita Zubieri (2016). This kind of environmental injustice is a dramatic example of the ways GIS can be an instrument for transformation.

Those critical of GIS attack it on epistemological grounds as a system that approaches physical space unproblematically and as an instrument of managerial interests, government and business entities, whose ethos is fundamentally opposed to that of the humanities (Harley 1989). While the positivist underpinnings of GIS make it less useful for understanding inhabitation and experience, its apparent objectivity makes for a powerful presentation of arguments. Important debates about whether technologies created within frameworks of hegemonic power can be turned effectively on the forces of oppression—or whether entirely new instruments need to be developed from radically different positions of power—are ongoing. But clearly, GIS is also being used in the service of public information and policy.

Critical assessment criteria

Maps are used most effectively when several crucial criteria are considered in the conceptualization and implementation of a project. These include choosing the right base map for the data and thinking about how the interpretation will be codified and presented. Including primary documents, narration, and interpretative frameworks guides the viewer through the argument, but allowing direct access to data can also offer useful insights for scholars interested in methods. Documentation of projects provides the way to understand how the design was arrived at, what decisions about technical methods were made, and why.

At the beginning of a GIS project, consider these factors:

- What is the base map and is it anachronistic in relation to the data? Does it show features of the landscape that would not have been present at the time of the events?
- Is the base map focused on roads, rivers, and other transportation routes? Or on geological and physical features? Does it map administrative boundaries? Or show cultural aspects of an area? Is the map suited to the project or was it merely a convenience?
- What layers exist and how do they support the base map? Are they concise? Is the data evident? Can you toggle the layers easily? What data belongs on which layer?
- What kinds of data are being mapped? Are they mainly coordinate points? Or do they have a spatial dimension in which the location is a dynamic aspect of the events shown?
- Is the map still working or are there notices about errors, missing plug-ins, or other absent functionality?
- Can you see the data and its structure? What elements were codified in the data? Was it created in a markup language, in GeoJSON, or a spread-sheet, and what custom fields were defined by the researchers?
- Was the data quantitative or qualitative and how were these given graphical expression?
- Does the map serve as a picture of a location or as an informative element of the research? If the map is a historical map, have its features been connected to a contemporary coordinate system?
- How are elements of spatial experience communicated in the project—through narration, visualization, or primary documents?
- If pop-up windows are used to display comments and/or documents (images, correspondence, newspapers etc.), do they block the view of the map? How effective is the connection between the depiction of space or geography and the display?

Takeaway

Geospatial information can be readily codified and displayed in a variety of geographical platforms. All mapping systems are based on projections that translate three-dimensional forms to two-dimensional representations and contain distortions. The assumptions built into the representations should be made evident within the arguments for which they are used, preferably with interpretative materials and documentation. Current research using GIS demonstrates that in spite of its origins within a positivist techno-industrial framework, its tools and platforms can be usefully put to work in serving to expose social injustice and to galvanize activism and awareness. All GIS systems will contain similar elements so understanding the basic vocabulary of these systems is essential.

Exercises

Exercise #1: QGIS and Leaflet applications

This QGIS (Quantum GIS) tutorial from finding, downloading, and installing, to use and print is clear and easy to follow: https://gisgeography.com/how-to-make-a-map-gis-free/ Leaflet is another popular, easy-to-use, platform and also has its own tutorials: https://leafletjs.com/

Exercise #2: storymaps

Embedding maps in a historical narrative can be compelling. Consider the advantages and some of the challenges or liabilities in such projects? https://collections.storymaps.esri.com/humanities/

Exercise #3: spatial scholarship

https://spatial.scholarslab.org/stepbystep/

For more resources along these lines, look at Anthony Sanchez, Storytelling, Spatialization, and Open Source Spatial Data https://libguides.library.arizona.edu/dighumantools/maps

Exercise #4: gallery of projects

https://anterotesis.com/wordpress/mapping-resources/dh-gis-projects/

Look through some of the projects in this list and see how they meet the criteria outlined above. Which are still working, which are not, and how effectively do they integrate research issues, data, maps, and arguments?

Orbis
http://orbis.stanford.edu/

Gulag Online
www.gulag.online/places?locale=en

Historypin.org
www.historypin.org/en/

Artists in Paris
www.artistsinparis.org/

Atlantic Networks Projects
https://sites.google.com/site/atlanticnetworksproject/

Legacies of British Slave-ownership
www.ucl.ac.uk/lbs/maps/

HGIS de las Indias
www.hgis-indias.net/cmv-app-master/viewer/

Yellow Star Houses in Budapest
www.yellowstarhouses.org/

Recommended readings

Bond, Sarah Emily. 2017. "Mapping Racism and Assessing the Digital Humanities." *History from Below.* https://sarahemilybond.com/2017/10/20/mapping-racism-and-assessing-the-success-of-the-digital-humanities/.

Elwood, Sarah, and Agnieszka Leszczynski. 2018. "Feminist Digital Geographies." *Gender, Place, and Culture* 25 (5). https://doi.org/10.1080/0966369X.2018.1465396.

Harley, J. B. 1989. "Deconstructing the Map." *Cartographia* 26 (2): 1–20.

McLafferty, Sarah. 2002. "Mapping Women's Worlds: Knowledge, Power and the Bounds of GIS." *Gender, Place, and Culture* 3: 263–69. www.researchgate.net/publication/233073842_Mapping_Women's_Worlds_Knowledge_power_and_the_bounds_of_GIS.

8b Critical issues in spatial humanities

As we have noted, maps are highly conventionalized representations that provide for the presentation of *geographical information* or data with spatial dimensions. While maps come with many distortions, learning how to use GIS (Geographic Information Systems) exposes the assumptions encoded in maps of all kinds. The digitization process reinforces certain kinds of attitudes toward knowledge, not only because of the formats of geospatial data, or the specific graphical properties of maps, but also built-in assumptions about space. How does one create a record of an embodied experience of space when maps often position the viewer above or outside of the geography?

In the humanities, GIS is used to show experience and cultural patterns that are encoded in geospatial information. For example, these might chart demographics, display historical events, or chart travel narratives. Other research might question the ways in which space is constructed as an effect of activity or experience, taking into account differences across populations with regard to gender, race, ability, class, and other factors. How do different individuals experience a neighborhood or transit route? What can we learn from mapping the affective dimensions of spatial knowledge? Whose memory is marked or recorded on a map, and whose is erased and rendered invisible? [See Exercise #1: Comparing historical records.]

Digital humanists understand that the "spatial turn" is not merely about mapping (Bodenhammer, Corrigan, and Harris 2017). Asking even the simplest question about space raises cultural issues and ethical ones immediately. How big is a particular city block and how is its location specified? Blocks differ dramatically in their metric dimensions, but also, in the way they are experienced. If the only system applied is that of latitude and longitude, then how are the cultural factors in an urban environment to be codified? A block might be extremely long for a woman walking alone at night and very short for a young man on a skateboard in the morning. On a cold day, a hot day, or during a protest, the space changes. Like all systems of measure, geographical instruments embody assumptions and values in their standards.

An entire subfield exists in geography—termed *non-representational geography* by one of its initial theorists, Nigel Thrift (Thrift 2007). The term refers to the idea of modeling space *from* experience, rather than making an assumption that space exists as a neutral container. Do the woman and young man mentioned above occupy the same space differently, or do they actually experience *different spaces*? For an ethical humanist, the study of social factors is a component of spatial experience. How would maps *look* if they were created from experience? These approaches have yet to find a full expression in digital graphics or data models. Spatial humanities is concerned with *inhabitation* and *experience*, not simply *location*.

Additionally, we have the question of what happens when mapping turns symbolic events or imaginative narratives into literal geography. When James Joyce wrote his novel, *Ulysses*, and had his character wander through Dublin, he did not describe the Irish city in literal terms. Metaphor and symbolic language abound in the novel and the place references play many roles, they are not reducible to points on a map.

Sacred spaces and their connections to ritual practices are also not able to be mapped simply by locating coordinates. The Kaaba in the Sacred Mosque at Mecca has geographical coordinates, but its symbolic value as a place expands across the globe, orienting daily rituals. The way a place is to be approached, who may or may not trespass on its terrain, and what behaviors are permitted in a particular precinct are all components of cultural space. The challenge of mapping aura and symbolic value remains. The symbolic impact of referencing all mile markers in the Roman Empire to their distance from the capital city is hard to ignore. Indigenous experience of the land does not match western mapping techniques (Watson and Yolngu community n.d.).

Mapping is done on a rational grid—no matter what form of projection it takes. This makes showing the impact of emotional experience—trauma, familiarity, or memory—difficult. Spatial experience is subjective, but much remains to be done to develop affective representations of spatial experience within humanistic frameworks.

A note about cartography

The field of cartography possesses critical and technical expertise in mapping. It has a long history, stretching to Egyptian and Babylonian mapmakers several millennia before the Common Era. The principle that unites the earliest mapmaking with cartographic practices in the present is the recognition that all maps are *projections*. The mapping of any section of the round globe of the earth onto a two-dimensional surface always results in distortion of one factor among several: distance, area, or shape. The study of cartographic conventions and their history is a field unto itself. But having some basic understanding of the implications of projection systems—how they distort—is helpful in thinking about maps from the most esoteric historical primary source to the banal but still problematic Google Maps application.

Maps are considered *conformal* if they preserve the shape of landmasses and water areas. This will always depend on the point of view from which the map is made. Different projections preserve shapes better at various latitudes. Some maps distort area to preserve other features: the Mercator projection, invented in the 16th century but still the basis of many maps, is created on a grid of lines that align with compass directions (true north, south etc.). In Mercator maps, the sizes of northern hemisphere land masses are particularly exaggerated. Other more recent innovations, such as cylindrical projection (invented in the 1960s by Arthur H. Robinson) have been invented to correct for various distortions.

Consider the features of Google Earth (satellite images)—that they show every area of the earth in daylight. Even in the satellite view of the earth, country boundaries are indicated as light lines imposed on the landmasses.[1] The photographic realism of the rendering suggests that we are looking at *the world* and not at a representation of it, but those lines don't exist on the earth. The omniscient view is also problematic. Google Maps, by contrast, is meant to provide support for navigation, travel directions, and daily use. It allows instant views of any place as if they were all equally accessible (Madrigal 2012). Google Maps is constantly being updated, which means that information about the built environment (street views, routes, etc.) is always being surveilled by Google.

Like all human artifacts, maps contain assumptions that embody cultural values. Even their orientation can have a symbolic value. For instance, maps common in the European Middle Ages positioned the known continents of Asia, Africa, and Europe with Jerusalem at their center. When we take a map of 17th century London or 5th century Rome, or an Aboriginal map drawing, and try to reconcile it to a digital map using standards that are part of our contemporary geographical coordinate system, we are making a profound, even violent, intervention in the worldview of the original. Whether we are working with materials in the present and forcing them into a single geographical representation system, or using materials from the inventory of past presentations in map formats, we are always in the situation of taking one already interpreted version of the world and pushing it into yet another interpretative framework. [See Exercise #2: Cartographic conventions.]

In western conventions, most maps portray the earth with the northern hemisphere at the top. Nothing in the physical world requires this to be the case. The earth turns on its axis, but this motion could be observed just as surely with the south pole at the top. Conventions become so naturalized that their ideological impact disappears. Researching map conventions provides insight into cultural differences and conceptions of space and geography. One of the challenges for humanists is to shift the perspective from that of *omniscience*—a viewpoint from a neutral outside position—to one of *experience*, situated within the conditions of lived persons.

Space and place

In environmental studies, a contrast is made between concepts of "space" as a physical environment and "place" as an experiential one. In addition, in the work of Edward Soja and others, the concept of space as an "artifact" or construction has arisen out of the already mentioned approach to "non-representational" geography (Blake 2001). In this approach, space is a construct, not a given, and comes into being through the activities of experience. These are not concepts that have found their way into digital projects to any large degree, and they pose challenges for the visual tools of mapping that we have at our disposal at present. However, the notion of space as an artifact versus that of space as a "given" that can be represented is profoundly important for humanistic work, even if the mapping platforms that come from more empirical sciences do not accommodate its principles. [See Exercise #3: Strange maps.]

One example of this constructed approach is the TubeMap made by Tom Carden (n.d.). Based on the famous schematic map of the London Underground, Carden's map distorts the length of each individual route to reflect the amount of time it takes to go from one point to another within the system. This is a finely defined project, and makes its point dramatically in the visual presentation.

Recent work on the relations between race and spatial experience address these issues more radically, building on the understanding of spatial constructed-ness as rooted in individual experience (Shabazz 2015). Work at

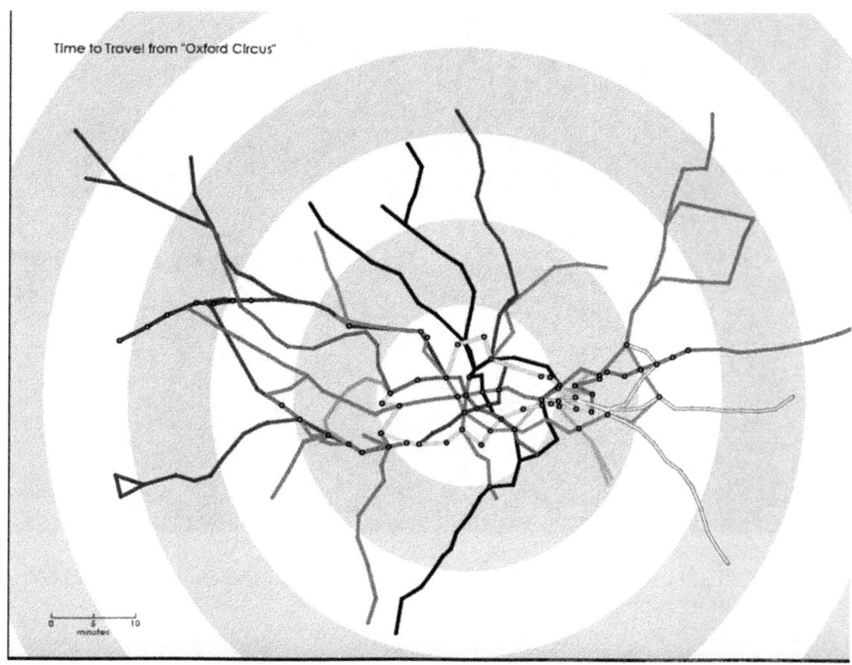

Figure 8.2 Tom Carden's Tube Map georeferenced for a time factor (Image by permission of Tom Carden.)

the cutting edge of such research grapples with ways to codify and structure data on topics of race (Teixara and Zubieri 2016). What constitutes the markers of racism, white supremacy, legacies of oppression, and how are they to be shown and seen in maps? How do settler maps erase Indigenous knowledge (Vélez 2017)? *Showing* the qualitative experience of space in a system designed for the display of quantitative information poses challenges. Information can be mapped, but how does the effect on space get shown? Feminist geographers have long advocated for a change in visualization techniques (Kwan 2002) (Lindeborg 2017). [See: Exercise #4: Mapping Indigenous knowledge.]

Laura Kurgan's *Million Dollar Blocks* project makes use of data from the criminal justice system to map the relations between incarceration and urban neighborhoods (Kurgan 2006). The project dramatically calls attention to the systemic inequities that racialize the criminal justice system and uses maps to connect this to urban demographics. While the maps are used to present data in the form of a graphic argument, they also de-neutralize the spatial presentation, turning the grid of city streets into a highly charged environment. Recognizing that spatial relations are active agents of social change and events, including social influence, cultural transmission, and

Figure 8.3 Laura Kurgan, Million Dollar Blocks, Prison Expenditures in Brooklyn (Image by permission of Laura Kurgan.)

epidemics, humanistic geographers are working to reconceptualize the role of space in every area of geopolitics. One project where these approaches have found considerable traction is in *Mapping Borderlands*, focused on charged arenas of cultural exchange whose shifting status emerges from and greatly impacts human populations.

Storytelling and narrative mapping

Spatial experience and maps are not always perfectly matched to each other. The individual connection to landscape and its effect on imagination often need to be expressed in narrative, not merely in maps. *Mapping the Lakes* is an experiment in showing the situated experience of two different English poets in the Lake District in northwest England (Gregory and Bushell n.d.). Journals of two renowned British poets formed the source texts: Thomas Gray's 1769 tour and Samuel Taylor Coleridge's 1802 accounts. Researchers developed a limited tag set for marking "visited," "unvisited," and "unknown" attributes for the sites. The researchers noted the need to develop a way for the GIS system to represent "the imagined, as well as the actual, experience" of these places.

One platform developed for narrative and mapping, Neatline, was designed specifically for the purpose of allowing documents and commentary to be embedded in a map. The project builds on Omeka, a platform designed for content management and web presentation, particularly within humanities work. The *Black Liberation Archive* project, "Mapping the Sit-In," used the same platform to link a narrative timeline linked to a base map and a collection of documents related to a 1969 protest of Black students at Swarthmore College. The map is meant to create a clear sense of location, and to track the activities of the students in activities related to their protest agenda. The conceptual challenge is to recreate the point of view of those who lived the experience. The other challenge is technical, which is to keep these resources updated and functional. Outmoded plug-ins, broken links, and obsolete, no longer functioning platforms condemn a great deal of research to oblivion.

Takeaway

Maps are highly effective instruments for locating data in relation to geography. However, they are less effective in showing the qualitative experience of space. Theoretical positions advocating recognition of the situatedness and specificity of spatial experience have been developed in critical race studies, queer theory, feminist work, and disability studies. But finding a graphic language to encode the embodied and situated experience of individuals across a wide array of diverse identities has met many challenges. The rational underpinnings of coordinate systems in maps and in their digital counterparts in GIS make it difficult to introduce methods of showing the subjective character of spatial experience. Humanities scholars continue to explore the possibilities of interpretative systems through which to analyze, narrate, and visualize spatial experience across a wide array of perspectives.

Exercises

Exercise #1: comparing historical records

Compare the maps of emancipation in the American Civil War with patterns of lynching in the United States. How do the maps assist in analysis? https://dsl.richmond.edu/emancipation/ and https://lynchinginamerica.eji.org/

Exercise #2: cartographic projections

Look at this gallery of projections and familiarize yourself with their distortions: www.icsm.gov.au/education/fundamentals-mapping/projections/commonly-used-map-projections

Exercise #3: strange maps

Look at these "strange" maps for inspiration: http://bigthink.com/blogs/strange-maps

Exercise #4: mapping indigenous knowledge

Compare these two projects for their approach to mapping Indigenous knowledge and experience: Maps are Territories http://territories.indigenousknowledge.org/

Perspectives on A Selection of Gabrieleño/Tongva Places from UCLA Mapping Indigenous LA (https://mila.ss.ucla.edu/)

Note

1 For a sobering experience, see the timelapse of GoogleEarth over the last thirty-five years. https://earthengine.google.com/timelapse/

Recommended readings

Rashad Shabazz. 2015. *Spatializing Blackness: Architecture of Confinement and Black Masculinity in Chicago*. Champaign and Urbana: University of Illinois Press. www.jstor.org/stable/10.5406/j.ctt16ptnhh.

Ljubicic, Gita J., et al. 2014. "Chapter 14 — The Creation of the Inuit Siku (Sea Ice) Atlas." In *Modern Cartography Series*, edited by D. R. Fraser Taylor, Vol. 5, 201–18. Academic Press. ScienceDirect. DOI: 10.1016/B978-0-444-62713-1.00014-3.

References cited

Blake, Emma. 2001. "Spatiality Past and Present: An Interview with Edward Soja." *Journal of Social Archaeology*. https://journals.sagepub.com/doi/abs/10.1177/1469605302002002964.

Bodenhammer, David, John Corrigan, and Trevor M. Harris 2017. *The Spatial Humanities: GIS and the Future of Humanities Scholarship*. Bloomington, IN: Indiana University Press. https://sarahemilybond.com/2017/10/20/mapping-racism-and-assessing-the-success-of-the-digital-humanities/.

Carden, Tom. n.d. www.tom-carden.co.uk/p5/tube_map_travel_times/applet/.

Fan, I-chun. n.d. "Chinese Civilization in Time and Space." http://ccts.ascc.net/framework.php?lang=en.

Gregory, Ian, and Sally Bushell. n.d. "Mapping the Lakes." www.lancaster.ac.uk/mappingthelakes/Research%20Outcomes.html.

Gregory, Ian, Niall A. Cunningham, D. C. Lloyd, Ian G. Shuttelworth, and Paul S. Eli. 2013. "Troubled Geographies: A Spatial History of Religion and Society in Ireland." www.lancaster.ac.uk/troubledgeogs/map_series.htm.

Gregory, Ian, Christopher Donaldson, and Andrew Hardie. 2018. "Modeling Space in Historical Texts." In *The Shape of Data in the Digital Humanities*, edited by Julia Flanders and Fotis Jannidis, 133–49. New York and London: Routledge. DOI: 10.4324/9781315552941-5.

Kelly, Jason M. 2018. "A Frankenstein Atlas." www.jasonmkelly.com/frankensteinatlas.

Kurgan, Kurgan. 2006. *Multiple Journalism*. http://multiplejournalism.org/case/million-dollar-blocks.

Kwan, Mei-Po. 2002. "Feminist Visualization: Re-envisioning GIS as a Method in Feminist Geographic Research." In *Department of Geography*. Ohio State University. http://people.ucalgary.ca/~rjacobso/W_PAPERS/Technology,%20community, polity/Kwan%20article.pdf.

Lindeborg, Elina. 2017. "Gendered Spatial Realities." Thesis. Department of Human Geography. https://pdfs.semanticscholar.org/d662/ddf4478c3d7534af c33f0ced4c648e156163.pdf.

Madrigal, Alexis C. 2012. "How Google Builds Its Maps—and What It Means for the Future of Everything." *The Atlantic*. www.theatlantic.com/technology/archive/2012/09/how-google-builds-its-maps-and-what-it-means-for-the-future-of-everything/261913/.

McElroy, Erin. 2018. "The Digital Humanities, American Studies, and the Anti-Eviction Mapping Project." *American Quarterly* 70 (3): 701–7, Johns Hopkins University Press. DOI: 10.1353/aq.2018.0055.

Pickles, J. n.d. www.geos.ed.ac.uk/~gisteac/gis_book_abridged/files/ch04.pdf.

Sack, C. 2017. "Web Mapping." In *The Geographic Information Science & Technology Body of Knowledge*, edited by John P. Wilson. DOI: 10.22224/gistbok/2017.4.11.

Teixara, Samantha, and Anita Zubieri. 2016. "Mapping the Racial Inequality in Place." *International Journal of Environmental Research and Public Health* 13 (9): 844. www.ncbi.nlm.nih.gov/pmc/articles/PMC5036677/.

Thrift, Nigel. 2007. *Non-representational Theory*. London and New York: Routledge.

Vélez, Verónica. 2017. "Spatializing Race and Racialzing Space." In *ISSUU*. Center for Critical Race Studies at UCLA. https://issuu.com/almaiflores/docs/vv_spatial_analysis.

Watson, Helen with the Yolngu community at Yirrkala, Aboringinal-Australian maps. n.d. http://territories.indigenousknowledge.org/exhibit-5.html.

White. Richard. 2010. *What Is Spatial History?* Stanford Spatial History Group. https://web.stanford.edu/group/spatialhistory/cgi-bin/site/pub.php?id=29.

XpMethod group. 2018. "Torn Apart." http://xpmethod.columbia.edu/torn-apart/volume/2/textures.html.

Resources cited

Anterotesis https://anterotesis.com/wordpress/mapping-resources/dh-gis-projects/.

Cartography https://sites.google.com/site/wadembere/cartography/cartography/introduction-to-cartography.

Converter KML-GeoJson https://mygeodata.cloud/converter/kml-to-geojson.

David Rumsey's Map Collection contains 10,000 digitized historical items www.davidrumsey.com/.

Geocoding http://mapninja.github.io/Tutorial-Geocoding-Crash-Course/ https://developers.google.com/maps/documentation/geocoding/overview.

Knightlab's tools are also quite useful https://storymap.knightlab.com/.

Leaflet https://leafletjs.com/reference-1.6.0.html.

Mapping Borderlands https://digitalhumanities.arizona.edu/news/mapping-borderlands.

Mullen, Lincoln, on Georectification https://lincolnmullen.com/projects/spatial-workshop/georectification.html.

Neatline https://neatline.org/showcase/.

Programming historian QGIS https://programminghistorian.org/en/lessons/qgis-layers or www.qgistutorials.com/en/.

Projections www.icsm.gov.au/education/fundamentals-mapping/projections/commonly-used-map-projections.

QGIS https://docs.qgis.org/3.10/en/docs/user_manual/preamble/features.html.

Raster and Vector https://gisgeography.com/spatial-data-types-vector-raster/ For a more technical discussion, see: https://gis.stackexchange.com/questions/7077/what-are-raster-and-vector-data-in-gis-and-when-to-use.

University of Arizona, LibGuide (Anthony Sanchez) https://libguides.library.arizona.edu/dighumantools/maps.

9 Three-dimensional and virtual models

9a Virtual space and modelling 3-D representations

The production of virtual and three-dimensional (3-D) models has provided scholars whose research focuses on the built environment with new intellectual and technical tools. These new modes come with challenges related to verifiability, truth, accuracy, and uncertainty. The creation of 3-D projects is time consuming, and also puts a hefty burden on storage and maintenance. Sustainability is an issue (think about out-moded games and what is required for playing them). The conceptual challenges are the same as in the use of any digital methods: are the intellectual questions of research served by these methods? The appeal of novelty effects intersects with scholarly argument in ways that are not familiar to most humanities scholars, so assessing the research value of this work is sometimes challenging. [See Exercise #1: Conceptualizing a project.]

The illusion that is provided by 3-D displays is almost always the result of extrapolation and averaging of information. They are frequently the creation of purely digital simulations, images that are not based in observed reality, but created from remains or records to provide an idea of what these might have been. The very capacity for an image to be complete, or even replete, makes it seductive in ways that can border on deception, inaccuracy, or promote entertainment values over scholarly ones. Many specific properties of visual images in a 3-D rendering work create overly finished and homogenous objects. They look may look artificial (too clean and schematic)—but that may be more honest than those that are realistically rendered (with photographic surfaces that create a stronger illusion).

The virtually rendered world is also often created from a single point of view, extending monocular perspective (invented in the Renaissance as a "realist" convention that is associated with a voyeuristic and objectifying gaze) and its way of depicting 3-D space (Mulvey 1975). This is not our visual experience of the world, which integrates peripheral vision and central focus, as well as the multiple pathways of information from our full sensorium. But the perspectival view is reinforced in digital production. Virtual models serve a purpose, but as with any representations, should be examined critically for the values and assumptions they encode. The force of interpretative rhetoric tends to increase with the consumability of images and/or simulated experience (Al Sayyad 1998).

Pioneering projects

Three-dimensional modeling takes spatial experience into a rendered representation that allows questions to be asked about the built environment that cannot be posed in other ways. Unlike maps, 3-D images are often immersive, though they do not have to be.

For instance, one early virtual project, created in 1998, brought the expertise of a structural engineer, Kirk Martini, to bear on a historical inquiry into patterns of building reconstruction in Pompeii (Martini 1998). The project focused on a single building in the market of Pompeii that was damaged in an earthquake in 62 CE a few years earlier than the famous eruption that buried much of the city in lava and ash from Vesuvius in 79 CE. Working with the archaeologist who was director of the larger Pompeii Forum Project, Martini analyzed patterns of damage and reconstruction using hundreds of photographs from which to extract the data for studying the chronology of the building's history of repair. Driving this research was a conviction that civic pride had pushed the reconstruction in the first century of Pompeii's history. But to prove that the building had been repaired required establishing the sequence of events preserved in the ruins—and extrapolating from this a hypothesis about the building in ancient times and between the earthquake and the eruption. Rubble patterns analyzed from an engineering standpoint combined with detailed study of the patches and repairs were keyed into a three-dimensional model of the building to assess whether these were ancient or more recent. Visual evidence, linked to a 3-D model, allowed for exploration of this hypothesis.

Research using models contributes to knowledge of cultural heritage sites at a very granular level, exposing building techniques and construction technology, but also, provides indications of the cultural value of these structures within their original society.

The Digital Karnak project, made more than a decade later, was created by a team of archaeologists and art historians. They reconstructed a major temple complex of ancient Egypt that existed for about two thousand years, from about 2055 BCE. During this period, the complex expanded into an elaborate site, including a massive main Temple and dozens of buildings and structures around it. Each element is constructed from information in drawings from the excavated site, and every pylon, doorframe, wall and other feature has to be created with scrupulous attention to historical accuracy. The elaborate models are shown mainly in video format, tracking the historical development of the site in animations.

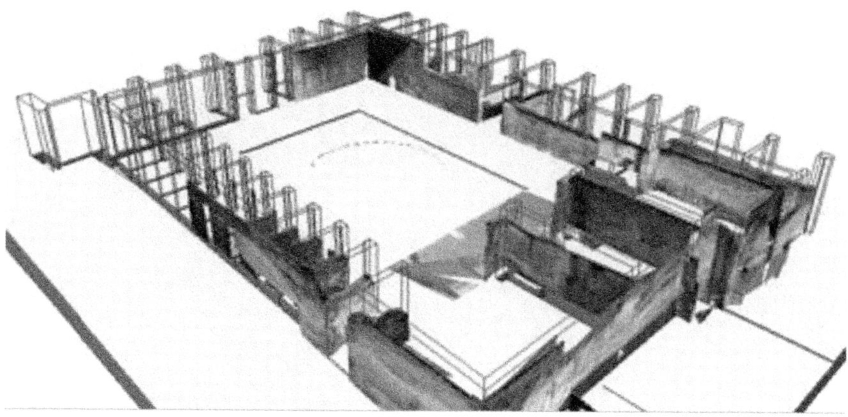

Figure 9.1 Kirk Martini, Pompeii project (Copyright 2010 Board of Visitors, University of Virginia All rights reserved.) http://www2.iath.virginia.edu/struct/pompeii/patterns/

The project directors, Diane Favro and Willeke Wendrich, were careful to point out that no amount of research would recover the experience of the site in antiquity. But the model allowed hypotheses about the ways ritual processions moved through the site, and other issues, to be tested. Understanding of these activities changes when they can be situated in a virtual space.

Note that many of the renderings were made from a very high and exaggerated angle, one that would never have been occupied by a viewer in antiquity. The point of view is omniscient, and the quality of the rendering is schematic by contrast even to photographs of the remains on the site, with their distinct signs of age and texture, variation in color of stone, and the dazzling light and deep shadows of the Egyptian sun. The model remains a digital rendering, even in its Google Earth fly-through version. The access provided by this technology contrasts dramatically with the experience contemporary persons would have had of the same site. The ethics of representational strategies are complex.

Virtual Pompeii was made to test an engineering hypothesis and Karnak was used to study ritual processions and spaces, and to test the accuracy of literary texts and references. Many other virtual projects, each with their own agenda, could be cited (Uotila and Sartes 2016). Some are archaeological projects for which only ruins remain, so the reconstruction, speculative as it may be in many respects, is the only way to visualize these monuments. Unlike artists' two-dimensional renderings of the past, these models can be

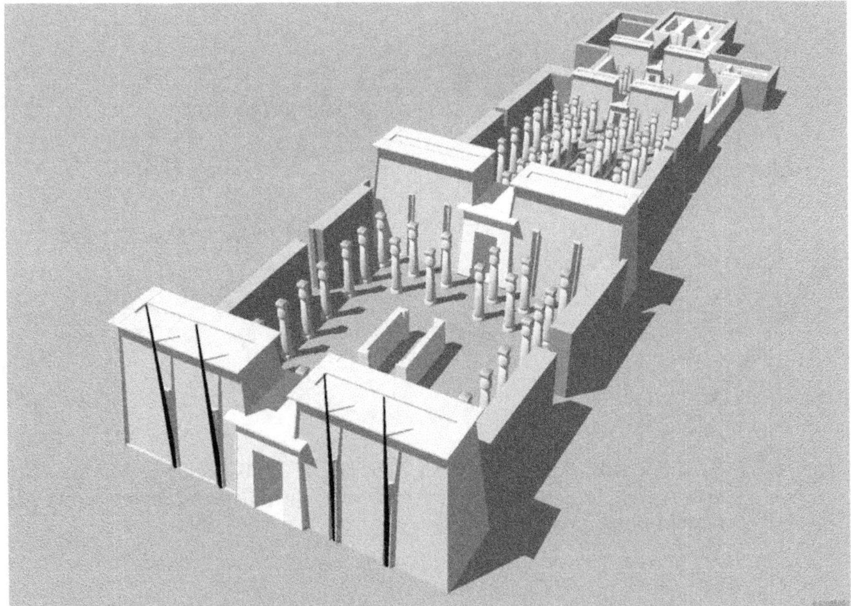

Figure 9.2 Virtual Karnak (Image with permission of Diane Favro and Willeke Wendrich.© Regents of the University of California, 2020.)

experienced in three dimensions and across time—and even be studied in a way that includes the remains.

Classical scholar Christopher Johanson developed a virtual project to study the use of space in public spectacles, including funerals, in the Roman Forum in the Republic, comparing architectural and textual evidence (Favro Diane and Christopher Johanson 2010). Johanson drew on concepts of refutability (could the argument be countered through evidence) and truth-testing (could the rendering be tested for accuracy to an original) within the virtual environment. This raises the question of whether "refutability" can be built into the visualization or virtual format. What does it mean to question an "argument" made in a model when the images are clearly reconstructions? Can another scholar access the evidence on which the model is made—not just the data underlying the virtual rendering, but the source materials on which that relies? The ethical issues around deception and truthfulness become more complex as the renderings become more realistic. Johanson added a useful distinction between "potential reality" and "ontological reality" of a monument. The first justifies the creation of virtual models as hypothetical objects, rather than representations of truth. The second argues for a pre-existing object against which the virtual model could or should be tested. As a humanist, Johansen was interested in interpretation, not just physical evidence. [See Exercise #2: Comparing Roman projects.]

An example of a virtual project with a different emphasis was created by Sheila Bonde to study life at the Abbey of Saint-Jean-des-Vignes in France (Bonde, Coir, and Maines 2017). Bonde's project focused on examining the site as a "physical expression of spiritual, social, and economic motives" in monasticism, not just a built structure. Bonde was interested in the interrelation of spatial form and social articulation. How did the monastic buildings structure gender relations, for example, limiting access for women to certain areas of the complex? What was the quality of life and the rhythm of work and seasons in a community in which "farms, mills, priories" and other components had to cooperate for their survival? Bonde also saw the web platform as a way to publish site drawings from the archaeological examination at the monastery—an undertaking that was too expensive to do in print.

By posting the primary evidence for her site she made it possible for the texts governing daily life in the monastery to be available for a fuller understanding of tasks and rituals. The title, *Sensory Monastery*, signals the link between the study of architecture and the experiences of sound, touch, taste, sight, and visual senses—all as part of a spiritual community. In order to keep issues like the problems of "incomplete data" or "uncertainty" in the foreground, Bonde used non-realistic photographic methods in her renderings. Discussions of the representation of uncertainty—of how reliable the evidence is or the hypothesis about the structure extrapolated from it—play a part in virtual archaeology (Zuk and Carpendale 2007). [See Exercise #3: Contrast the cathedral and the monastery.]

Making 3-D models

The concept of a *virtual* 3-D model suggests immersive experience, or, at the very least, the possibility of moving through an on-screen display in real time (and also in simulation of historical time and events) (Wendell, Altin, and Thompson 2016). To make such a model requires a few basic components: modeled objects drawn as forms in a design tool and a rendering engine to add surface texture, color, and the representation of materials. For these to have behaviors they need to be put into a platform that has what is known as a physics engine, that allows attributes like weight, flexibility, bounce, or other physical attributes to be attached to the models. This is the process of design that is used in architecture and industrial design, or for theater sets or special effects.

The basic steps in making models (details below) are these: 1) create a wireframe object with a 3-D drawing program, 2) give it properties (surface texture, color, or other attributes), 3) put it in a scene and 4) add interactive features. Many 3-D modeling programs access "libraries" of objects to aid in design work. For architects, the standard platforms work with CAD

(Computer Aided Design), but for humanities work, an early tool Sketch-Up has a low threshold and easy learning curve. It also has a library of objects to build on. Blender is a free tool for similar work.

Checklist for making a model

- Source material: What documents or sources do you have to work with? These can include architectural plans, photographs, measurements, information about materials and surface textures, paint or stucco or other finishes, decorative details, furnishings, window openings, and wall thickness and other information about the physical form.
- Platform: Use a platform like Sketch-Up, Blender, or a CAD (Computer Aided Design) program made for 3-D models. Many of these come with libraries from which you can pull existing models of objects, buildings, and landscapes with which to work. Always read the documentation and examine the feature set. Some programs may allow 3-D modeling, but not surface treatments or lighting. Others may allow a full scene, but no animation or interaction.
- Textures: The question is what evidence is available for ancient or destroyed buildings. For existing monuments, accuracy of lighting, conditions in which photographs are taken, and other considerations of accuracy (like showing wear and deterioration) are crucial. Which moment in a structure's time is being rendered? What material types are able to be rendered? What do surfaces record that may not appear in virtual versions?
- Actions: If the rendered object is going to move, bounce, fly or have any capacity for action, this will need to be built in a physics or game engine environment.
- Interaction: Interaction might include allowing a viewer to walk or fly through the model, move around in it, or change the point of view from which they are seeing the model. It might also allow modifications or changes, or game activities and narrative.
- Documentation: Does the program or platform allow documentation to be embedded in this model, or at least, included with it in some way? Consider ways of effectively linking evidence, including textual descriptions, to the visual model. Also reflect on how you might indicate uncertainty about the design decisions.

Modeling depends on source data. Primary sources include maps, drawings, or field notes from archaeological sites. On-site techniques for taking automatic measurements using a laser pointer create usable data. Extracting measurements from photographs requires more skill and remediation. But a model will be built with specifications for each form, shape, and element. The researcher draws each component—door, window, column, roof feature, etc.—directly in a 3-D modeling environment. These can be stored for duplication and re-use.

An alternative approach called *procedural modeling* works with text-based instructions or specifications, that contain instructions and information for shapes and for the surface rendering of color and texture. The set of instructions tells the program what to draw in lieu of doing the sketching directly (e.g. make a box of certain dimensions and cover it in a concrete texture from a library of surface patterns). The advantage of the procedural approach is that modification of any component is done at the level of the textual specification and that makes it easier to make global changes. Both are a considerable amount of work.

Platforms for modeling 3-D space are environments for creating simulations. The cultural specificity of space and spatial relations is neutralized in these platforms. They treat all space as if it were simply an effect of physical measure. Virtual renderings are immediately replete and pristine. They do not show or acquire marks of use, wear, or human habitation. They are stripped of the dimensions that engage the sensorium in analog space but can be useful for testing and modeling hypotheses about how movement, eye-lines, use, and occupation occur. Unity is a popular game-engine for working with 3-D models for a wide range of purposes, including digital humanities projects (Jones 2015). (Unreal engine is a freely available alternative to Unity.)

Rendering is one of the crucial features of 3-D projects. The issue is whether a *simulation* or a *model* is being made. A *simulation* attempts to pass for the thing it represents, to mimic it in many details. In our visual culture, photographic codes are the ones that are associated with simulation, and they read to our eyes as realistic. Because 3-D digital objects have a compelling quality to them, the ethics of rendering should be taken into account. What is being put on view, and on the basis of what evidence?

File formats

Data for 3-D models comes in a variety of formats. Early virtual models were created in a markup language called VRML, Virtual Reality Markup Language, which has largely gone out of use. Many early models and records of them made use of Flash, another once-popular program that has become obsolete (in browsers). These are familiar cautionary tales. Applications, programs, and formats are all subject to expiration. Even current formats with large user-bases are subject to uncertain futures (Flash was widely used). Conceptualizing the various components—shapes, surfaces/textures, behaviors, and scenes/settings—independent of the platform for user experience provides more flexibility for reuse and repurposing of the data.

Many platforms output only in proprietary formats, and this creates issues, particularly if the company fails or if they decide to issue updates on their software that are not retro-compliant (meaning that they do not read older versions of files). STL (STereoLithography), OBJ, and COLLADA (an XML variant) are non-proprietary formats that can be exported from most programs and used to transfer data between them. X3D, which succeeded VRML as an open-source standard, is also widely used and supported by the W3 consortium. You already know that is a good sign.

To create files of 3-D objects, two main approaches are used. One understands forms as a combination of many polygons—think of this as a map of the contours of the shape by using many smaller shapes (often triangles). This "mesh" approach is like making a mold of a complex form by stretching a tight hairnet over it and then recording every shape made by the strings in the net. The other approach is to use geometrical forms, objects, whose shapes are readily described in mathematical terms (spheres, cubes, and so on). These two approaches are roughly analogous to the distinction between pixel-based and vector-based graphics. One (mesh) stores specific, point-by-point information at a very granular level (with varying degrees of resolution) and the other (geometry) stores shapes that are described as geometric forms. Are you making a mold or combining basic forms? Texture mapping and scene information (including lighting, point of view, distance, etc.) complete the look of the object. Many considerations come into play in making decisions about formats and design features—will the objects need to be rendered on the fly, how quickly, will they be moving or animated, and will they need to be edited over time?

A note on VSim

Three-dimensional models, once built, need an environment in which to be used. VSim is a framework built specifically to meet the needs of scholars. Developed by Lisa Snyder, director of the *Chicago Columbian Exposition* project, it is a presentation environment (Viele 2015). VSim allows production of narratives to frame that experience. In addition, it supports embedding source documents within the model itself. Since many historical models built in three dimensions draw on primary sources for their information, the capacity to add annotation, metadata, and commentary into the models allows a user to see what has been extrapolated, what has been copied, and where decisions about the model do and do not rely on historical documentation.

The contrast between the rendered model, with its highly studied and carefully constructed forms and surfaces, and the primary sources in the form of postcards, photographs, and memorabilia, makes for a useful critical dialogue between evidence and representation. Questions of what we see and how, which features of visual experience become significant over time, and the distance from the perceptual capacity of individuals in different periods or locations, becomes vivid as a result. The historical context of viewing, experiencing a building or object, cannot be recovered—but at least, it can be noted as an absent feature of the dynamics of modeling. Presentation of evidence legitimates the scholar's work so it can be assessed by

Figure 9.3 VSim showing embedded resources for the 3-D model of the Chicago Columbian Exhibition. The image is a screengrab from a real-time simulation model of the Street of Cairo installation on the midway at the World's Columbian Exposition held in Chicago in 1893. The model was begun under the auspices of the Urban Simulation Team at UCLA and is now supported by UCLA's Office of Information Technology and Institute of Digital Research and Education.

Source: (Image courtesy of Lisa Snyder. © Regents of the University of California, 2020.)

others. Argument and evidence are not the same and keeping both in view in a virtual environment is an important scholarly principle.

Ethics of spatial modeling and critical race studies

The question of who authors a model of a space or building is as important as whose experience is represented. The right to speak about experience cannot be assumed, and in any work that focuses on a particular community, the ethics of authorship and design appear. This is true across communities, but is particularly charged in modeling experience across racial, gendered, and able-bodied boundaries. The presumption of understanding is just that—presumptuous—and engagement is required. Doing this with a living community poses one set of challenges. Addressing the participation of a vanished one raises others—are there descendants? Where and how are cultural records preserved and where is memory stored? Who has the right to speak about experience?

A set of conversations about Black Spatial Humanities brought these issues into focus. Kim Gallon's work has galvanized the relationship between Africana/African American/Black studies and the digital humanities, along with projects that make use of geospatial technologies (Gallon 2016). The framing questions, posed by Gallon and others, are whether digital humanities can be in any way transformative, and how to use these technological methods as social forces.

Taking racialized bodies into account in spatial modeling requires conceptualization from within an embodied perspective. Racial experience is a dynamic feature of the unfolding of events in space, central to a recognition of perceived and lived identity. The design of data always carries values, and the crucial initial intervention in digital work takes place there, in the classification and identification of information about spatial experience.

The Virtual Harlem project provides some useful insight as an example. A project of primary documents and networked resources, Virtual Harlem also extended into an immersive environment (as a CAVE projection). These activities occurred around 2000–01, but the project's visualizations are preserved in a video format (Johnston 2015). The representation preserved images of the Harlem Renaissance Ballroom, demolished in 2015 (Meier 2015). Bryan Carter, the project's director, drew extensively on archival materials—photographs and texts—to create an environment in which the cultural activities of the vital African-American neighborhood in New York in the 1920s can be experienced.

The questions of who should, or can, make such representations—and how they can be used and populated—are not easily answered. They raise concerns with vicarious experience as a form of exploitation and cultural tourism. Can objectified presentations of individuals guarantee their authority as subjects and agents—or does representation itself pose a problem in

Figure 9.4 Virtual Harlem, Cotton Club interior, 2017. Center for Digital Humanities, University of Arizona.

Source: (Image courtesy of Dr. Bryan Carter.)

the way it positions women, people of color, and others? Is the experience merely voyeuristic? Who has warrant to do such work? Years ago, the Black British art historian Kobena Mercer described the difficulty of being made to speak for his racialized identity, calling it "the burden of representation" (Mercer 1990). But the problems that arise by being spoken—positioned as an object of representation—may be at least as burdensome. How thin is the line between historical documentation and display created for uncritical consumption? The challenge is to keep the viewer experience and research framed in a critical mode, not make it simply entertainment and distraction.

Takeaway

Virtual models of historical and cultural sites can create credible versions of absent or vanished environments. But the work of making objects, putting surface textures on them, and positioning them within frameworks for viewing and exploration is labor intensive. Components have to be built one at a time, and assembled, or else created using procedural modeling approaches from a set of programmatic instructions. In either case, the production of virtual materials immerses a viewer in an experience that raises questions about authenticity and deception, simulation and modeling, that raise ethical concerns when the visual credibility of an object is at odds with its accuracy (Bakker et al. 2003). The development of virtual experiences also raises issues about whose voice and perspective are doing the narrating—and whether objectification in 3-D simulacra can ever escape the problems of vicarious engagement with cultural practices and communities.

Exercises

Exercise #1: conceptualizing a project

Using this lesson as a guide, conceptualize a project in AR.

https://programminghistorian.org/en/lessons/creating-mobile-augmented-reality-experiences-in-unity

Exercise #2: comparing Roman projects

Apply Bakker's criteria of refutability and truth-testing to one of these projects about Rome.

Why do different kinds of historical evidence require different criteria for assessment—or do they?

www.romereborn.virginia.edu/

http://etc.ucla.edu/projects/augustan-rome/

http://etc.ucla.edu/projects/romelab/

www.digitalmeetsculture.net/article/rome-reborn-original-project-and-new-apps/

Exercise #3: contrast the cathedral and the monastery

Look these two projects and contrast the ways they use 3-Dmodeling: www.wesleyan.edu/monarch/index.htm
Compare with Amiens: www.learn.columbia.edu/Mcahweb/indexframe.html

Recommended readings

Bonde, Sheila, Alexis Coir, and Clark Maines. 2017. "Construction-Deconstruction-Reconstruction." *Speculum* 92 (S1). www.journals.uchicago.edu/doi/full/10.1086/694169.

Nieves, Angel David, Kim Gallon, David J. Kim, Scott Nesbit, Bryan Carter, and Jessica Johnson. 2017. "Black Spatial Humanities." *ADHO Abstracts*. https://dh2017.adho.org/abstracts/285/285.pdf.

Papdopoulos, Costas, and Susan Schreibman. 2019. "Towards 3D Scholarly Editions: The Battle of Mount Street Bridge." *Digital Humanities Quarterly* 13 (1). www.digitalhumanities.org/dhq/vol/13/1/000415/000415.html.

9b Photogrammetry

Photogrammetry and other 3-D visualizing techniques create images of existing objects, sites, monuments, and phenomena. Artifacts as varied as fragments of ancient pottery, sculpture from collections around the globe, ruins of structures buried in the earth, and anything else that can be "imaged" with one technique or another are able to be made into a digital surrogate. These surrogates are still modeled, made as virtual objects, but they are constrained by their relation to existing physical evidence. Photogrammetry is a way to make a 3-D image of something in digital form.

Virtual models and photogrammetry have in common that they can store data about an object as a mesh of small shapes, as a set of geometric forms, or as a picture made from data sources. Photogrammetry is used most frequently to make a digital rendering of an existing physical object for purposes of study or display. Photogrammetry can also be used for analysis—particularly with regard to formal features. However, much of the work done in this field is linked to museums for creating virtual displays, or to cultural heritage sites to create surrogates for sites that are threatened, vanishing, or otherwise at risk. Photogrammetry always records existing evidence. Three-dimensional models can be built from imagination, physical evidence, existing records, or some combination of these. When no other record will exist, and a site is underwater, bombed, or collapsed, then photogrammetry might be the only way to experience it. Relying on these methods as if they are preservation formats is problematic at best. But sometimes it is all that will remain.

Another aspect of 3-D imaging is its use in non-invasive techniques for archaeology and art history. Conflicts around the work of excavation and the irrevocable damage done by careless—or even careful—digging make archaeology a fraught field. Evidence once disturbed or destroyed can never be recovered. Some of that evidence might seem insignificant at the time—who in the 19th century was attentive to pollen counts and layers of organic material as part of an ecological timeline for a region? Our agendas change over time. Non-invasive archaeological methods are increasingly gaining traction. Techniques like Lidar and ground-penetrating radar have become a regular part of initial surveys of sites.

Other interventions are carried out regularly in the work of conservation, the act of restoring a surface or part of an artifact to restore it to its "original" condition, though establishing that can be difficult. Did the Renaissance artist Michelangelo anticipate that smoke would alter the finish on his painting of the Sistine Chapel, toning the bright vivid colors into subtler tones? Or did he choose his pigments as if they would remain as intense as those of a modern abstract painting? The historicity of vision, style, and taste are not easily recovered, if at all. So, the notion that restoration might always be virtual, done as a projection onto an object, recognized as an act of interpretation has opened the door for speculation in digital format that leaves the object (damaged or not) intact. Virtual reality, augmented reality, and mixed reality are all modes frequently referenced in the use of imaging technologies.

Imaging processes

At its simplest, photogrammetry involves taking multiple images of a 3-D object and stitching them together automatically. The software to do this ranges from high-end professional platforms capable of handling hundreds of high-resolution views, to freeware that works on a phone (Graham 2018). For display purposes, the lower end technology can work to create objects that can be rotated, viewed, and examined. For analytic work, advanced programs that can analyze features of the images are pressed into service for archaeological or anthropological study. A small fragment of a work, a bone chip, or part of an artifact can be measured in three dimensions and extrapolated based on curvature, strength, load-bearing, or other features. The capacity to regenerate artifacts from such computational analysis is an aid to many fields of humanities research in which physical objects are an integral part of the scholarship. The ease of production of this mode of representation, which was originally dependent on very expensive and rare equipment, has made it possible to extend its use for many functions, including virtual conservation.

Three-dimensional viewing

The Louvre in Paris, the Metropolitan Museum in New York, the Dunhuang caves in China, the National Museum of Anthropology in Mexico City, and the National Museum of Modern and Contemporary Art in Seoul, Korea are just a handful of the (literally) thousands of museums that have mounted virtual exhibits (UNESCO n.d.). Many have partnered with Google Earth to offer a viewing experience online. The advantages are many, but some reflection on partnerships of this kind should be taken into account, since the work stands to vanish if the corporation pulls out. (For instance, Google has previously stopped supporting various platforms used for production and presentation of digital scholarship.)

When we reflect on the values of virtual exhibition, some benefits seem obvious. The experience is available without travel, the cost of admission is generally free, and many objects can be approached for close-up viewing in ways that would not be possible in an actual museum setting. But, the ecological costs of creating, storing, and providing access to such materials are considerable, and rarely considered as part of the ethical consideration of the value of these exhibits.

Aside from these touristic experiences, 3-D photography is used for analysis and study of at-risk sites. The Dunhuang Grottoes in China have several threats that make in-person viewing no longer feasible, and so the caves and their murals have been photographed for online access and an immersive exhibit experience online. Carved and painted statues, wall-paintings, and frescoes suffer from the effects of climate change, including rising water levels near the grottoes. But more damaging in the immediate moment is the presence of tourists whose body heat and breath create humid conditions that put the painted murals at risk. The paintings and sculptures date from the 4th to 14th century, and in order to make them accessible to a broad public, they have been photographed using ultra-high resolution digital imaging (at a billion-pixel resolution) (Liu 2012). In the virtual exhibit, a "magnifying glass" feature allows viewers to examine details that would not be perceptible in the physical space. In partnership with the City University in Hong Kong, the project filmed dancers whose presence was added to the virtual presentation, bringing features of the culture preserved in the paintings to life (Janzekovic 2017). Or do they? We have to reflect on questions about how the technology meets expectations for entertainment rather than meditative engagement with the iconography of the paintings. [See Exercise #1: Dunhuang caves.]

The use of digital photography in production of virtual sites has extended worldwide. Some of these projects are simply high-resolution photographic presentations, like the Mayan Temple at Chichen Itza. Some, like the Chavín de Huántar site in Peru, were photographed using drones. Mixed reality and augmented reality are increasingly popular modes of imposing layered information onto photographic or actual experience. An in-person visit to a site can be augmented by information accessed through a phone or tablet that puts historical information back into an existing physical space. This work has found its way into tourism, and of course entertainment, where simulation of smell, sound, and even touch are increasingly touted (Soo 2016). But at their most instructive, augmented reality applications, like the Tour of Cahokia Mounds, the site of an elaborate Mississippian city from about 1000 CE, allows features of the past to be exposed in the present without disturbing the ground (CMMS n.d.). An augmented reality application reveals features of objects in the mounds or in the landscape that simply are not visible otherwise.

Imaging techniques such as magnetic imaging and underground radar are being used to study other archaeological sites without any excavation. For example, a group working at Stonehenge in England has discovered a number of previously unknown structures in the vicinity of the famous monument (Cumming 2017). As tools, these imaging processes create breakthrough discoveries that would have been difficult, if not impossible, in an earlier era. The ability to "see" into unexcavated ground and produce an image of what remains, as well as to project from that what might have been present, opens new frontiers in archaeology and digital humanities.

The high-end imaging techniques needed for a project of this scale are expensive and require technical teams with expertise and infrastructure support. But the use of photogrammetry at the smaller scale permits 3-D representations of objects in online publications and web exhibits. Being able to interact with an object, turn it, and see it from multiple points of view and at various scales supports study of the details of making and design. In some cases, the images offer more detail than any in-person view would afford. As photogrammetry has become more affordable and easier to use, models of cultural objects are increasingly available online. A rare object can be embedded in a publication without permission, raising issues of intellectual property and ethics of use. Provenance of the objects is often unclear. Metadata for the digital artifact may be missing or inaccurate, and professional standards of curatorial work are not always observed. [See Exercise #2: Sketchfab.]

Analysis and study

For purposes of research, photogrammetry can be used to reconstruct a lost or destroyed building or monument from historical records. One such project worked from a repository of historic photographs of the Kronentor gate in Dresden (Maiwald et al. 2017). The goal of the project was to see if a 3-D model could be constructed from the information in historical photographs. Using a technique called SfM (structure from motion), the researchers put together a model by using images taken from different viewpoints. These photographs were themselves archival objects, not images produced for this purpose. The gate was destroyed in the 1945 bombings, and though later reconstructed, the goal of the research was to recover the earlier structure. The account of the project documents the process, use of the software Agisoft-PhotoScan, and the derivation of the point clouds (data points aggregated to create an image) from the photographs—on which the specific features of the model are built.

In archaeological research, the labor-intensive task of matching fragments of pottery with possible original shapes benefits from digital models and renderings (Zvietcovich et al. 2016). The idea of automatic matching involves extrapolation of information from a fragment to compare it with an "implicit" form (Maiza and Gaildrat n.d.). Matching a "shape model" and a fragment and building a hypothetical object of which it is a part involves computational processing of thickness, angles, and every detail of the form to try to guess what the original larger object looked like and where in that overall shape the fragment belonged. This reverse engineering of a form based on assessments of "distance" between the fragment and its place in the original object is rendered using the same kind of meshwork as that in virtual reality techniques. The hybrid of analytic photogrammetry and virtual modeling can produce remarkable results, even if they must be treated with requisite caution with regard to authenticity.

Digital imaging techniques promote methods of analysis through formal contrast and comparison, as well as in their application to individual objects. *Mapping Gothic France*, a pioneering work in digital architectural history, contained laser-drawn wireframes of all the cathedrals in the database. These can be compared feature by architectural feature—nave height, aisle width, floorplans, and sections (Murray n.d.). Without a way to digitize the physical structures and make them into data models that can be manipulated, this work would be impossible. Is there a risk that this approach reduces complex cultural artifacts to positivist renderings of their physical properties? The argument can be made that the research allowed new questions to be asked about style, influence, and symbolic qualities. A project carried on at Duke University used crowd-sourcing to generate enough images for a high-resolution photogrammetric model of its neo-Gothic chapel. The contrast between the rendering of Duke's chapel in cloud points and that of the Gothic France project stresses the difference between a special-effects rendering and a systematic project conceived from a scholarly perspective that made use of 3-D models for analytic purposes. [See Exercise #3: Gothic France and Duke's chapel.]

In another, very different, project, some "mutant" artifacts, or hybrid objects, have been produced by an experiment carried out by the Metropolitan Museum in New York and Microsoft. GenStudio, the name of the project, is an environment in which features of 3-D representations of artifacts can be selected and combined to produce new artifacts. The novelty effect of this platform quickly wears, but it offers ways to think about style and form, and texture and surface, as components of material history and culture. Are the resources invested in such a project worth the outcome? As manipulation and hybridization become familiar, they emphasize superficial approaches to the study of cultural artifacts, losing sight of the symbolic dimensions of artifacts in use. When the history of human production becomes an inventory of objects to be played with, they lose their connection to the fabric of social relations. The artifacts may become autonomous objects, more likely to be appreciated for their formal qualities than for the more complex aspects of their cultural role and identity. [See Exercise #4: Cultural artifacts.]

Virtual restoration and non-invasive archaeology

The restoration of art historical objects often generates controversy. The physical alteration of remains of statues or monuments relies on interpretation and speculation. The act of making changes to the remains of a once-intact object—or even cleaning an artifact that has accumulated so much discoloration or dirt from wear—can involve changes that do damage of their own. Altering any historical work of art involves risks. So, the possibilities of doing this virtually, even allowing for multiple restorations that reflect different opinions, offers one solution to this dilemma. [See Exercise #5: ALiVE.]

Bernard Frischer's digital sculpture project offers one case study in this area. Focused on a statue of the Roman Emperor Caligula, the project committed to scanning, digital restoration, and multiple hypotheses on the original coloration of a single statue (Frischer n.d.). The research team wanted

Figure 9.5 Two views of Caligula

Source: (Courtesy of Bernard Frischer. Copyright 2010 Board of Visitors, University of Virginia. All rights reserved.) www.digitalsculpture.org/papers/frischer/frischer_paper.html

to be able to indicate degrees of uncertainty about their historical hypotheses. Since most classical marble sculptures were originally polychromed, the recovery of small bits of pigment from the existing object can be used as a guide in digital restoration. Such remains are not always sufficient. Base coats and preparatory layers might be what remains, rather than final surface tones. Extrapolating from existing evidence involves informed guesswork. One challenge is to provide visual cues to indicate degrees of uncertainty about the features of the restoration. This can be difficult in the technology of photogrammetry since its photo-realistic renderings offer a sense of repelete-ness and finish. The solution proposed by the Caligula team was to present variant alternatives of the restoration in order to demonstrate their hypothetical character. The argument from within a conservation community involves a distinction between an intervention that conserves a physical artifact and one that imposes an artistic judgment. Digital restoration allows the physical object to be stabilized independently and theories of its original appearance to be produced anew into perpetuity.

Takeaway

High-resolution digital photography is being used to capture information from cultural heritage sites that are at risk, while many sites damaged in the past by human or natural disasters are being "restored" virtually by a combination of imaging techniques and speculative work. Imaging technologies that use radar and magnetic imaging have been able to create vivid 3-D models of archaeological sites, and lend their techniques to the creation of augmented reality applications that can provide vivid reconstructions of a historical past without any invasive excavation. The use of photographic and other imaging techniques makes monuments and artifacts available in ways that would not have been possible even a generation ago. As this activity increases, so should the respect for the cultural property and intellectual provenance of the original artifacts and their digital surrogates. One challenge will be to keep all cultural experience from becoming a form of tourism. Scholarship has a role to play in keeping critical considerations of argument and evidence in play. [See Exercise #6: Open Heritage Project.]

Exercises

Exercise #1: Dunhuang caves

What features of the caves are readily understood from this online imaging? What are not?

www.e-dunhuang.com/

http://idp.bl.uk/pages/technical_infra.a4d

www.researchgate.net/publication/326804961_Usability_Evaluation_of_E-Dunhuang_Cultural_Heritage_Digital_Library

Exercise #2: Sketchfab

Compare the commercial part of this site with the section curated by a University of North Carolina Research Lab. https://sketchfab.com/ and https://sketchfab.com/rla-archaeology. Be sure to go back to the Lab and look at their cataloging standards, documentation, and record-keeping, here: https://archaeology.sites.unc.edu/home/rla/collections/#3D

Exercise #3: Gothic France and Duke's chapel

Contrast these two projects. https://sketchfab.com/3d-models/duke-chapel-8-million-point-cloud-8ec8b87123814ca4be3a38c6035efb2b

Be sure to use the "comparisons" tool in Mapping Gothic France. http://mappinggothic.org/comparisons

Exercise #4: cultural artifacts

Explore the possibilities of this site and consider how the effects created do and do not increase understanding of the artifacts in the collections. What alternatives to this approach might be more instructive? https://gen.studio/ Compare with https://artsandculture.google.com/ (Google) and think about the line between entertainment and scholarship.

Exercise #5: alive

www.vi-mm.eu/2017/12/20/alive-project-city-university-of-hong-kong/

Imagine possibilities for these developments to be useful in a research project.

Exercise #6: Open Heritage Project

Look through the Open Heritage Project, CyArk (California), and consider the implications of virtual cultural tourism.

www.evolving-science.com/information-communication/virtual-reality-00732

Recommended readings

Mafkereseb Kassahum Bekele and Erik Champion. 2019. "A Comparison of Immersive Realities and Interaction Methods: Cultural Learning in Virtual Heritage." *Frontiers in Robotics and AI*. www.frontiersin.org/articles/10.3389/frobt.2019.00091/full.

Reconstructing Journalistic Scenes in 3D | The New York Times—Research & Development. 2020. *New York Times*, July 27. https://rd.nytimes.com/projects/reconstructing-journalistic-scenes-in-3d.

References cited

Al Sayyad, Nezar. 1998. "Virtual Cairo: An Urban Historian's View of Computer Simulation." *Leonardo* 32 (2): 93–100. www.jstor.org/stable/1576690?seq=1#metadata_info_tab_contents.

Bakker, Geeske et al. 2003. "Truth and Credibility." *The Journal of Visualization and Computer Animation* 14 (3): 159–67. https://onlinelibrary.wiley.com/doi/abs/10.1002/vis.314.

Cahokia Mounds Museum Society. n.d. "Back to the City of the Sun." https://cahokiamounds.org/augmented-reality-project/.

Cumming, Vivien. 2017. "We May Have Cracked the Mystery of Stonehenge." *BBC*. www.bbc.com/travel/story/20170713-why-stonehenge-was-built.

Favro, Diane, and Christopher Johanson. 2010. "Death in Motion: Funeral Processions in the Roman Forum." *Journal of the Society of Architectural Historians* 69 (1): 12–37. www.jstor.org/stable/pdf/10.1525/jsah.2010.69.1.12.pdf.

Frischer, Bernard. n.d. "Digital Sculpture Project." *Caligula* www.digitalsculpture.org/papers/frischer/frischer_paper.html.

Gallon, Kim. 2016. "Making a Case for Black Digital Humanities." In *Debates in the Digital Humanities*, edited by Matthew Gold and Lauren Klein. Minneapolis, MN: University of Minnesota Press.

Google, Arts and Culture Exhibits. n.d. https://artsandculture.google.com/exhibit/OgLSnnqWE9B_IQ. https://artsandculture.google.com/exhibit/VwLyaBwv7bFPKA.

Graham, Shawn. 2018. "3D Models from Archival Film/Video Footage." *hcommons.org*. https://hcommons.org/deposits/item/hc:17869/ purl: http://dx.doi.org/10.17613/M60V7D.

Janzekovic, Petja. 2017. "Alive Project: City University of Hong Kong." *Virtual Multimodal Museum*. www.vi-mm.eu/2017/12/20/alive-project-city-university-of-hong-kong/.

Johnston, Jessica. 2015. "An Archive for Virtual Harlem." https://scalar.usc.edu/works/harlem-renaissance/index.

Jones, S. E. 2015. "Ch. 6 New Media and Modeling: Games and the Digital Humanities." In *A New Companion to Digital Humanities*, edited by Susan Schreibman, Ray Siemens, and John Unsworth. Wiley and Sons. DOI: 10.1002/9781118680605.ch6.

Liu, Melinda. 2012. "Virtual Tourism: China's Dunhuang Buddhist Caves Go Digital." *Newsweek*. www.newsweek.com/virtual-tourism-chinas-dunhuang-buddhist-caves-go-digital-63615.

Maiwald, F., T. Vietze, D. Schneider, F. Henze, S. Münster, and F. Niebling. 2017. "Photogrammetric Analysis of Historical Image Repositories." https://d-nb.info/1143876547/34.

Maiza, Chaouki and Véronique Gaildrat. n.d. "Automatic Classification of Archaeological Potsherds." https://www.researchgate.net/publication/228355481_Automatic_classification_of_archaeological_potsherds.

Martini, Kirk. 1998. "Patterns of Reconstruction at Pompeii." *Universitiy of Virginia, IATH*. http://www2.iath.virginia.edu/struct/pompeii/patterns/.

Meier, Allison. 2015. "Virtually Visiting the Harlem Renaissance." *Hyperallergic*. https://hyperallergic.com/229303/virtually-visiting-the-harlem-renaissance/.

Mercer, Kobena. 1990. "Black Art and the Burden of Representation." *Third Text* 4 (10): 61–78. www.tandfonline.com/doi/abs/10.1080/09528829008576253?journalCode=ctte20.

Mulvey, Laura. 1975. "Visual Pleasure and Narrative Cinema." In *Visual and Other Pleasures*. New York: Palgrave Macmillan. www.asu.edu/courses/fms504/total-readings/mulvey-visualpleasure.pdf.

Murray, Stephen. n.d. "Mapping Gothic France." http://mappinggothic.org/comparisons.

Soo, Daniel. 2016. "A New Age of VR Involving All Five Senses." *ISPR Presence*. https://ispr.info/2016/08/02/a-new-age-of-vr-involving-all-five-senses/.

UNESCO. "Magao Caves." n.d. https://whc.unesco.org/en/list/440/.

Uotila, Kari, and Mina Sartes. 2016. "Medieval Turku, Finland—the Lost City." *Virtual Worlds in Archaeology Initiative*. www.learningsites.com/VWinAI/VWAI_Turku-home.php.

Viele, Nico. 2015. "World's Columbia Exposition of 1893 Comes Alive on Computer Screens." https://newsroom.ucla.edu/stories/worlds-columbian-exposition-of-1893-comes-alive-on-computer-screens.

Wendell, Augustus, Burcak Ozludil Altin, and Ulysee Thompson. 2016. "Prototyping a Temporospatial Simulation Framework." *Complexity & Simplicity: Proceedings of ECAADE* 2: 485–91. http://papers.cumincad.org/data/works/att/ecaade2016_144.pdf.

Zuk, Torre, and Sheelagh Carpendale. 2007. "Visualization of Uncertainty and Reasoning." https://innovis.cpsc.ucalgary.ca/innovis/uploads/Publications/Publications/Zuk_2007_VisualizingUncertaintyReasoning.pdf.

Zvietcovich, Fernando et al., 2016. "A Novel Method for Estimating the Complete 3D Shape of Pottery with Axial Symmetry from Single Potsherds Based on Principal Component Analysis." *Digital Applications in Archaeology and Cultural Heritage* 3 (2): 42–54. www.sciencedirect.com/science/article/pii/S2212054816300078.

Resources

Blender www.blender.org/.

GenStudio https://gen.studio/.

Non-Invasive Archaeology. https://digdays.org/non-invasive-archaeology-methods/.

SketchFab. https://sketchfab.com/3d-models/buddha-point-cloud-5b43e8455ec349bdb3726dcb02813c19 and https://sketchfab.com/3d-models/duke-chapel-8-million-point-cloud-8ec8b87123814ca4be3a38c6035efb2b.

SketchUp www.sketchup.com/plans-and-pricing/sketchup-free.

Three-D modeling. www.web3d.org/getting-started-x3d.

Three-D printing. https://all3dp.com/3d-file-format-3d-files-3d-printer-3d-cad-vrml-stl-obj/.

Unity. https://programminghistorian.org/en/lessons/creating-mobile-augmented-reality-experiences-in-unity.

Virtual Harlem. www.evl.uic.edu/cavern/harlem/.

Vsim. https://vsim.library.ucla.edu/xmlui/.

10 Interface

10a Interface basics

Interface is the embodiment of the contents of the project, a guide to how a visitor can move through it, and a support for actions that can be taken for use. A schematic sketch of the interface is one of the first steps in the planning process. Decisions about content, functionality, and audience are reflected in the interface design. Interface is not just the style or look added as an afterthought to a project (font, background color, images, or layout). Design features, functionality, and intellectual content must be fully integrated.

What is an interface?

An interface is a zone of exchange. An interface can connect a person with a computer (as with the screens on our devices), a computer with a computer (as in an API), or a network of multiple systems and agents with each other. The fob of a vehicle that automatically opens car doors and allows an engine to start is a form of interface. So are faucet handles and radio knobs and many other features of the physical world. Interface design organizes our experience and, very simply, if something is not "on the menu" it cannot be found or acted on. While we tend to think of interfaces as screens, they also include the peripheral devices such as the mouse, touchpad, joystick, and voice-activated tools, as well as smart devices (Norman 2010). The "internet of things" has extended the ways in which systems are connected to each other through interfaces (Burgess 2018). But in the realm of digital scholarship, the function of an interface is often to communicate with a viewer what the contents of a project site might be and how to access and use it effectively.

Screen interface conventions have solidified very quickly since the invention of the GUI (Graphical User Interface) in the 1980s. The familiarity of their format and structure and make it hard to see the ways our thinking is constrained by the interfaces we use. In the early years of mainframe computing, the "interface" through which operators provided programming instructions consisted of huge banks of switches. Later, punch cards contained program information as well as data to be analyzed for researchers who dropped them off at service centers and waited for a place in a queue for "run time." Real-time interaction with computational operation only became possible in the late 1960s.

When Doug Engelbart was first working on the design of the mouse (the first working prototype was built around 1968), he was also considering foot pedals, helmets, and other embodied aspects of experience as potential elements of the interface design (Engelbart 2008–2020). Why didn't these catch on? Or will they? Various augmented reality applications for handheld devices, VR glasses, and helmets have also come and gone, but sensor-based and distributed technologies are increasingly present in the built environment. What happens to interface when it moves off the screen and becomes a layer of perceived reality? The possibilities for the use of cultural heritage materials are constantly unfolding. [See Exercise #1: History of interface.]

As scholars, our tasks are to understand how interface organizes an experience for those using our work digitally. In addition, we need a critical understanding of what interface can and cannot do—and how to read it as a cultural artifact.

Basic types of interface

The most basic interface is the Command Line Interface. Almost all desktop computers have a "terminal" utility that allows you to work in this mode. The command line interface is direct and powerful as a way of doing things within your own computer, but it requires learning commands that are typed directly, line by line (hence the name). Early PCs *only* had command line interfaces, so all work was done in this mode.

The invention of the GUI increased ease of use. The GUI made use of icons—file folders, trash can, and so on—that performed the work of the object they represented. Drag and drop capabilities combined with these icons to give someone the impression they were "throwing away" a file or "storing it in a folder" by moving it around. The illusion works even though the actual computation is enacted with binary code.

The TUI, or Tactile User Interface, dominates phones and personal devices. Touch and swipe functionality has become part of some computer screens, particularly kiosk-type installations in public places.

The NLI or Natural Language Interface is an aid to the sight-impaired or physically limited patron, and the use of voice activated software and devices extends capability. When designing for an NLI, keep explicitness in mind. Commands should be clear and unambiguous: "Open," "close," "select," "up," "click," "next," and "back" as opposed to "Show me the next," or "Go back to the last one." For scholarly purposes, an interface is not likely to use much more than links, search boxes, some buttons, and pull-down menus, all of which will conform to well-established conventions. Tricky or over-designed thematic interfaces can undermine a site. The famous case of Microsoft Bob—considered an industry disaster—is a case study in bad design.

Responsive design

Designing content to work across platforms and devices, with their different displays and modes of interaction, has become a necessity if you want your materials to be available in anything but a standard desktop. The concept of "responsive" design is simple, the features of the interface (particularly dimensions, layout, and aspect ratio) are reworked to suit the dimensions of the screen display on which it appears. Most design platforms will take this into account for testing as your project develops. If you are working directly in HTML5, you will need to build these capacities into your project with code.

Contents or behaviors

In the design community, UI (User Interface) and UX (User Experience) are distinguished. Though the line between them is not always clear, it is helpful to think of the interface in terms of the graphical structure—the features, layout, behaviors, and actions it supports, and the activities that will be engaged through its design. User experience can be thought of as the way someone engages with that design to accomplish or achieve something—is it easy, hard, or frustrating?

Another crucial distinction is useful to keep in mind: Does the interface *reveal the contents* of a site (repository, system, exhibit, or other content) or does it structure *the use* of a site through cues for human actions and the behaviors of the design elements? Some combination of these two—showing what a site contains and giving instructions or cues for use—are at the basis of all interface designs. This is true whether you are giving voice instructions or navigating with a tactile device. Showing contents and supporting use need to function together for the interface design to be effective. For the sake of clarity in description, the term "interface front-end" will be used to describe the ways use is structured into the design accessed directly by individuals. The term "back-end" will be used to describe some of the contents, organization, and functionality accessed by the design. Some of this material will also be taken up again in the discussion of web presentation formats and networked resources. [See Exercise #2: Jesse James Garrett.]

A couple of examples of scholarly sites, one large and one small in scale, help illustrate this distinction between showing *contents* and supporting *actions*. The Tibetan and Himalayan Library is a mature digital humanities project with considerable content and a well-organized interface. The masthead, menu bar, and lower information bar form a stable frame. The masthead communicates the site's identity. Though the masthead image is small, it has been chosen to represent the mountain region on which the scholarship focuses. The top-level navigation bar structures the site with menu buttons labeled to identify the intellectual content. When clicked, a menu button changes color and opens a new window, as expected, thus supporting the use of the site. Each category is distinct, and the navigation and masthead remain visible wherever the viewer is in the site, keeping the frame intact. The site is dense and informative and communicates its *contents* directly. The *labels* in the menu bar identify *contents*. One clearly labeled "action" item in the interface is the option to "hide" or "show" the sidebar menu on the upper right. All *actions* taken by the visitor result in *behaviors* on the screen—clicking the "hide" action results in the collapse of the sidebar information and clicking a menu button opens the tab. Accessing content takes several steps (in part because of the amount of material the site contains). The Collections link opens a page describing four main collections: Images, Maps, Audio-Visual Materials, and Texts, and these in turn each have their own page with search and menu options.

For a contrast, consider *De Heresi*, a unified collection of documents from the "Early Medieval Inquisition." On the front-end, the screen space is well-used. The top bar identifies and brands the site and offers entry to

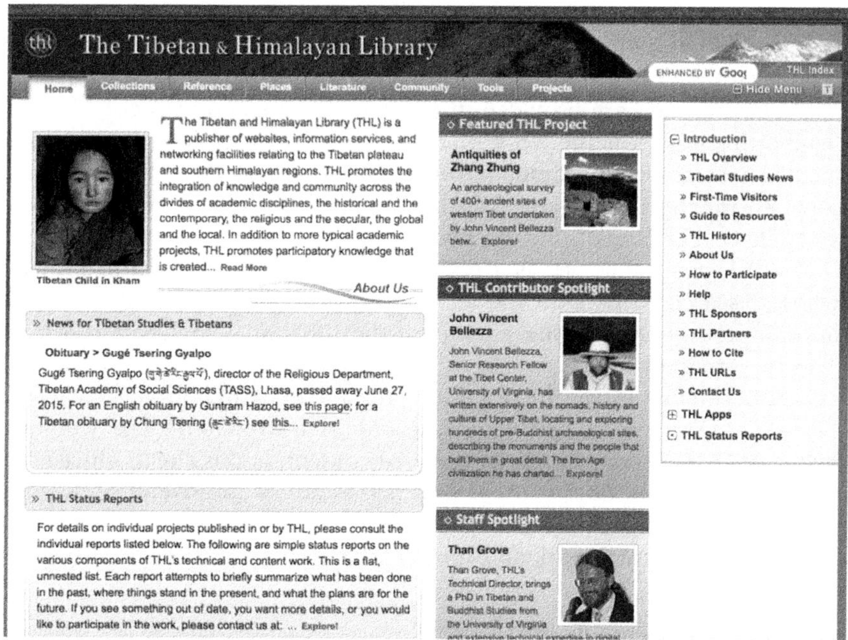

Figure 10.1 Tibetan Himalayan Digital Library interface (Provided for unrestricted use by the Tibetan and Himalayan Library)

Source: Courtesy of David Germano.)

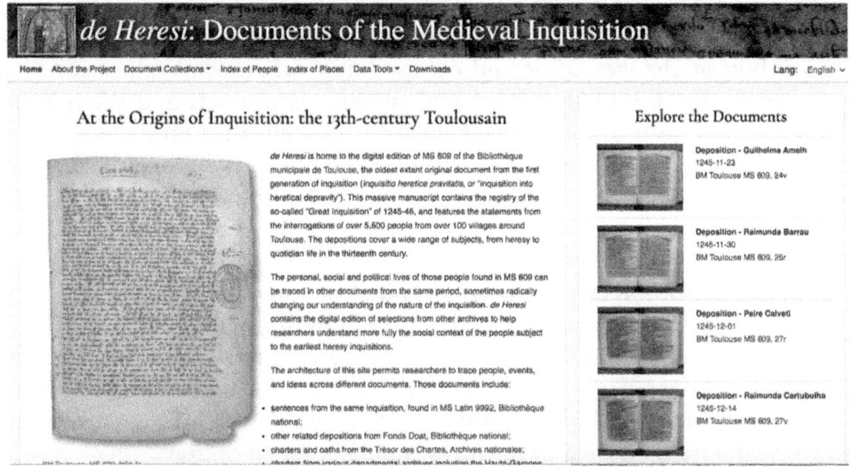

Figure 10.2 de Heresi: Documents of the Medieval Inquisition home page

Source: (Image by permission of Jean-Paul Rehr, Université Lumière Lyon 2/CIHAM.

the contents (overview, downloads, tools, and documents). The main action item is the invitation to "Explore" the documents. The project goals are to create a full index of the people and places identified in a well-defined set of documents that are provided in facsimile images and transcribed texts. Behind this project is the work of digitization, transcription, markup, and metadata creation—all familiar from earlier discussions. But in addition, some information architecture has been employed on the back end to hold and deliver the materials for display.

The Pelagios site serves as a point of entry to a consortium of projects whose research focuses on the ancient classical world. Almost all of the information on the landing page is in the form of invitations to action. This is a group of sites networked together for common search and discovery, rather than a single site organized around a research topic. So "Join," "Read," "Discover," and "Find" are crucial instructions. The windows below offer immediate access to featured content. Is this site as efficient as the two others and does it use screen real estate as effectively? How clear is the branding and navigation? This is also a mature site with rich content and much intellectual work and considerable resources behind it.

How an interface works

An interface is a set of cognitive cues. It may look like a screen full of pictures of things inside the computer, but in fact, the interface *mediates* between an individual the computational activity. By definition, an interface

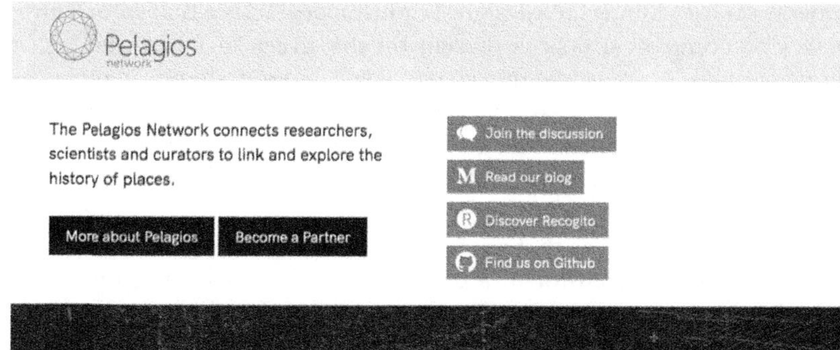

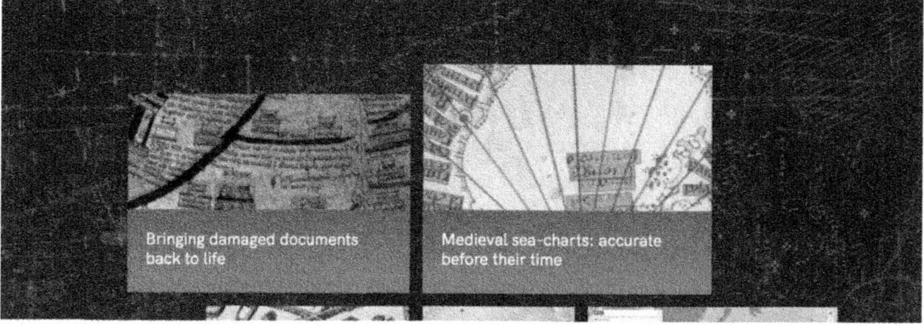

Figure 10.3 Pelagios Portal (Image of the Pelagios Network home page, website design by Agile Collective, header image by Emma McNally. The Pelagios Network is an association of equal and independent Partners and a wider community of members, coordinated by a Chair, a General Secretary and a Partnership Secretary.)

is an in-between space of communication and exchange, a place where two worlds, entities, or systems meet. Because interface is so familiar to us, we forget that it was built on metaphors like "windows" we can look through and a "desktop" on which we work.

As just noted, an interface is not a picture of what is "inside" the computer and does not show us the way the computer works or processes information or data. In fact, the screen often makes such processing invisible. It is an obfuscating environment as much as it is a facilitating one. As the GUI developed, icons were made to provide intuitive visual cues on which to perform actions and give instructions to the information architecture and programs. These icons—like file folders, trashcans, and the tools in our applications (pen, printer, eraser, etc.) allow us to perform activities in the digital environment that mimic those in the analog environment. This requires elaborate back-end engineering. Front-end experience becomes seamless through training and experience. Dragging and dropping are standard moves in an interface, but not really in an analog world. Early engagement with GUI was not necessarily intuitive. We had to learn how to interact with computer systems through an interface.

The notion of "cognitive load" (how much mental work is required) is a consideration for all interface design. For instance, be sure that information necessary to complete a task is present on the screen in which the task is being performed. A point like this is very basic, but you do not want someone to have to remember a specific string of words or numbers, specialized vocabulary, or other information and carry it in their mind from one screen to another. Errors creep in and so does frustration. For scholarly projects, a useful feature is the creation of drop-down menus and pick lists of specialized vocabulary (keywords that guide the visitor to specific content). Would you know what to search for in a catalog of ancient artifacts from Mesopotamia? Offering a researcher a free-text field, one in which they can type anything, is only useful for those already familiar with the domain.

Many humanities projects developed substantial research content but did not have effective interfaces. A project sponsored by the American National Endowment for the Humanities, "Digging into Data," was created to make these contents available through new interface designs. One of these, the records of the Old Bailey court, the longest continuous record of legal activity in Britain, was enhanced when a list of crimes, date spans, gender and age of criminals, and punishments was provided. The result was a filtered search that guided researchers into the specific cases. The Old Bailey project had been in development for years, but its humanist scholars were not accustomed to thinking in terms of interface design.

Designing an interface

The process of interface design involves creating the look, structure, and activity for the project. It also should involve writing use-case scenarios that are quite specific for the project. After the interface is mocked-up in a wireframe (a schematic outline of the landing page and linked pages within the site) with functionality, it needs to be user-tested. The process of interface design is: 1) sketch the concept (what contents and functions need to be in the layout); 2) write specific use cases linked to specific profiles or personae of visitors; 3) create a mock-up and walk through it step by step using the personae; 4) create a prototype of the design; 5) test with actual visitors; and 6) connect the back-end information architecture and contents to the front end (Nielsen 1994). A few iterations of this cycle will be needed before the project is finished. [See Exercise #3: Eight Golden Rules.]

Sketching an interface does not require any particular tools or platforms—it can be done on paper or at a whiteboard. An interface can be designed using HTML and CSS by structuring the divisions, columns, and other layout and style features. However, to mock-up functionality—the relation between human actions and screen behaviors—some design tools are helpful. Once you have thought through how you want your interface to be organized, using a platform like Balsamiq, Figma, Proto.io, or FluidUI will allow you to create wireframes and basic functions (Cardello 2019). Unlike commercial sites in which you may need to handle business transactions—ordering, scheduling, processing financial information, etc.—a research site will usually have static content (even if it is updated or extended on a regular basis). The main design decisions you make for a scholarly site are how to communicate clearly what it contains and how to use the contents.

A few basic principles should be kept in mind with regard to the design:

1) Brand your site and be sure to put an icon/logo into the tab so it is visible whenever the site is open; have a vivid and clear masthead that immediately identifies the project.
2) Use screen real estate effectively—the top part of the site should contain all of the essential information for navigation. Do not fill the top of the screen with a single image or lots of blank space or decorative elements that are not related to functionality.
3) If you put functionality into the lower part of the screen, it should be administrative information, not information for navigating the site or understanding its contents.
4) New, changing, or featured materials should be in the top part of the screen.
5) Keep navigation elements visible at all points within the site so that someone using it can always return home or move to another place within the site.

When designing a project, create specific personae and use cases. Use cases should be specific and each persona should have goals, needs, and behaviors through which to test the site. Write a step-by-step scenario for a persona from the moment they arrive at the landing page. How do they know what is in the collection? How do they find it? What are the easiest ways to inform and guide their actions?

Components

The components of an interface are structural (layout and organization) and activity oriented. The structural features are the familiar navigation bar, menus, pages, and sidebars. The activity-oriented components are buttons, links, search boxes, and drop-down and swipe or arrow forward/backward elements.

Structural components:

Navigation: This is usually a top or side bar that provides an overview of the site for movement through it. Depending on the complexity, the site might be several levels deep, or it might consist of pages meant to be moved through in a particular sequence. Signals for how to use the site should be clear in the navigation bar. This is the top-level conceptual organization of the site and should contain a label or marker for every subdivision of the site that a visitor needs to know about. Together, the navigation and menu bars reveal the *contents* of the site and also how to *use* it at the highest level of conceptual organization.

Orientation: Giving a viewer a sense of *where* they are in the site is called *orientation*. The *breadcrumbs* (file pathways displayed in the browser) that show in a browser bar will also orient a viewer, but it is important that you provide a sense of where a researcher is in the whole project as well as how to move within the site through the navigation. Do not let a visitor get lost.

Menus: Drop-down or collapsible menus are an excellent way to show more detailed contents. Be sure they are organized appropriately. If they are indexes, alphabetic order makes sense. If they are topical and part of a thematic study, they will be more like a table of contents. Creating drop-down menus that go more than one level becomes difficult for navigation—and does not translate well into swipe interfaces.

Pages: The size of an individual page and its role in the overall structure of the site will depend on the material being presented. While scrolling presents no difficulties, chunking material into consumable, screen-sized pieces, has advantages. These design decisions are specific to each project, but too much information is just that—too much.

Sidebars: Sidebars provide an alternate method of navigation. They should be built into the frame of the site so they stay present throughout.

Links: These can be internal, offering a way to move around the site, or external, to other sites, references, social media, and so on. If they are internal, be sure links go both ways. If they are external, be clear about whether you want your reader to leave your site or simply have a second site open at the same time. You cannot link back from someone else's site.

Indexes: These are used more rarely in websites for research than in printed books, but they serve an important purpose, which is to guide a reader into the intellectual material.

Activity-oriented components:

Keep your viewers' expectations in mind. When they click on a link, they expect to be taken to an area of the site. When they enter text in a search box, they expect results.

Buttons: Easy navigation instruments, buttons in a conspicuous or subtle format guide the researcher to the materials most relevant to their interests. They should click easily and transfer the viewer swiftly.

Links: Make sure links go both ways. A forward and backward link needs to be embedded in each page to which the link refers. Don't lose

your viewers by forgetting to give them a route of return. They should be legible as links.

Search boxes: As noted, free-text search boxes should be supplemented with a pick list or controlled vocabulary list. This guides the experience and allows a novice to become familiar with the intellectual content of your site. Too many "no results" returns will frustrate anyone.

Drop-down/expandable menus: One level of expansion is good, a second is acceptable. Beyond that, the viewer is likely to lose their place, have the window snap shut, or become frustrated trying to understand these multiple levels of argument. Make sure the windows stay open in a non-fussy way—by clicking rather than hovering. Menus that only stay open on hover are likely to be harder to navigate.

Swipe or arrow-forward/backward navigation: For slide shows, visual materials that are sequenced for an argument, or to show a resource that has multiple pages/parts, a swipe or arrow-forward action is required. Keeping these materials within the larger frame, rather than in a separate window, will help the viewer stay focused on the site. Automated or timed arrows for forward motion can be annoying. Researchers have different rates of absorption and different levels of interest in materials. Best to let them take their own time. At least, put a pause button on any automated or timed display. [See Exercise #4: Compare interface designs.]

Takeaway

An interface can be a model of intellectual contents or a set of instructions for use, but it should be part of the initial development of any project, not a "style feature" added at the end. Interface is always an argument, and combines presentation (form/format), representation (contents), navigation (wayfinding), orientation (location/breadcrumbs), and connections to the network (links and social media). Interfaces are often built on metaphors of windows or desktops, but they also contain assumptions about users. The difference between a consumer and a participant is modeled in the interface design. While a consumer wants to get to a targeted result, a participant becomes engaged in the site and its materials.

Exercises

Exercise #1: history of interface

Look at the major milestones in the development of interface design and think about which features have been preserved and which have become obsolete? These are merely the physical/tactile features of the interface. Here are two useful sites: https://faculty.washington.edu/ajko/books/uist/history.html

https://medium.theuxblog.com/a-short-history-of-computer-user-interface-design-29a916e5c2f5

Exercise #2: Jesse James Garrett

https://uxcollection.com/the-elements-of-user-experienceby-jesse-james-garrett/

Analyze Garrett's diagram, then relate to examples across a number of digital humanities projects such as Perseus, Whitman, Orbis, Old Bailey, Mapping the Republic of Letters, Animal City, Codex Sinaiticus, Digital Karnak, the Roman Forum Project, Civil War Washington, and the Encyclopedia of Chicago.

Exercise #3: Eight Golden Rules

Ben Shneiderman is one of the major figures in the history of interface and information design. He has Eight Golden Rules of interface design. Use these rules to assess a website of your choice and then consider whether you would modify the rules or the site. http://faculty.washington.edu/jtenenbg/courses/360/f04/sessions/schneiderman/GoldenRules.html

Exercise #4: compare interface designs

Contrast this with the ways in which Civil War Washington and Valley of the Shadow organized their navigation. Consider the floorplan image in the Valley project and decide if it is too strong a metaphor or a helpful organizational concept. http://valley.lib.virginia.edu/ http://civilwardc.org/

Recommended readings

Kaur, Avinash. 2018. "Accessibility Guidelines for UX Designers." *UX Collective*. https://uxdesign.cc/accessibility-guidelines-for-a-ux-designer-c3ba775539be.

Kirschenbaum, Matthew. 2004. "Ch. 34: So the Colors Cover the Wires." In *C2DH, Companion to Digital Humanities*, edited by Susan Schreibman, Ray Siemens, and John Unsworth. Oxford: Blackwell. http://digitalhumanities.org:3030/companion/.

Thoden, Klaus, Juliane Stiller, Natasa Bulatovic, Hanna-Lena Meiners, and Nadia Boukhelifa. 2017. "User-Centered Design Practices in Digital Humanities—Experiences from DARIAH and CENDARI." *ABI Technik* 37 (1) (January). DOI: 10.1515/abitech-2017-0002.

Waddell, Kaveh. 2017. "The Internet of Things Needs a Code of Ethics." *The Atlantic*. www.theatlantic.com/technology/archive/2017/05/internet-of-things-ethics/524802/.

10b Understanding interface design

An interface constructs a narrative. This is particularly true in the controlled environment of a project where every screen is part of the design. We imagine the user's experience according to the organization we give to the interface. Of course, a user may or may not follow the structure we have established. (Readers don't go through books or print publications in a linear way either.) Thinking about what the narrative is and how it creates a point of view and a story is useful as part of the project development. In many cases, narrative is as much an effect as it is an engine of the experience. Odd juxtapositions or sequencing can disrupt the narrative. We are familiar with the ways in which frame-to-frame relationships create narrative in a film environment, or in graphic novels, or comic books. One of the distinctive features of digital and networked environments is that the number and types of frames are radically different from in print or film. The kinds of materials that appear in those frames is also varied in terms of the kind of temporal and spatial experience these materials provide. A video can play in a window next to a pop-up window while multi-level text displays vie for attention and images scroll along in a sidebar. This is a lot to process and requires many changes of mode—reading, viewing, listening, and selecting.

A few examples are useful for understanding these concepts. Look at each of these sites about writing: The Poetess Archive, focused on 18th and 19th century women poets writing in English; the Walt Whitman Archive, focused on a single American author and his works; the Iraqi Jewish Archive; and Invisible Australians, a cultural project. How does each tell a story? What is the narrative of the content as well as the site organization?

The Poetess Archive uses graphical motifs to establish its tone—delicate color, the songbirds, a serif typeface, and background frame tint. It starts with a "Welcome" statement, speaking to the viewer. News items are posted, to give a sense of where the project is in its own development (note that the last updates were in 2017), and then the tabs invite the viewer to search the materials in the site. The story is mainly contained in the welcome frame, after which, viewers are free to search and browse. A new interface is in design production in Fall 2020, so comparing it with the example above will be useful to see what new functionalities are indicated and how it guides the experience of a researcher.

The Whitman Archive brands its identity with a steel engraving of the American author. The image speaks of a time and also a personality. The engraving is skilled, the product of a practiced technician in an era when these images were a part of visual culture. The style of the site looks dated, very early 2000s. The site is organized by types of things relevant to the poet's work—published materials, manuscripts, biographical material, and so on. The story of the site is the focus on an individual figure, a monumental personality of American letters in the 19th century. Included are

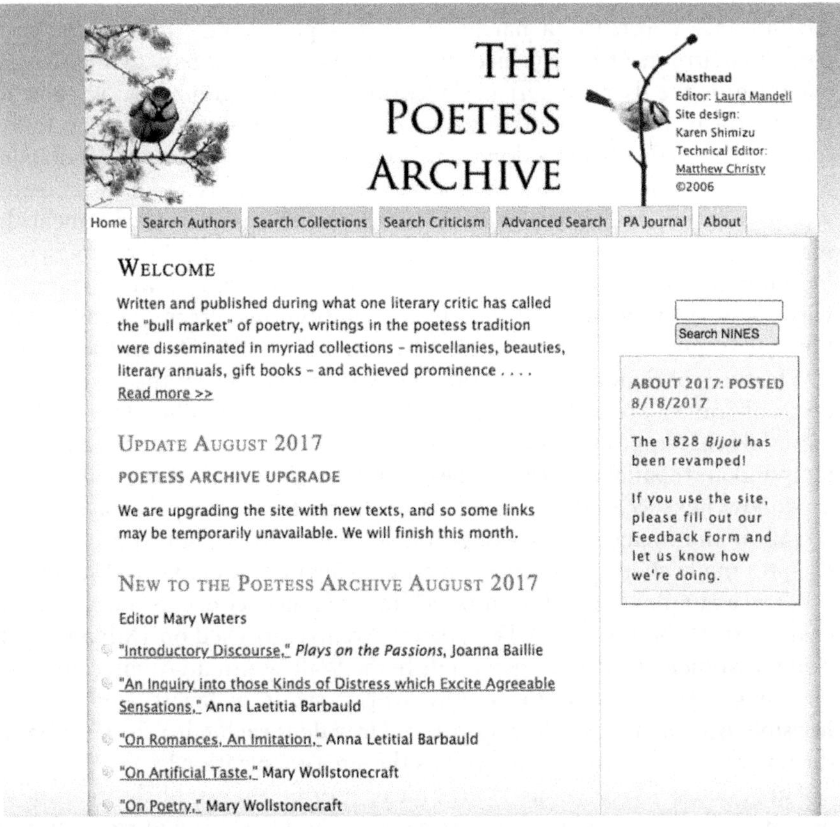

Figure 10.4 poetessarchive.org

Source: (Image courtesy of Laura Mandell, project Director and Principal Investigator.)

studies of such unusual materials as an enormous geographical scrapbook put together by Whitman. A special Scrapbook Page Viewer argues, by its presence, that this is a very important object. The ability to move through the entire scrapbook, zoom into its details, and examine the many pieces of its composition reinforces this argument.

The Whitman and Poetess archives are repositories, their "narrative" is mainly a framework for discovery. But in an exhibit a narrative is explicitly organized by the sequencing of pages. The Iraqi Jewish Archive exhibit tells a succinct tale that is structured as a series of panels moved through with an arrow. Each panel has a vivid image, a clear informative text, and the whole exhibit sits within the larger framework of the repository. Viewers can return to the archive and explore the other themes in the menu bar, such

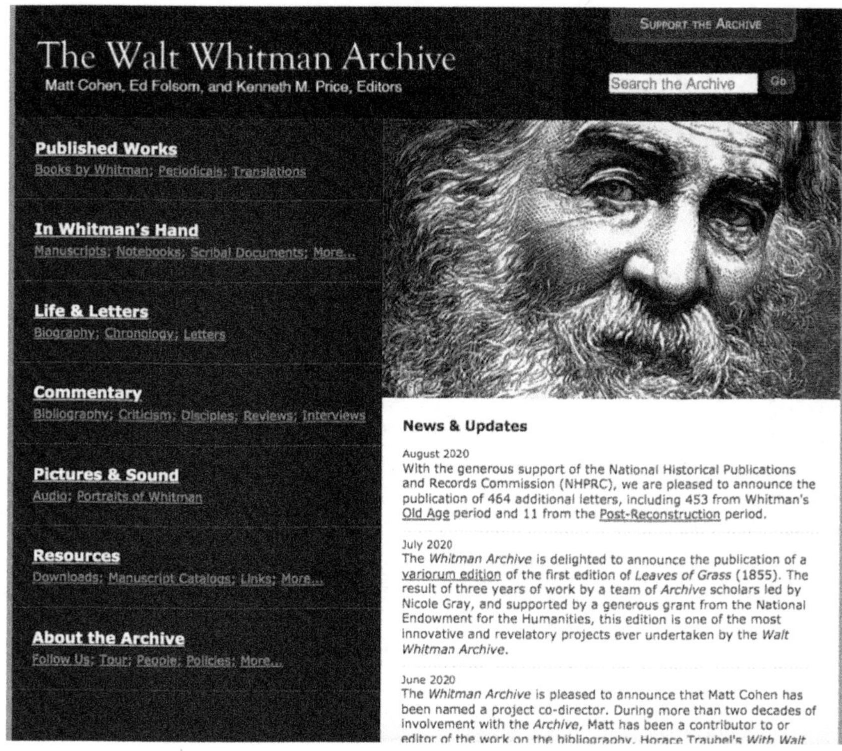

Figure 10.5 Landing page of the Whitman Archive

Source: (Reproduced courtesy of The Walt Whitman Archive. Gen. ed. Matt Cohen, Ed Folsom, and Kenneth M. Price. Accessed 30 August 2020. <www.whitmanarchive.org>.)

as Text & Heritage, or Personal & Communal Life. This is a structured narrative experience. The narrative is kept in view by the consistency of the framing, color backgrounds, the directional arrows, and a single directed experience of viewing.

Invisible Australians is a repository of powerful stories. These are "discovered" through a gallery of faces, and each individual story is presented as a profile of someone whose identity was erased.

These four projects are each distinct in their format, their contents, and their design. While digital storytelling is appropriate in some projects, the presentation of a repository might need for its contents to be available without a framing narrative. Note other components of interface design, in addition to the identifying masthead and menu bar for navigation. The sidebar posts, directions to Faces, Resources, and administrative parts of the project such as Contact and Home are clearly labeled.

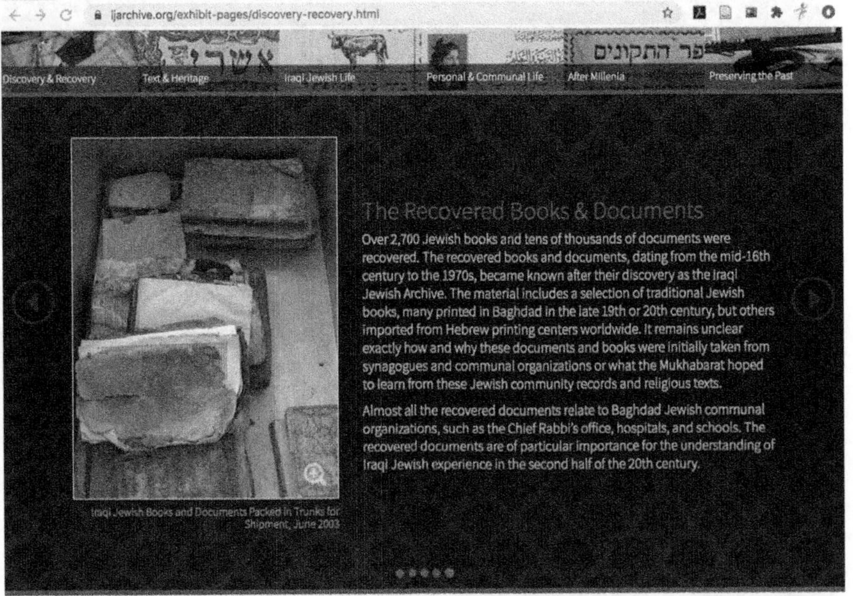

Figure 10.6 Iraqi Jewish Archive exhibit, from the *Preserving the Iraqi Jewish Archive* website

Source: (Featured photo courtesy of Harold Rhode; screenshot courtesy Council on Library and Information Resources.) https://ijarchive.org/exhibit/exhibit

Note the components of interface design, identifying the masthead, menu bar for navigation, elements of the navigation internal to the exhibit, and consistency of format and style.

Non-linear site design

Hyperlinking creates multiple pathways through a project in ways now so familiar we don't consider them. A site design should be developed with the recognition that someone might enter the site and move around at will, not necessarily following a prescribed path. In fact, many sites—particularly repositories or collections—do not have a path. Those that do create an overarching narrative for the viewer. This illusion of continuity might conceal even more of the back-end operations.

Explicitly non-linear arguments require careful design. A platform that was specifically designed to create narratives with multiple, non-linear or not-necessarily linear navigation are Scalar and Twine (slightly more game-like). Developed from within a community that wanted to embed media, particularly time-based media, within scholarly work, Scalar has built-in capacities for forking-path design that are very well suited to creating non-linear arguments. As in all online projects, the conceptual approach required

Figure 10.7 The Invisible Australians project (Image with permission of Tim Sherratt and Kate Bagnall, Invisible Australians: Living under the White Australia Policy, http://invisibleaustralians.org/)

is modular—what are the logical pieces and chunks, and how might they fit together in a variety of ways? Scalar supports many scholarly—and creative—projects and has a strong commitment to argument. The innovative design offers alternatives to a single linear organization or pathway and encourages branching and networked structures. [See Exercise #1: Scalar showcase.]

One consideration for all interface design is how it will wear over time. This is true from a technical standpoint, of course, as many plug-ins go obsolete and other features cease working. But it is true from a style standpoint as well. Consider the longevity factor and whether viewers will find novelty features annoying or rewarding, integral to the project or layered on top of it for effect. Also consider how tightly linked the digital assets are to the platform—will you be able to migrate these forward if the authoring platform disappears? All styles will age, some will do so more conspicuously than others. This is not always negative.

Rapidly changing concepts of what constitutes a good or bad design, a workable or functional model, and a stylish or "contemporary" one shifts daily. A final exercise that provides useful insight into design principles is to look through the Best and Worst Interfaces (these appear on various sites) and analyze the disasters that are collected there. Someone designed each of those thinking they worked. [See Exercise #2: Best and worst interfaces.]

Cultural issues

Interface designs often depend upon cultural practices or conventions that may not be legible to users from another background. The most obvious point of difference is linguistic, and language use restricts and defines user communities. But color carries dramatically different meanings across cultures, as do icons, images, and even the basic organization and structure of formats. Concepts of hierarchy, of symmetry, and of direct and indirect address are elements that carry a fair amount of cultural value. Creating designs that will work effectively in globally networked environments requires identifying those specific features of a project or site that might need modification or translation in order to communicate to audiences outside of those in which it was created.

The ethical issues in interface design are significant. The design should take into account the widest range of possible viewers. While a personal site is not legally required to be compliant with the Americans with Disabilities Act (ADA), any site hosted by an institution that deals with the public—school, museum, library, and so on—should follow these guidelines. Color blindness affects many adults, so using schemes that will be legible to a broad readership means avoiding contrasts that disappear to those with visual limitations. The concept of *inclusivity* is used to describe practices that will make a site useful for the most viewers, including those with different abilities. Cultural differences in attitudes towards hierarchy, direct address, greeting, and formal vs. informal behaviors are worth considering if the site is to be used in wide contexts. What might give offense? Or be off-putting? Consider embedding interface options that expand usability. Testing a site is the best way to understand how it will affect individuals with different capabilities (Tognazzini 2014).

Because interface is so integral to our access and use of networked and digital materials, the complexity with which it operates is largely obscured by its familiarity. Taking apart the literal structure of interface, identifying the functions and knowledge design of each piece, and articulating the conventions within a discussion of narration, navigation, and orientation is useful. So are the exercises of trying to think across cultures and communities. The fluency and flexibility of interface design is an advantage and a challenge.

In their "Critical Interface Manifesto," the Catalan activist group outlines a number of key principles for thoughtful and ethical interface design. They stress the extent to which interfaces conceal their ideology and value systems. In particular, they focus on how navigation in an interface contributes to a sense of "freedom"—the viewer feels they can move anywhere, that everything is accessible, available, and equally open to all. They make many other points as well and make a cogent argument for the need to *read* an interface for what it conceals as well as how it works in the visually present form. [See: Exercise #3: Critical Interface Manifesto.]

Access: not always uniform

Who should see what on a site? And how does the interface indicate levels of permission and access? This point has been discussed before, but it comes into design and implementation in an interface. Password protection is one way to keep some materials from view. So is participant-registration. Consider the liabilities of the materials in your research. Are you at risk of violating someone's privacy by making public work or projects they may have authored in an early stage of their career or development? Are you allowing materials specific to a particular community and made for circulation within that community to become more public than their authors had imagined? This is often a question with digitization of 'zine materials, activist publications, or documents made to circulate among a self-identified group. They were "publications" only in the sense that they were multiples that were part of building a community. Does their existence in print format justify their digitization and presentation in an online environment? How are they identified and are authors who wrote pseudonymously being "outed" by the digital presentation?

Indigenous communities often have a need for self-documentation and archival production without a desire for these materials to be fully available

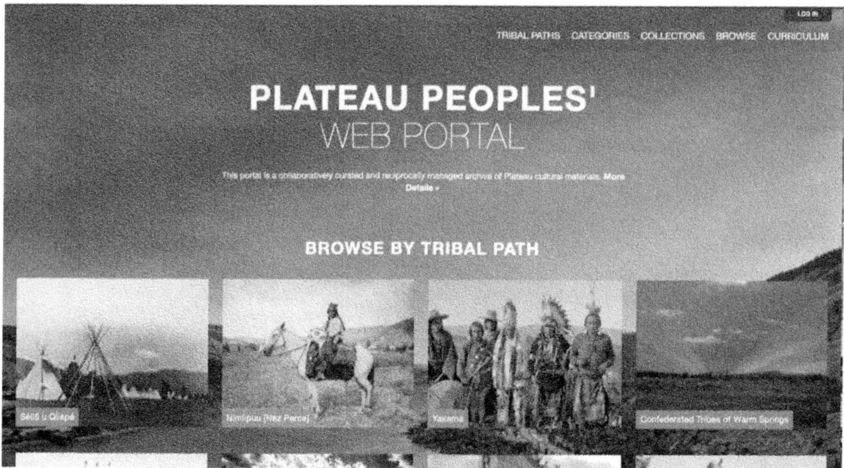

Figure 10.8 Plateau Peoples' Web Portal is built using Mukurtu, a platform designed for Indigenous knowledge. Here the designers have already structured the narrative by calling for visitors to "browse" in a particular way, "by tribal path." However, the menu at the top is organized by contents (paths, categories, collections, curriculum) as well as by behavior (browse). The visual identity is clear.

Source: (Image courtesy of Kimberly Christen, Center for Digital Scholarship and Curation, Washington State University.)

to a broad public. The Mukurtu project, already referenced, was designed to provide degrees of access to different constituencies. The designers of Mukurtu created cultural access protocols that were structured into the interface as well as the back-end design of sites. The showcase of Mukurtu projects provides a useful introduction to these issues, as does the other documentation on their site. Whose voice "speaks" in the interface and whose values and cultural identity does it represent? The Plateau Peoples' portal identifies the collaborative character of the project. At the very least, this provides assurance that the materials are presented with permission of the tribal peoples involved. [See Exercise #4: Cross-cultural design.]

Takeaway

Critical readings of interface require considering their organization, narrative, and functionality—but also, the ways in which interface conceals workings and back-end structures. Most interfaces assume a "universal" reader and an "omniscient" viewer. But no such person exists, and each individual will respond to the contents and the organization of a site in accord with their own background, experience, and expectations. Narratives are structured into the user interface and also into the relation of information in a digital project. The "narrative" of an exhibit, archive, or online repository may or may not correspond to the narrative of the information it contains. To analyze the *argument* of a digital project requires combining visual and graphical analysis with textual and navigational assessment. The interface can be assessed for *how* it engages with a viewer, not only for what it *contains*. How does it identify the place from which it speaks and the person, institution, or community whose values it embodies?

Exercises

Exercise #1: Scalar showcase

Scalar is an experimental publishing platform meant to provide multiple points of entry to a project and various pathways through it. It extends work that was done in Vectors where every interface was custom designed to suit the projects. Look through the Vectors archive and think about narration, navigation, and orientation conventions in these projects.

http://scalar.usc.edu/

http://vectors.usc.edu/issues/index.php?issue=6

Exercise #2: best and worst interfaces

Do a search for recent "best" and "worst" interfaces (even "worst interfaces of all time" produces interesting results). Sort out whether the judgment is being made on style or functionality. Do you agree with the assessments?

Exercise #3: Critical Interface Manifesto

The Critical Interface Manifesto makes thirteen strong statements. Walk through these one at a time and see how they provide a framework for reading an interface like the examples described in the text. https://crit.hangar.org/toolbox/

Exercise #4: cross-cultural design

Extract the principles from Cynthia Risse's article, "Cross-Cultural Interface Design," 2017, and consider how your project will read cross-culturally.
https://medium.com/@cynthiarisse/cross-cultural-interface-design-1f259a8fbcdc

Recommended readings

Burgstahler, Sheryl. n.d. "Designing Software That Is Accessible to Persons with Disabilities." *Disabilities, Opportunities, Internetworking, Technology*. www.washington.edu/doit/Brochures/Technology/design_software.html.

Shah, Nehal. 2013. "Cross Cultural Considerations for User Interface Design." *Human Factors International*. www.humanfactors.com/newsletters/cross-cultural-considerations-for-user-interface-design.asp.

References cited

Burgess, Matt. 2018. "What Is the Internet of Things?" www.wired.co.uk/article/internet-of-things-what-is-explained-iot.

Cardello, Jeff. 2019. "17 Useful Tools for UI/UX Designers." *Webflow blog*. https://webflow.com/blog/ui-ux-design-tools.

Engelbart, Douglas. 2008–2020. www.dougengelbart.org/content/view/162/000/.

Nielsen, Jakob. 1994. "10 Heuristics for User Interface Design." *Nielsen Norman Group*. www.nngroup.com/articles/ten-usability-heuristics/.

Norman, Don. 2010. "Natural User Interfaces Are Not Natural." *Interactions* XVII (3). https://interactions.acm.org/archive/view/may-june-2010/natural-user-interfaces-are-not-natural1.

Tognazzini, Bruce. 2014. "First Principles of Interaction Design." *Ask Tog*. https://asktog.com/atc/principles-of-interaction-design/.

Resources

ADA, Americans with Disabilities Act. www.w3.org/WAI/standards-guidelines/wcag/.

Bad Websites. https://blog.rankingbyseo.com/bad-websites/.

De Heresi: Documents of the Medieval Inquisition http://medieval-inquisition.huma-num.fr/.

Digging into Data https://diggingintodata.org/.

Invisible Australians. http://invisibleaustralians.org/.

Mukurtu https://mukurtu.org/. And https://mukurtu.org/showcase/.
Old Bailey Online. www.oldbaileyonline.org/.
Plateau Peoples Web Portal. https://plateauportal.libraries.wsu.edu/.
Poetess Archive. www.poetessarchive.org/index.html.
Scalar. https://scalar.me/anvc/scalar/features/ and https://scalar.me/anvc/showcase/dna-seven-interactive-essays-on-nonlinear-storytelling/.
THDL (Tibetan Himalayan Digital Library) www.thlib.org/places/.
ToastyTech. http://toastytech.com/guis/bob.html.
Walt Whitman Archive https://whitmanarchive.org/.
Web Content Accessibility Guidelines www.w3.org/WAI/standards-guidelines/wcag/.

11 Web presentation formats and networked resources

11a Web presentation formats

Not all digital scholarship ends up online. The use of computational methods can be effective in producing research results without being on the Web. Data mining, text analysis, and other forms of automated processing of information in digital formats are often carried out as primary research investigations whose results are funneled into publications. But online publication formats and presentation modes are also a crucial part of the work in digital humanities. Presentation formats take various forms, as was already evident in the discussion of interface. The most common are repositories, exhibits, theme and topic-specific sites, or digital publications. In addition, digital projects that create tools and platforms, or document pedagogical techniques and best practices, are also major contributions to emerging scholarship.

This section will describe some of the most common web presentation formats to examine what they share in terms of functionality. The section is meant to address the basics of making intellectual content available in a networked environment. It focuses on a fairly high-level description of the components of these presentation tools, rather than on the details of setting up server environments or configuring platforms within them. The assumption is that a scholar working in digital modes will either have access to web hosting through a home institution (university, museum, library, or company or foundation of some kind) or purchase commercial hosting services, not mount their own servers. The following section will address some of the current best practices for sharing resources within a networked environment.

Basics

The time to consider the web presentation format of your project is at the beginning of the planning process before development begins. The creation of digital assets will then serve the project's overall design. Are you making a collection and repository—as in the case of an archive like Walt Whitman, or the Old Bailey? Or are you making an exhibit, as in the case of The Smithsonian Museum or the National Library of Russia? Or is your goal more of a publication of scholarship and research that might contain embedded maps, analytics, images, or audio-visual materials, like the project on Landscape Change in Southern Brazil from 1953 to the present? To reiterate, the basic formats are repository/collections, exhibits, and publications. Many projects are combinations of these but understanding the infrastructure requirements of each is helpful as a guide to design. We will begin by describing these different modes of web presentation, the activity they support, and their design requirements from a functional technical standpoint.

Another crucial distinction to understand is the differences among *collections* management systems, *content* management systems, and *digital* asset management (DAMS) components. *Collections management systems* are used by institutions to manage their materials—registrars need condition reports, loan records, descriptions of the assets, and their location and any restrictions on use. *Content management systems* provide a set of pre-packaged tools designed to support interpretation, presentation, query/search/retrieval, and use of digital assets. In large institutions, the two may need to connect with each other. In an individual project, a content management system can be used to create digital assets and provide the services needed to make them useful. In an individual, small-scale project, the collections management may be built into the platform (as it is with Omeka and Drupal, for instance, discussed later). *Digital asset management systems* are designed to store substantial quantities of assets for shared use and are generally found in large-scale institutions or business environments where content sharing across units is essential.

Decide if your presentation will be static or dynamic. In a static site, all of the content is essentially "held" by the HTML framework through links to files. This works well for content that is not interactive and is edited for presentation of information and argument. In a dynamic site, user queries and other interactions will "call" resources from a repository. This works for a site that customizes experience for researchers seeking specific contents from a collection.

Publishing on the web involves several elements. A URL and domain name will be required. This is the "web address" through which your materials are found. The actual contents (files, frameworks, and style sheets) have to be on a server that is live and linked to the Web. The server will hold the materials for you, but your domain name is what tells a browser where to look for them. Your files can be developed on a desktop but must be transferred to a server. The easiest way to do this is with an FTP (File Transfer Protocol) application. Many such applications (like Filezilla) are drag and drop or have a graphical interface to make this process intuitive. Be sure files are named properly, nested properly in folders, and that their pathways are specified so that images, videos, sound files, and other materials can be found by the browser.

Web presentation formats and platforms

This is a brief overview of three kinds of web presentation formats. In actuality, their boundaries blur, but for the sake of description, they have been separated here to give some idea of what they do, how they work, and what a few popular applications are for each. The question is whether you want to build functionality into a customized platform, whether you can use a generic one, or whether you can modify an existing tool.

Collections and/or repositories

- Description: These are projects that consist of large collections of material—documents, photographs, audio-visual materials, and so on. These include large, institutional projects. But scholarly work might take place in community archives, or regional museums, or a study of a single author's papers. These are projects well within the scope of a single researcher or a small team. Classroom projects are sometimes focused on making collections as an exercise, putting together materials from a neighborhood, or working with materials in a local library, university archive, or other repository.
- Activity: Within the web environment, these materials will need to be able to be searched, retrieved, and presented to viewers for study or analysis.
- Specifications: Metadata will need to be attached to each digital asset (image, document, video, etc.) in a record in the system. This is work done by the scholar, without automation. If metadata exists already, it can be reused, though for an individual project, new fields and content may be added.
- Popular applications for this work include Omeka, Drupal, Joomla, and various alternatives. Check features such as export functions (if you write a long interpretative statement for an object, can it be exported? If so, in what format? What about the metadata?). Is the platform retro-compliant so that if you build a project in one year and the platform is upgraded your project will still be supported and viable? Is there a broad user community that supports the platform and helps fix bugs, adds features, and provides help through listservs or other social media sites? These are important issues. Also, consider the hosting options. Omeka will host your project on its site, but the version has limited features. Installing an Omeka instance on an institutional server is advisable. Drupal is a high-powered system that is highly flexible and customizable—but with a much steeper learning curve.
- Implementation: A content management system provides a set of services built on top of the repository. This allows you to use the assets in your collection to make exhibits, display the materials online, or have

them served to scholars for use. The content management system builds in the code to *do things with digital assets*. Without this, you will have to custom-build all of these features into your site. By analogy, if you have a warehouse full of physical artifacts, you need a catalog, shelving system, and a way to find and handle the objects for study and display. [See Exercise #1: Omeka.]

Exhibit

- Description: Many projects that are based on digital assets are most suited to creation of an online exhibit on a particular topic or theme. Exhibits are built around a framing narrative while a repository provides direct access to digitized artifacts, documents, or resources. An exhibit often draws on a repository, but it could embed all digital resources directly in the HTML or presentation. A church group or community organization might want to make an exhibit to document its history. A local historical society might be interested in commemorating an anniversary. Museums, galleries, historical societies, and artists are likely to post exhibits on a rotating basis. A whole back-end repository might not be needed for this, simply a presentation format for content.
- Activity: The content might simply need to be organized, designed, and presented. A simple HTML page with a style sheet in CSS would be sufficient, but a platform like WordPress will also provide an easy way to create pages, themes, and sub-themes within a site. The main activity being supported is viewing with some navigation (tabs, links, and sidebars).
- Specifications: You need a way to hold the digital assets—images, text, audiovisual files, and so on—so they can be displayed. You may want to be able to increase image size in a roll-over or click, to navigate to subthemes within the exhibit, or to show more or less material. A platform that allows intuitive organization of the path through the exhibit is crucial—this is true in physical exhibits where the viewer is directed through the material as it is laid out in the spaces of a gallery. The sections of the site provide an online equivalent.
- Applications: WordPress is one common platform for exhibit building, but so are many commercial applications like Wix or Squarespace. Concrete5 is an open-source freeware platform with modular functionality so that it can be used easily without much prior training and yet is customizable. Omeka can be used for exhibits but requires creating an asset repository first.
- Implementation: That they are simple, easy to use, and low-maintenance as well as having a very short learning curve are the benefits to using an exhibit builder. These generally make use of WYSIWYG, or "wisiwig"

approaches—what you see is what you get—that are graphical in format and show you immediately what your work looks like. [See Exercise #2: WordPress.]

Publication

- Description: The basic currency of scholarship is publication. Articles, books, reviews, and essays of all kinds form the core of scholarly knowledge production and dissemination.
- Activity: From an individual *scholar or writer's* point of view, what is required is a flexible authoring platform that allows for creative and intuitive use. In particular, the ease of hyperlinking modules of the argument provides structure, offering non-linear pathways, and custom design features (graphic as well as functional). From a *publisher's* point of view, what is needed is a way to manage workflow from submission to publication, including a way to track peer review, corrections, proofing, and other stages of the process. One feature to consider is, as always, the export function. Can the publication be readily repurposed as a PDF? Make it easy to do this or consider including an already-formatted PDF for download.
- Specifications: These can be as simple as a platform that supports writing, embedded media of any kind, and some options for structuring arguments using digitally specific capabilities like navigation, menu bars, and links. Or they can be as elaborate as the management of workflow and design.
- Applications: In addition to WordPress, mentioned above, which is widely used by individuals, applications for publishing within scholarly communities make use of elaborate systems that manage workflows from submission to review, proofing, and final publication. Some of these platforms are referred to as "manuscript management systems" designed for the use of professional journals and scholarly communities (Kim et al. 2018). ScholarOne and PubMed are high-level publishing platforms. Scalar, designed from within the humanities community, provides considerable flexibility and creativity as an authoring platform. Do not forget the ubiquitous Wiki format, which is a highly adaptable format for group work and multiple contributions, and has an intuitive page and navigation structure.
- Implementation: Authoring and publishing are the core of academic scholarly work. Creating innovative digital formats has been slow, and many online platforms replicate the structure of analog print media, rather than considering potential alternatives. Can the familiar mode of linear argument that is central to print—even with marginal commentary, footnotes, and other features—be expanded in ways that extend argument structures in a meaningful way?

Using web presentation platforms

There are several ways to use web presentation platforms. Some of these are free, or have free trials, and a graduated pay scale depending on the client's needs and profile. Many of these platforms (Drupal, Omeka, and WordPress) can be downloaded and installed on a local server. Instances can even be installed on a desktop for development purposes. For the content of your project to be available online, it has to be stored on a server that has a publicly accessible URL. Even if your computer is online and networked, it is not a server. (It has an IP address, but not a web-address, and making it into a server requires serious work.) Commercial service providers like Amazon and GoDaddy provide this service for a fee.

In an educational institution, web hosting is generally provided for small scale projects and research. Larger projects that pressure the limits of resources may need to be supported by grants or other funds—or even hosted "off-site." Keep in mind that a project that is live online will need to be maintained into perpetuity. Even if its content is stable, the platform will become outmoded and features of its functionality will no longer work in upgraded browsers. It may be liable to spam attacks or other automated or deliberate hacking. And the costs of maintaining the project will, at the very least, consist of paying for hosting. While this may be a minimal fee, attention to these matters is best built into the project budget and planning process. [See Exercise #3: Preparing your materials.]

To install a web presentation platform "instance" on your desktop or on a local server, you may need to configure the environment so the platform runs properly. Familiar formats are the WAMP, MAMP, and LAMP configurations. These acronyms all refer to "Apache, MySequel, and PHP" software that support the running of the code in a W=Windows, M=Mac, or L=Linux environment. Installing MAMP or LAMP on your desktop is not difficult—you download it from the web—but understanding how to work with it and how to connect the presentation platform may require some assistance.

A few tips

- Always follow the tutorial, read the documentation, and look at the demos, examples, and export options. [See Exercise #4: Export Functions.]
- Check to see what degree of customization is possible. Are you limited to the themes and templates provided or can you re-style and restructure?
- Figure out how modular the platform is. Can you extend it easily, and add features and functions?
- What is the security record for a platform? How often will you need to update plugins to keep it secure?

- Who is going to maintain the platform and make sure it has not been spammed?
- Who will be responsible for updating content?
- What level of participation and what kind of community interaction do you envision? Monitoring comments and feedback is an ongoing task.
- Consider the intellectual property issues and what kind of license you are putting onto your online work (see the section ahead on IP).

Takeaway

Digital scholarship is frequently (though not always) presented in an online environment. Knowledge of the existing tools and platforms for this aspect of research is important. Many platforms are powerful but rigid, requiring a fairly high level of investment for learning in exchange for greater customizability. The basic trade-off is going to be simplicity of use vs. customizability and flexibility. Picking a platform requires making a list of the design specifications and functions your project requires and then finding the tool that will support this. Always be sure to check the export function. Building intellectual content directly within web presentation software that cannot be ported to another site or file can result in lost labor and considerable frustration. A platform with a broad user community is more likely to last—and to provide help support in the form of list-servs and other venues. Pretty much any problem you encounter—or any way you wish to customize a platform—someone else will have addressed. User groups for software host advice sites that can be very helpful.

Exercises

Exercise #1: Omeka

Read through the Omeka site and consider whether or not it would suit your project. Look at examples. Try this tutorial by Miriam Posner:

https://programminghistorian.org/en/lessons/up-and-running-with-omeka

Exercise #2: WordPress

Look at the WordPress documentation and compare it with Omeka. Why would you choose one over the other? Create a grid of features and compare them.

Exercise #3: preparing your materials

What are the assets you have digitized and how are they organized, described, and named? How will they be used and how much flexibility do you want in your site? Should scholars be able to access the entire set of assets, or only see them in the interpretative frameworks you have created?

Exercise #4: export functions

Look at some of the tools and platforms you use regularly for word processing, image viewing, presentation authoring, or audio editing. What export formats do they each have? How about a spreadsheet program? How much interoperability is there among data types?

Recommended readings

Jacobson, Daniel. 2009. "COPE: Create Once, Publish Everywhere." *Programmable Web*. www.programmableweb.com/news/cope-create-once-publish-everywhere/2009/10/13.

Yuri Gasparyan, Armen, Marien Yessirkepov, Alexander A. Voronov, Anna M. Koroleva, and George D. Kitas. 2019. "Comprehensive Approach to Open Access Publishing: Platforms and Tools." *Journal of Korean Medical Science* 34 (27). www.ncbi.nlm.nih.gov/pmc/articles/PMC6624413/.

11b Networked resources, standards for data sharing, and platforms

Resources, services, and platforms are three separate topics, but will be treated together here as additional concepts. Resources that use standards to assist sharing assets are increasingly common as online repositories grow and individual collections are made interoperable with others. Services are sites that offer support for projects, coding, and work in the online environment. Platforms provide a pre-set framework to enable specialized activity on a desktop or laptop with relative ease of use.

Most individual scholars will not be involved in setting up institutional infrastructure without technical support. But having a knowledge of the kind of infrastructure that is part of the broader scholarly community allows informed decisions about the design and long-term sustainability of projects. One particularly important issue is the connection among projects and resources. An ethical consideration is attached to this issue, since making materials digital involves considerable investment of resources—human, technical, ecological, and economic. Not every project needs to be preserved, but if it is, how can benefits be optimized?

If a project is going to have a long-term future, building it on resources that meet professional standards within library, museum, and archive repositories makes sense. These institutions are staffed by information professionals whose expertise builds on communities and consortia in which such standards are established and implemented. These are the people who help establish best practices for the creation and management of cultural resources. They are trained in understanding the needs of researchers and ways to provide for information access and retrieval across a wide range of disciplines. Every sector from private companies and government organizations to community groups and educational institutions has need of this expertise—which includes an understanding of the ways networked resources are designed to be shared and maintained. This group is not simply composed of "programmers." Information professionals span the full range of expertise in project design, development, and management. They are the people to consult to see if you need Omeka or Drupal, should create a custom interface and metadata, and whether you will need to pay for hosting.

This section contains a very basic introduction to some of the activity that supports networked resources, services, and platforms designed to support online work. The concept of a "framework" will be useful here since it describes an infrastructure that provides functionality and services. Precisely what that means will hopefully become clear below. But in essence, these frameworks anticipate the needs of people who will want to use digital assets for research, publishing, exhibition, analysis, and other purposes. In the analog world, this might be compared to a distinction between a service center and a warehouse. A warehouse might contain cultural materials (vinyl records, lantern slides, rare drawings, sculptures, and documents of all kinds). A service center supports access through devices for listening, projecting, viewing and accessing these materials, and information about who made them, when, where, and other crucial details of media, provenance, and intellectual property conditions for use.

In the first instance, the warehouse, the assets are preserved, but not necessarily accessible. Many impediments to access would be present if every individual scholar had to come equipped with the right record players, tape deck, or video equipment. When accessing streaming content made from formats as diverse as silver nitrate film prints and Betamax video, each individual viewer does not need to set up an emulation instance on their desktop. In the process of digitization, the materials have been standardized for use. For scholarly purposes, a considerable amount of extra metadata and infrastructure is required since the materials are being managed for long-term cultural memory, not just entertainment within a commercial sphere.

The purpose of standards for formats, metadata, services, and other features is to make materials more accessible to more communities over a longer period of time. Many people will never think about infrastructure. In many cases, the infrastructure that supports access to digital assets and services only becomes apparent when it breaks. A little bit of knowledge goes a long way toward ensuring that resources remain usable. Nothing substitutes for professional expertise and projects should be designed from the outset with advice on best practices. Applications and platforms that allow you to "dock" projects and simulate the application environment for their development have emerged. Docker and Heroku are two applications that support this work, extending the capacities of desktop computers to engage with a range of platforms.

LoD linked open data standards and the concept of interoperability

The scope and scale of online resources grew in the last decades, creating a realization that making material "interoperable" posed certain challenges (Blaney 2020). The principle of *interoperability* is that resources described and stored in one networked environment ought to be able to be integrated and used simultaneously with materials in other environments. If the Museum of Modern Art in New York classified its assets with one set of terms and the São Paulo Museum of Modern Art and one in Seoul Korea used others, how could they be searched in aggregate? What if they used different digitization standards and file formats? The legacy data in collection management systems (the "back end") is considerable. Though increasingly there are standards for the cataloging of cultural objects, the problem of differences remains. One perceived solution to this problem was to create a structured information format that would be applied to all of these collections and allow them to be searched at the same time.

Many scholarly projects were built in siloed environments. This means that while considerable discipline-specific expertise went into these projects, they could not "talk" to each other or share information. Gradually, consortia began to form, such as NINES, the Networked Infrastructure for Nineteenth-century Electronic Scholarship. Another, ReKN, the Renaissance Knowledge Network, performed similar functions for scholarship in that period. And the Pelagios Network was created to integrate geographical work on ancient places, including cartography, archaeology, codicology, and other fields. These organizations would create metadata "wrappers" for projects so they could all be found within a single search environment or portal, but they were still not accessible within standard search engines. These are a handful of discipline-specific consortia trying to integrate materials from a variety of projects. But large-scale interoperability efforts are also underway. A project called Europeana created a networked infrastructure in Europe. In Canada and Australia, networked infrastructure has been built with the goal of exposing collections to greater access. The documentation in these projects shows their shared recognition of the need for aggregation and sharing.

Linked Open Data (LoD) takes these issues to a higher level of aspiration for data integration by creating a standard for libraries, museums, archives, and other cultural institutions that is legible to machines. The goal is a standard metadata vocabulary that can be universally adopted, including application to legacy information. For instance, one feature of LoD is an International Authority File—a single index of all named entities such that every individual person, or place, who might be referenced in any data source has a single unique ID called a Uniform Resource Identifier (URI). The structure used in LoD allows for considerable analysis of relations (the data is structured in what are known as "triples" of subject/predicate/and object). Think of the challenges of names spelled many ways, in different languages, and using different transcription conventions—the difficulties of aligning these is daunting.

LoD uses a data standard known as RDF, Resource Description Format. Like many of the standards already mentioned, it is supervised by the W3C as part of the development of Semantic Web Technologies. These are approaches that were meant to make data machine-readable, and thus analyzable, across sites and repositories. Keep in mind, all of this grew up without precedents or standards, as multiple and varied institutions began to move their assets into online formats.

By this point you may feel lost in acronyms and references to standards with which you are not familiar. But some principles discussed multiple times here are useful to keep in mind, among which the most important is that standards only work when they are applied and applied consistently and across a substantial portion of data. (Refer to the Dublin Core examples in Chapter 4.) This requirement has been a sticking point since the application of data standards to existing data within cultural repositories is, like so many digital processes, very labor intensive, time consuming—in a word, expensive. Whether LoD will succeed depends on the extent to which it is adopted and whether alternatives arise that can be automated to do some of the same work of integrating information that was created in a wide range of formats and structures.

One example of a project that is built on LoD principles is LOUD. The acronym stands for Linked Open Usable Data and promotes usability. By contrast, LoD's publishing data is meant to make it easy to exchange information among systems. Usability implies other activities—for instance, is a file really usable if it can only be displayed at one size? What if a video has no fast-forward button? Or an audio file cannot be bookmarked? By now you will not be surprised to find that a common standard is JSON-LD, a JSON format for linked open data. LOUD is meant to be more useful for consumers, including curators and individuals working with art objects. The LinkedArt site contains useful documentation, including information on projects and consortia (PHAROS consortium of Photo Archives, Linked Conservation Data, American Art Collaborative, etc.) and a long list of prestigious institutions with broad international representation. The descriptive metadata on the site (accessed under the Model tab) gives a clear sense of the community from which it derives, and the specific domains in which it is useful. LOUD is related to IIIF, which will be taken up immediately in the next section. [See Exercise #1: LOUD's metadata.]

IIIF, International Image Interoperability Framework

IIIF, the International Image Interoperability Framework is important because it is integrated into the operation of so many institutions worldwide, and because it serves as an exemplary model of the "framework" concept mentioned in earlier sections.

Each of the words from which the acronym IIIF is taken is suggestive: *International* shows that this is a project that has many global partners. A glance at the map of participating institutions confirms this, and though the majority are in the northern hemisphere and in Europe, Canada, the UK, and the United States, participants from the global south are also present. *Image* is perhaps misleading, because though the project began with focus on image management, it has expanded to audio and video formats as well using the same principles. *Interoperability* points to the commitment to make resources usable across institutions and platforms in ways that are reliable (links will remain, references are stable, and the assets have standard formats and metadata). *Framework*, the final term indicates that the project is designed to provide standards for storage, access, delivery, and use through a number of APIs (you remember these, applied programming interfaces).

The main APIs in this framework are for Image (viewing specifications) and Presentation (metadata and sequencing of images). More on both of these below. But the concept of the *framework* is important because it is designed to anticipate use and integrate standards and services into a single environment. For example, it imagines that a scholar might want to take images from more than one institution and work with them in a common environment, adding custom notes and organization. Or, that if someone were looking at a video, you might want to be able to fast forward or put in bookmarks for later reference. These two examples describe an integration of digital resources (or assets: images and videos) and services for their use (annotation or search).

IIIF was initiated to "give scholars an unprecedented level of uniform and rich access to image-based resources hosted around the world."[1] This includes support of various features that add considerable value. All materials for IIIF compliant repositories are prepared with the same standard. It guarantees that when repositories make images available, they should be able to be used in certain standard ways: as thumbnails, for zooming, or as regions for detailed viewing. The *derivatives*—versions of the image in various sizes for onscreen viewing, detailed study, print publication, and so on—are already built into the collection as sized image files. The format allows the images to be scaled, rotated, cropped, and manipulated in other ways while keeping them as part of web linked data. Annotation layers can be stored—and shared—on images, thus making detailed scholarship and analysis available. By standardizing the ways that objects are represented in repositories, as well as the formats in which they are stored and accessed, the IIIF makes image access easier and more reliable. It also means that institutional repositories can make their resources available *once* for reuse by multiple individuals or other institutions, rather than having to answer requests for image download and use on a repeated basis. The savings to institutional repositories are considerable, and benefits to those accessing the images are that they know what to expect. Reliability and consistency add value to the assets but preparing these digital materials requires an investment of resources. IIIF assets can be accessed without a high-speed internet connection because of their reliable standards for availability.

To be used effectively, the resources in IIIF have to be accessed in a *viewer* installed in a local environment such as a desktop or web page. The viewers are programs (not people), and many off-the-shelf products exist. Some are open-source and others are proprietary. Leaflet-IIIF, for instance, is made to work with images. IIIF has its own vocabulary to describe the way its framework is organized into what are termed *manifests*. Understanding these technical details is essential for those *building* IIIF repositories. But for those *using* them, tutorials are more immediately valuable.

Note that the information about IIIF can be found on GitHub, a useful open-source repository for programming code (it was recently bought by Windows, but still operates), about which more will be discussed later. (Gitlab is an alternative.) GitHub provides a service by hosting projects and code and supporting version control. Learning all of the new terminology, acronyms, technical back-end pieces can feel overwhelming, but finding a viewer with which to work is an easier way into the experience. Scholars do not have to be developers but gleaning the basics of a framework's design from tutorials allows for more effective use of these tools. [See Exercise #2: Evaluating image viewers.]

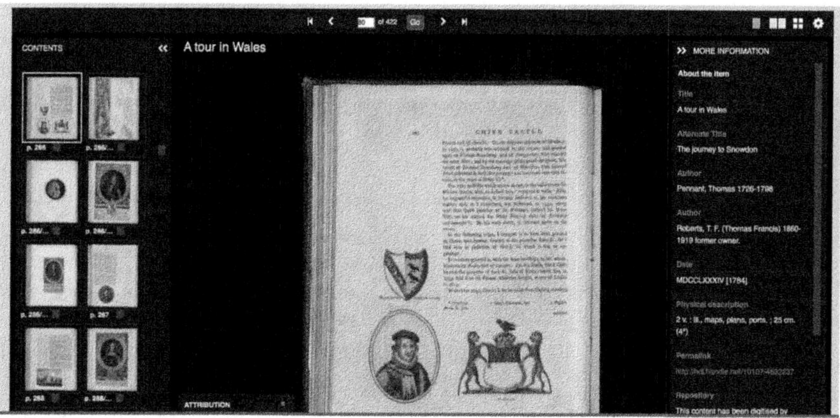

Figure 11.1 IIIF information in *Tour of Wales* by Thomas Pennant, digitized by the National Library of Wales

Note the sidebar of information. (By permission of Llyfrgell Genedlaethol Cymru/The National Library of Wales)

IIIF offers considerable support for its framework, including tutorials and demonstrations of its capacities. Above is an image taken from one such tutorial, showing the "sidebar" column with metadata next to the image of the resource. Keep in mind, for a complex resource like a book, the images in the repository are stored as individual files, but the experience of viewing requires they be sequenced correctly. This is just one tiny detail of the kind of back-end organization that IIIF standardizes. The difference between accessing images through IIIF and finding them in a random search engine result is that the institutional source, and information about the dimensions, materials, authorship, and other significant data are included (Look at the sidebar in *Tour of Wales* above). Search engines offer image results that are often far from the original materials, remediated multiple times, and do not have information for tracking owners for permissions and use. Inaccuracies in the image resource itself, such as cropping of important information (signatures, frames, dates, or other contextual elements) also occur. Other functionality for research is also built into IIIF repositories, including the ability to manage workflows and also to search within resources (OCR readable book page scans, for instance, might be available for full-text search from inside the repository). Professionally managed assets presented in a framework are the gold standard for digital scholarship. [See Exercise #3: Tutorials introducing IIIF and also a playspace.]

CIDOC-CRM a framework for cultural heritage

Every domain of knowledge and different discipline has its specific needs and demands when it comes to metadata and standards. Over several decades, the cultural heritage field has developed a "theoretical and practical tool for information integration" in its field. This is known as CIDOC-CRM. CRM stands for Conceptual Reference Model, a phrase that does not bode well for easy uptake of what it is (sorry). However, translated into the language of digital scholarship, this means that it is a way to describe cultural heritage materials using a formal, structured, and standard language. As with many of these standards, it was developed to be useful for information systems, rather than human readers. A look at the use cases that are part of the documentation on its site is instructive. They are institutionally based projects, mostly with library or museum technical support, and contain substantial intellectual contributions by a team of scholars as well as technical experts. With CIDOC-CRM we are squarely in the realm of professionals whose expertise has helped to build standards for infrastructure. Because it is such a widely used and powerful model, and is an ISO (International Standards Organization) standard, knowing about the role it plays in museums and other repositories of cultural heritage materials is useful.

What you need to understand about CIDOC-CRM at this point, given the discussions previously, is that standards have been created for data in networked cultural heritage environments, and that any project that is being conceived at this point in time in digital scholarship benefits from being built within these standards and frameworks.

GitHub a programming code repository

LoD, IIIF, and CIDOC-CRM are all built around standards for data access and use. By contrast, GitHub is a *repository* for *sharing programming code*. It provides a service. The main feature of GitHub is a "distributed version-control" system. This means that multiple program developers using the same code can create versions of it at the same time in a "non-linear" manner. This allows for a broad community of individuals to post and access programming code in the GitHub repository, and each use it without creating conflicts or problems. Each version is stored. Because source code might be adopted, modified, and customized many times, developers working on large projects need to be able to work independently but later access updated versions of each other's code. The larger community of GitHub users works independently and posts their code for the benefit of others. The ethics of using GitHub are readily apparent as it promotes a culture of sharing and building. Anyone can join GitHub. Settings in the creation of a repository ("repo") allow access to be controlled by a developer. Most repositories include a "README.md" file, which introduces the project and is a good place to start. Always read the README to familiarize yourself with the project—and include a README on your own repository if you publish. The community has created its own vocabulary to describe practices like "forking" (making changes to someone else's existing code) and "pulling" (asking the original developers to include your changes in their project) and so on. GitHub is designed to encourage sharing of data and code so that collaboration can occur remotely and in a non-linear fashion.

Git, on which GitHub was built, was invented by Linus Torvalds, a Finnish software engineer with a sense of humor. He picked the term Git because the word means "a disagreeable old codger" but he suggested it could mean any number of things, depending "on your mood." To be specific, Torvalds listed several possibilities: that it was a "random three-letter combination that is pronounceable, and not actually used by any common UNIX command," or that it meant "Stupid. Contemptible and despicable." Or it could mean "global information tracker" since when it works "Angels sing, and a light suddenly fills the room." His final definition, for when it breaks, was less polite. Torvalds was the inventor of Linux, an open-source version of the ubiquitous operating system Unix. His aspirations in creating GitHub as a version control system came directly from his experience in software development and understanding the challenges in its workflow. Any project that has a programming component to it can benefit from GitHub's basic functions and learning how to read files on the repository is a useful skill. One final note: look through GitHub's pricing structure and think about how it embodies their ethical values. Be sure to compare several categories. Perhaps keep in mind the extent to which many proprietary and open-source projects alike are built on infrastructure developed with government funding for military and other research—such as GPS and Wi-Fi. These histories are not apparent in our daily use. [See Exercise #4: Exploring GitHub.]

Takeaway

By creating standard formats for data sharing and networked resources, large-scale organized frameworks like LoD, IIIF, and CIDOC-CRM are promoting access and use of digital assets in ways that are more efficient and effective than one-off or custom approaches. The benefits for institutional developers of these assets are considerable, but so are those for individual scholars for whom the resources and services attached to them make work possible. The pressure to use standards and the expense involved in executing these frameworks mean that larger, better-funded institutions are more likely to be able to implement them. This reinforces certain inequities, but more significantly, puts pressure on communities to conform to the standards within the larger professional projects even when they do not have adequate resources. Will less-well-funded institutions be left out of integrated systems and consortia? Obviously, benefits and liabilities have to be assessed. But a repository like GitHub (though, actually, there are not many "like" it) is an invaluable resource for anyone working on digital project development.

Exercises

Exercise #1: LOUD's metadata

Look at the descriptive metadata on this site. https://linked.art/model/example_index.html The contrast with TEI, the Text Encoding Initiative, is useful to consider.

Exercise #2: evaluating image viewers

Look at the list of viewers available for IIIF and see what you learn reading their descriptions. Build a vocabulary for understanding open-source and proprietary formats. Note that some are built in JavaScript and HTML5, others make use of JSON formatted data (the suffix .js is frequently present). Learn to evaluate feature sets for these applications in relation to your project needs: comparison, annotation, sequencing, high resolution image displays, and so on.

Exercise #3: Tutorials introducing IIIF and also a playspace

Read through this workshop to understand IIIF. Ask yourself what you do and do not understand and whether you think you can use this resource within your research. http://ronallo.com/iiif-workshop-new/image-api.html

See also the play space for seeing how images can be accessed and manipulated from IIIF while remaining linked to their networked resource. www.learniiif.org/image-api/playground

Exercise #4: exploring GitHub

Take a look through the materials on the GitHub site. https://github.com/collections

Look, for instance, at https://github.com/collections/pixel-art-tools and think about working with these. GitHub is designed for ease of use and has a very low threshold of entry.

Note

1 A look at the map of participating institutions raises immediate questions about what "global" means https://iiif.io/community/#participating-institutions.

Recommended readings

Braunstein, Laura. 2017. "Open Stacks: Making DH Labor Visible." *Dh+lib*. https://acrl.ala.org/dh/2017/06/07/open-stacks-making-dh-labor-visible/.

A Digital Infrastructure for Humanities (Report on the activities of DARIAH). *European Commission*. https://ec.europa.eu/research/infocentre/article_en.cfm?&artid=50093&caller=other.

References cited

Blaney, Jonathan. 2020. "Introduction to the Principles of Linked Open Data." *The Programming Historian*. https://programminghistorian.org/en/lessons/intro-to-linked-data.

Kim, Soon, Hyungwood Choi, Nayon Kim, EunKyung Chung, and Jae Yun Lee. 2018. "Comparative Analysis of Manuscript Management Systems for Scholarly Editing." *Science Editing*. www.escienceediting.org/m/journal/view.php?doi=10.6087/kcse.137.

Resources

CIDOC-CRM. www.cidoc-crm.org/ and www.cidoc-crm.org/useCasesPage.

Europeana. www.europeana.eu/en.

Git https://guides.github.com/introduction/git-handbook/#basic-git and https://github.com/kirschbombe/learngit.

GitHub www.howtogeek.com/180167/htg-explains-what-is-github-and-what-do-geeks-use-it-for/, https://github.com/git/git/blob/e83c5163316f89bfbde7d9ab23ca2e25604af290/README and https://github.com/pricing.

IIIF.https://docs.google.com/document/d/1h9SPg9nlLA3TAdzkYxkyaFFNNf8m4PsbaIExcYwVLyo/edit#heading=h.q7mmne7d3bk2, https://github.com/IIIF/awesome-iiif; www.learniiif.org/image-api/playground and https://resources.digirati.com/iiif/an-introduction-to-iiif/, https://resources.digirati.com/iiif/an-introduction-to-iiif/, http://ronallo.com/iiif-workshop-new/beginnings.html.

IIIF Viewers. https://iiif.io/apps-demos/, https://github.com/IIIF/awesome-iiif#image-viewers.

Linked Art Model. https://linked.art/model/example_index.html.

National Library of Russia Online Exhibitions http://expositions.nlr.ru/eng/.

Nines. https://nines.org/.

Pelagios. ttps://pelagios.org/about-us/.

RDF www.w3.org/RDF/.

REKN https://rekn.org.

Smithsonian Libraries Online Exhibitions https://library.si.edu/exhibitions/online.

Stanford Spatial History Project. https://web.stanford.edu/group/spatialhistory/cgi-bin/site/index.php.

12 Project design and intellectual property

12a Project design and management

All serious research in digital scholarship is driven by intellectual questions from within a field or discipline, even if the use of technology changes the methods, scope, or presentation of the work. In beginning a digital project, the first consideration should be the level of your own expertise and its fit to the project design and development. Will using computational processes or web-based tools allow you to raise new questions, ask existing questions differently, or just add special effects? Are you willing to invest in learning computational methods well enough to think with them?

Subject area expertise is essential, but does the topic lend itself to digital work? You may be very knowledgeable about an author (Jane Austen), a period of time (the Kamakura period in medieval Japan), or a historical event (the Bambatha Rebellion of 1906 in South Africa). But what are the materials that can be digitized and what kind of data will you extract from your sources? We are back to where we began, analyzing the research problems to assess their connection to digital methods.

Consider the context carefully. You may be working with a group such as a class, or in an institutional setting with a community archive, a museum collection, or a library unit, or you may be working entirely on your own. You may have funds to pay for some of the work to be done as a start-up or prototype. If you will be dependent on grant support for start-up, development, or expansion, this should be taken into account. The granting institution's guidelines may shape your project and proposal. You should carefully define the scope of your project and whether it is finite, narrow enough in scope to reach a state of completion, or whether you will want to build on it over time.

All of these considerations play a part in the way you conceive of the project. Having a sense from the outset of where the project will be hosted and how it will be maintained is important. This will also guide the design and its development. Now each of these aspects of project design and management will be looked at in a bit more detail. [See Exercise #1: Documentation.]

Project design

Project design should address each of these issues systematically by defining the goals, scope, resources, and location at the outset. The parameters for each of these include the following:

- Intellectual goals: Define your project goals from the outset. What are you making and why do you need digital tools to do it? You may be building a digital repository to make materials and content available from a collection or around a theme. You might believe that analytics and data mining will provide insight into an issue. Perhaps you are creating a platform to serve an agenda or engage a community. Once you define the project, you can consider what materials will be used and how. Analog materials require digitization and rights clearance. Data will need to be modeled and produced, or re-purposed. The outcome should be considered from the beginning, so you know if your goal is publication, online display, analysis, or something else. Project design should be iterative, and frequent prototyping will inform the work, even changing some of its methods or approaches. Keeping a focus is important (try not to add new features without justification) but designing a project to be extensible (added to as it matures) is also a useful consideration. Extensibility might include new features for interactivity or use built on the existing infrastructure, or it might include participation in a consortium or the aggregation of projects or collections.
- Administrative structure: Understand what needs to be done and who will do what in the project. If digitization of materials is going to take place, who is going to scan, photograph, re-type, or otherwise remediate the artifacts? Who will attach the metadata and set up a repository, and who will design the interface and suite of services behind it? Every piece of the project needs someone responsible and knowledgeable to take care of making it happen. Make a workflow and then think about each piece and who will do it. Who will coordinate and do quality control? Digital projects involve enormous amounts of time and a wide range of expertise and effort.

    - Labor—roles, responsibilities, and credits

      As you consider the roles and responsibilities of all involved, also consider the credit that each individual deserves. Students who are digitizing materials usually have *not* contributed to the intellectual conceptualization of the project. But a student who designs the implementation and helps make decisions about the platform and functionality *is* guiding its development. Writing out a clear understanding of roles and responsibilities for all partners will help clarify these matters. Intellectual property generated in work for hire agreements, which is often what students or freelancers do, does not belong to the worker, but to the person who paid for the work. Someone can still be thanked and credited, even though they do not own the intellectual property from work for hire. [See Exercise #2: Roles and responsibilities.]

- Documentation

A designated documentarian is essential. If you are the director of the project, keep a journal and make notes for every meeting, every decision, and every activity. If the project grows and you are holding group meetings, designate one person, at least each time if not permanently, to take minutes and create a record. Personnel are likely to change on a long-term project and without documentation, it will be very difficult to know what decisions were made, why, and how to replicate workflows. All workflows should be documented in step-by-step instructions or they will not be able to be replicated by new members of a team. The documentation of workflows is essential—even if you are the only one working—so that they can be repeated.

- Institutional site: Where is the project being developed? If you are starting from within an educational institution (university or school) then talk with your library and any other technical support unit. You need to know if your institution will offer hosting services, any other technical support (advice on software, platforms, or assistance in installation of these), and whether they are going to serve as partners in the project. Be explicit about the scope of your project (e.g. in phase one you will be digitizing 1500 photographs, creating metadata, and a web presentation framework for scholars to search and use this repository, and you are thinking of working in Omeka). If you expect the project to be finite, say so, and if you think you might want to build on it for some time, be clear about this as well. You want to have institutional partners. The library and educational technology units understand the local infrastructure and its resources. If they are not going to be partners, and you are working independently, you will need a hosting service and a domain name. These can be set up using any number of commercial services (GoDaddy is one). Be sure to formalize any institutional agreements with a Letter of Understanding that includes roles and responsibilities and also plans for what happens if you leave the institution.
- Financial resources: What are the resources you have to create the project? Students need to be paid, programmers as well, and hosting services and equipment for digitization, though not prohibitively expensive, will need to be maintained over time. Who pays for the equipment? Software? Consulting? And the ongoing hosting of a site? Do a cost analysis in advance of beginning. Make a budget and list everything that will

involve financial resources from purchasing software licenses to paying fees and travel for a consultant or collaborator. Surprises should be kept for other parts of your life.

- Sustainability concerns: Digital projects are costly to the environment. The myth of the "cloud" as an "immaterial" environment is just that, a myth. Digital technology runs on chips and processors that involve rare minerals and metals. These are mined in dangerous circumstances, often by individuals who are exploited and mistreated. The toxins involved in this work can be lethal. Likewise, the ecological costs of server farms are enormous because of the heat they produce and the water used to cool them. Waste from the digital industry—cast off equipment, devices, and materials—is a serious pollution problem. Do not be deceived into thinking that "digital" means "ecological" or "immaterial." Digital activity is heavily material. Just as you might cringe to see paper misused because of the trees sacrificed, so you should be aware of the impact of digital production lifecycles on the world we live in. For the project itself, sustainability involves consideration of the longevity of the project. Who will maintain it? Will all of the intellectual investment be lost if the site goes away? How long will the software used in its construction remain viable? How do you know? Building for sustainability is important, and open-source tools and platforms with a larger user community are more likely to last than proprietary formats, no matter how well these perform. However, some proprietary products have a strong market share and are also likely to continue to be used. Consult with experts such as your technology advisors in your institution. Make your work conform to their environment if you can. This will serve everyone's interests in the long run.
- Outcomes and assessment criteria: How will you know if your project has been a success? What are the criteria of assessment? If you know that you want to digitize 1500 photographs, add metadata, and make them available in a repository, then you can easily say when that has been accomplished, and even mark milestones along the way. But if you say that you are tracking the influence of the work of the Italian poet Dantë on the English Pre-Raphaelites, then what are the metrics of success for the analytics you are going to perform? Modularize your assessment criteria. For instance, in this Dantë project, you might include the following milestones: 1) successfully learned to use Mallet; 2) located full-text materials for 20 of the most significant (most cited) poets and a broader corpus of about 15 more who were affiliated or published in the same journals; 3) demonstrated success at extracting data from the texts in relation to specified criteria; 4) established metrics for gauging the percentage of materials in this corpus in relation to once-extant materials and/or those in a comparable sample size of another group. And so on. The point is that you need to be able to demonstrate that you will know *how to assess your own success or failure*.

These are all components of a project's design that would need to be specified in a grant application or project proposal. The intellectual research goals will drive the project, but the apparatus of digital scholarship is far more cumbersome than that of analog work. Many working parts have to be coordinated for the project to be successful.

Be realistic about time commitments—your own and that of others—and the extent to which start-up will consume more hours than imagined (a safe estimate is to double the time you imagine each task will take and add another ten percent). Make sure the work you are doing is work you enjoy. Creating a team, getting up to speed, having planning and design or development meetings is exciting and fun. Learn to delegate responsibility—but responsibly.

Prototyping is a crucial aspect of digital project development. An iterative design process will assure success since initial results or stumbling blocks may suggest a need to rethink tools, scope, or methods. These reworkings are not failures, they are part of the process. [See Exercise #3: Workflow.]

Afterlife of a project

Key points to remember are that creating the project may be the most important aspect for your research. A project does not have to endure, and if it does, the institutional context will be crucial. Is the project preserved in a static state (repositories and publications often are), in an ongoing condition of change (in different versions or serial issue, like a journal), or is it merely documented and then abandoned. In any case, resources will need to be found to sustain or terminate a project. The time to think about how to export intellectual content is at the beginning—what formats are available for outputting the research? Web-based projects are not easily transformed into print projects (images are not high enough resolution, links don't work, many features become obsolete or irrelevant). But if you have spent several years creating a project with rich intellectual content, you might want to have a plan for preserving it that does not simply involve a tedious cut-and-paste of texts and images. If data input has been involved, are there export formats for it? Common formats for structured data, like .csv or .json still have to be factored into the design. XML data? RDF? And text? Where are the images, media, or sound files stored? Can you save the interface? If not, then how is the argument preserved? Merely saving files of content, without the organizational structure and presentation, can result in stripping away the very things that made the digital project distinct. Making a plan for the afterlife of a project is a crucial part of design development.

Takeaway

Every digital humanities project involves intellectual, administrative, technical, and financial considerations. The success or failure of the research will depend on being realistic about the amount of support required and the commitment that is possible. The intellectual goals should drive the project, but most humanists are surprised by the amount of time involved in digital work. Work backwards from the final output and realization as well as planning each step from the beginning. Consider the institutional context and long-term maintenance of projects. Not all projects need to endure, and documentation of a project may be the best contribution to research in a discipline or to digital scholarship as a field. Unless you enjoy the process of learning new methods and processes, digital work is not worthwhile. Keep the goals in mind and the focus clear. Manage expectations realistically. Start with something that can be done. When that is finished, then consider additions. Build with extensibility in mind, but not with constant support as a requirement. You may love doing digital work, but you will still want to have a (little bit of a) life.

Exercises

Exercise #1 documentation

Look at several digital humanities projects and see what level of documentation they have about their process, methods, and development. Recommend a set of guidelines for this work.

Exercise #2: roles and responsibilities

Write a letter of understanding that outlines specific roles and responsibilities for your project.

Exercise #3: workflow

Write a step-by-step workflow for asset acquisition and digitization for your project. Be sure to include all specifications necessary for replication of the workflow (file sizes/dimensions, settings for scanning or otherwise uploading, details of data formats or conventions, definitions of tags for markup, file naming and folder organization, and any other details).

Recommended readings

Project management guidelines from various institutional teams:

Emory University. https://scholarblogs.emory.edu/pm4dh/.

Princeton University. https://cdh.princeton.edu/research/project-management/.

Reed, Ashley. 2014. "Managing an Established Digital Humanities Project: Principles and Practices from the Twentieth Year of the William Blake Archive." *Digital Humanities Quarterly* 8 (1). www.digitalhumanities.org/dhq/vol/8/1/000174/000174.html.

12b Intellectual property issues

Anyone working in scholarship or pedagogy, publishing, or the management of cultural materials needs to understand the basics of intellectual property law. This is true in all areas and media. But the ease of appropriation and re-use of existing creative and intellectual resources in the digital environment makes it all the more important that researchers be informed about the legal and ethical issues guiding their work. Guidelines for use should not be restricted to whether it is allowed legally, but whether it embodies ethical behavior. Understanding the following core concepts in intellectual property is crucial:

1) Respect for the principle of copyright
2) Knowledge of the concept of "Fair Use"
3) Familiarity with Creative Commons licenses
4) A sense of property vs propriety—something may be legal and still not ethical
5) Privacy and liability issues
6) The definitions of open source, freeware, and proprietary systems

When peer-to-peer networks sprang up for file sharing, particularly in the area of popular music, the questions of how rules governing analog media were going to apply in an era of easy endless copying arose immediately. Considerable grey area continues to exist with regard to appropriation of materials found online, and how they can be embedded in sites without any formal procedures for permissions. A few basic, common sense guidelines are worth keeping in mind. The first is how you would feel if what was appropriated was *your* intellectual property—a song, photograph, painting, or video. How do you want to be acknowledged and credited? Always put yourself in the position of the person who created the material. Second, promote a culture of citation. When in doubt, always cite. Provide attribution and credit for any artifact you borrow or embed in a site or publication. Print publication requires permission, formal and in writing. Online citation is easy—note the source and credit the author or creator.

Copyright—rights, reproduction, take-down

The best source of information on copyright law in the United States is the government office responsible for jurisdiction over these matters. However, the United States is a signatory to international agreements as well, and copyright laws vary considerably around the world.

Copyright laws protect works that are in "fixed, tangible form." They do not protect ideas, methods, or concepts. If you have an idea for a project, you cannot copyright it. If you write a proposal about the project in which your ideas are expressed in language, images, or recordings, this can by copyrighted. Since the 1976 Copyright Act, copyright is automatically assigned in the United States. The intellectual property does not have to be registered with an official government agency. Using the copyright symbol is useful, but it is no longer necessary. In a legal dispute, you would need to be able to demonstrate you were the author of a work. In the case of this book, for instance, an earlier PDF publication carried authorship attribution and a publication date to indicate it was this writer's intellectual property. It had a clear tangible instantiation. One of the rights of copyright holders is to create derivatives, later editions, and versions of a work. This protects a publication from being plagiarized by opportunistic individuals who might feel they have a right to work they did not author merely because they wish to use it in some way.

Keep in mind that joint authors hold shared copyright, and that work for hire is excluded from copyright protection on the assumption that the person who hired that individual guided the intellectual development of the project. Copyright can only be transferred in writing. Copyright was extended in the Copyright Act to the author's life plus seventy years. This can be quite a long time.

Copyright is not automatically an international protection. The laws of each nation are specific, but some international agreements exist. The United States Copyright Office is, again, the most authoritative source for information on this topic for authors and artists under its jurisdiction. Those working in other countries need to know the laws of their land and also which international treaties have been signed. WIPO, the World Intellectual Property Organization, is the organization that oversees many international agreements, such as the Berne Conventions, first established in Switzerland in 1886. These were established in part in recognition of the vast industry of literary piracy, particularly across national boundaries, without paying the authors. (In the 19th century, publishers' agents used to meet shipments of new bestselling books from foreign countries at the docks, run them up to the printers, and issue unauthorized editions for profit.) The Berne Convention guidelines were updated regularly into the late 20th century, but then in 1996 WIPO created a Copyright Treaty in recognition of changes brought by networked technologies. The WIPO portal contains useful and interesting resources, many of which are specific to digital technologies, such as WIPO Proof, designed to give date-stamped, tamper-proof, evidence of the existence of data or files to help "safeguard the many outputs" of an individual work.

One interesting story in United States copyright law is that of Mickey Mouse and his history as intellectual property (Escovedo 2016). The original Mickey Mouse will soon pass into public domain, but many commonly recognized icons and images cannot be used without express permission. This is true of brand identities and famous figures—like Charlie Brown or Superman. These were creative works with individual authors. Strangely enough, you cannot copyright your own image—someone can use your face in a photograph and they own the rights to the image. They do not own your face. That is all yours—at least for now.

Public domain works can be used without permission or fees. Materials that are in the public domain have had their copyright expire or else were never intended to be copyrighted by their authors. If something is in public domain—such as the works of William Shakespeare, Buddhist texts, the Vedas, and writings of Confucius, they cannot be owned or copyrighted by anyone. Copyright can be renewed for up to 95 years. Then materials pass into public domain. This statute is particularly important for scholars working on materials that are coming into public domain but which were formerly subject to copyright. Keep in mind that a surrogate may be copyrighted even when an original cannot—so the Louvre can hold copyright on reproductions of the Mona Lisa (and prevent unauthorized copies from being made), even if the original work is in public domain (Deazely and Meletti 2016).

A note on plagiarism: While copyright and plagiarism are not precisely aligned, any scholar or teacher should be able to guide their own work and that of others with regard to correct citation practices. Many excellent resources exist for this that help to define paraphrase, direct and indirect citation, and other parameters within which plagiarism can be avoided. The key point to keep in mind is that even if you do not use someone's precise words, copying their argument, its sequence and framework, and ideas is an act of plagiarism and could even be a violation of copyright law. Always cite anyone whose work you are using. This will spare you difficulties ahead. When in doubt about permissions, ask, but also, be acquainted with Fair Use guidelines and defend them through proper use.

Fair use

Fair use guidelines set legal terms on which copyrighted materials can be used. The concept exists largely, but not entirely, within educational domains where many materials may be included in courses and teaching. Fair use is governed by a few very straightforward principles. Copyright material can be used for non-profit educational purposes *without permission from the copyright holder* provided the activity follows certain guidelines. All scholars should know these and know if they can make an argument for fair use when appropriating works. Here are the four principles:

Purpose and transformative activity: One crucial criterion in fair use arguments is whether the individual or entity is involved in commercial or non-profit activity. Transforming a work so that it provides new insight or meaning is within fair use guidelines. So, if you radically alter an original work of art by making it into a parody or putting it into a very different framework, you may be able to justify it as fair use. Note that several musical figures have sued political campaigns for appropriation of their work, and the music industry is particularly vigilant with regard to rights. Many artists sign away rights in an early phase of their career, taken advantage of by agents or producers. The rights holder of a work may not be the artist.

Nature of the original: If the original material is factual or historical material it is more likely to meet fair use guidelines. So, if you are embedding citations and quotes from a source that is largely informational, citation should suffice. If, however, you are using a work of creative expression—music, literary text, performance, film, video, painting, or other image—the guidelines are more restrictive.

Amount and significance of appropriation: You can take a small sample of a work, but not the entire work. Using a chapter from a book might be legitimate for teaching purposes, but in general, keeping to less than 10% of an original is a good way to stay on the safe side of copyright violations. For time-based media, no single rule exists for the number of seconds that are permitted as fair use. If the original copyright holder sues, the smaller the amount of the percentage of the whole used the more likely your defense will hold. The significance of the borrowing also matters—if you appropriate an iconic image, a narrative summation, or other crucial moment or part of a work, that is more likely to constitute an infringement.

Impact on market value: If your use has an impact on the market value of the original material, you can easily be sued. Copying an entire textbook for a class and providing it free of charge is a clear violation of copyright. Copying an article or chapter and offering it free to students behind a firewall is generally not. Under no circumstances should you ever sell or market someone else's intellectual or creative property. That is a clear violation of copyright.

Fair use is meant to assist in the circulation of ideas and promotion of scholarship and creative work—it should not be abused, but it should be upheld aggressively.

Creative Commons licensing

Creative Commons licenses help regulate use of materials with innovative agreements designed specifically for use of digital materials (though they can be used for analog works). Creative Commons licenses were developed by three individuals, Lawrence Lessig, Hal Abelson, and Eric Eldred, who founded the organization Creative Commons in 2001. Their goal was to support the notion of the Web as a "commons"—an arena for open and shared exchange of intellectual work in the sciences, humanities, and other arenas of scholarly expertise and cutting-edge research. Their goals were utopian, in the best sense, seeking support of ways to ensure that knowledge could be protected and transferred equitably. With this in mind, they created a set of licenses that have been widely adopted and used for intellectual property within networked environments. Their claim is that more than 1.6 billion projects have used their licensing conventions. These are very commonly adopted for digital humanities purposes and are widely respected within scholarly communities. Creative Commons licenses were in part inspired by GNU, a General Public License concept invented by computer scientist Richard Stallman, who also coined the term "copyleft" as part of his work.

The Creative Commons licenses are differentiated by their features. Do you allow your work to be shared? Adapted and changed? Used commercially? The combination of choices you make will determine the type of license. This will be indicated by a phrase and a set of icons. The work of the group at Creative Commons goes way beyond the specification of licensing agreements and extends into widespread advocacy for intellectual exchange. Their work is ongoing and benefits the entire scholarly community. Using these licenses is good practice. [See Exercise #1: Creative Commons.]

Property and propriety

Discussion of degrees of access and control have come up several times in the previous sections. Not all materials should be accessible to all viewers. Limited access has justifications that include the rights of communities and individuals. Legal rights and ethical rights are not the same—access need to be constrained by law in order for it to be controlled by intellectual rights holders (Sonderholm 2010). But unlike legal limits, which, though sometimes unclear, are at least spelled out and established with precedents, ethical limits have to be carefully negotiated. What are the guidelines for "propriety" (good behavior) rather than "property" (respect for ownership) in dealing with intellectual content? Concepts of "moral rights" over property are centered in discussions on the values of an individual and of a community with respect to use. For instance, one consideration is that artists, musicians, designers, and others need to make a living. If you steal a font from an online source, or borrow it from a friend, you have cheated the designer from a fee. Is this ethical? Again, the peer-to-peer sharing culture made access to content so easy that many individuals do not stop to ask who is being cheated in the process. [See Exercise #2: Managing permissions.]

If the research that a scholar does is supported by public funds, then they may have an ethical obligation to be sure that outcomes from that research are made available to the public. The counter-argument is that incentives to create new breakthroughs in certain areas (probably more in sciences and applied technology than in the humanities) will be diminished if researchers have to make their discoveries public without monetary reward. Even if the work cannot be turned into a commercial product, the scholar may feel they have the right to recognition as a reward through attribution. Philosophers, lawyers, and ethicists have argued every side of these questions, but scholars creating analytic and discursive insights within networked environments will want their contributions identified, cited, and recognized—not appropriated.

One last point on which to be informed is libel—defamation of character. To be sued for libel, an individual must have made *false* statements demeaning to the image or reputation of another person. True statements are not subject to libel, no matter how damaging they may be. Fact-checking is essential in any situation in which the work, character, or behavior of another person is being disparaged or negatively characterized. The criticism may be justified, but it must be based on facts and evidence.

Privacy issues

The right to privacy is a protection from intrusion into personal matters or domains, including one's home. Another form of privacy includes the right not to be surveilled in public space. Privacy also involves the liberty to make decisions over areas like religious faith, political affiliation, moral values and such without government coercion or intervention. In the United States, the Fourth Amendment of the Constitution prohibits searches in someone's home without a warrant. But what this means in a networked culture becomes more difficult to define. Computers are porous spaces; they are linked in upload and download systems that make it difficult to define boundaries. If downloads to your computer are tracked, has your domestic privacy been breached? What about your personal phone when you are in a public space? Would you track user activity on your research or personal site by IP addresses? Other information?

Eavesdropping, searches, and public scrutiny are all activities that are limited by privacy statutes, but these become more difficult to control in an era of electronic surveillance. Many websites and companies collect data about purchase, activities, sites visited, medications, and many other details of individuals. "Cookies," common on many websites, are small packets of information exchanged between your browser and site's server to track use. Will you install this system on your site? Public libraries have been aggressive in protecting patron profiles and refusing to turn over their records. Should computers in their spaces disallow cookies? Many companies and sites are interested in monetizing the data collected on visitors. The European Union has passed stricter regulations on the collection of information in online environments than most nations. Any site that uses "cookies" to track usage is required to have explicit agreements, not implicit ones. If you decide you are going to collect data of any kind from visitors to your site, considering how it will be stored, protected, and used is important.

The question of who owns a "digital avatar," that is, the personal profile created by online activity is continually being debated. Also, when you use a cloud-based service or hosting site to store your data, you should know who has access to the information. Is the hosting service monitoring content, traffic, or financial transactions? Since domain names are all registered, the owner of a site can be found and identified. Such information can be protected with privacy settings. Distinctions exist among categories—deliberate consent to having data collected versus implied consent. Settings can require either an "opt-in" or "opt-out" action with regard to informed data collection in exchange for more limited access (Elliott 2019).

The concept of "openness" is often touted as a universally positive feature of data repositories and online sites, particularly in the public or government sector. The definition of "openness" is not uniform—open to view, open to know about, open to search, or use for analytic purposes?

Finally, any use of intellectual or creative property created by others should protect information about an individual's personal life that they themselves have not revealed. The digitization of correspondence, for instance, can be a liability if information contained was not sanctioned for public consumption. Romantic, medical, family, or financial information may be contained in these documents. In the planning phases of a project, review these issues and consider the guidelines for use of materials that will protect the privacy of all concerned.

Freeware, open source, and/or proprietary systems

Freeware is software that can be used without payment. It is just what it sounds like, free. Open source software developers make the code available for use and modification by others, including developers. Open source materials can have proprietary systems built on top of them, they do not guarantee that every application developed from the code remains available for appropriation and re-use. The ethos of the open-source community strongly advocates for keeping code available, but many applications have used these building blocks as the foundation for commercial products. Linux and Git, both discussed earlier, are open source projects, but proprietary projects can be built on top of their open source code. Proprietary software, such as the operating systems for Apple and Microsoft, are carefully guarded so that developers cannot imitate them and build systems that run their products on other competing platforms. Keep in mind, something can be commercial without being proprietary (Gehman 2019). An application or platform can generate revenue and still be built on open source code and allow its code to be used. Open source code is generally protected by licensing agreements, so knowing the types of licenses (GPL—General public license, AGPL—allows download, LGPL—allows linking, etc.) and terms of these is essential (Kulkarni 2018).

From the point of view of scholars and researchers, open source has an ethical advantage. It is supported by communities of developers. It is responsive to the needs of the members of those communities. It is not secret. But it is also not always stable, and it can disappear without much prior warning. Open source code allows for rapid development and prototyping since many of the basic operations are built into the software. Imagine you are trying to make a viewer of the kind discussed in an earlier section for working with IIIF image repositories. Suppose you have some specific needs for your project—microscopic imaging for instance—but the major features of your platform are fairly standard. Should you build from scratch or modify the code for an existing viewer? The answer is obvious. And even if the code is free, the development is not—this will need to be paid for and maintained. Also, open source software may be vulnerable to security risks.

In 1985 the computer scientist Richard Stallman created the concept of *copyleft*. The concept has strict guidelines and was attached to his GNU operating system and the GNU Manifesto he published (Stallman 1996–2018). Stallman created licensing agreements that conform to the principles of copyleft: the rights to use, study, share, and modify. The most important principle is that derivatives of open source materials *inherit* the rights of the source. For instance, if the source code is protected by a Creative Commons license that requires attribution, that must be given. If the license specifies no derivatives, then using the code would be in violation of the agreement. Stallman was the founder of the Free Software Foundation and, like several other early internet pioneers, was an advocate for community-based, rather than commercial, development of the Web.

Takeaway

Digital technology makes it extremely easy to copy intellectual property. Behavior of this kind should be guided by informed understanding of the legal *and* ethical dimensions of one's actions. A basic understanding of copyright, fair use, distinctions among licensing agreements, concepts of openness, and considerations of privacy are all central to working ethically. Citation is an essential aspect of scholarship and should be practiced in all circumstances. The practice of linking does not require permission, and building rich resources in networked environments does not always involve ingesting and storing materials, many of which can be "called" into a window for display without being stored on the server of your site. If ever there were a place for the Golden Rule to be invoked, it is in the area of intellectual property—from the smallest snippet of code, a style sheet, to a large-scale project and its detailed contents. Treat the work of others as you wish your own work to be treated.

Exercises

Exercise #1: Creative Commons

Identify the features of a Creative Commons license that seem most appropriate for your own work.

Exercise #2: managing permissions

Write a workflow for managing permissions for intellectual property in your project.

Recommended readings

Sonderholm, Jorn. 2010. "Ethical Issues Surrounding Intellectual Property Rights." *Philosophy Compass*. https://onlinelibrary.wiley.com/doi/abs/10.1111/j.1747-9991.2010.00358.x.

References cited

Deazely, Ronan, and Bartolomeo Meletti. 2016. "CREATe Working Paper: Copying, Creativity and Copyright." CREATe Blog. https://www.create.ac.uk/blog/2016/02/02/create-working-paper-copying-creativity-and-copyright/.

Escovedo, Josh. 2016. "Disney's Influence on United States Copyright Law." *The IPLAW Blog* (Intellectual Property Law Blog). www.theiplawblog.com/2016/02/articles/copyright-law/disneys-influence-on-united-states-copyright-law/.

Elliott, Deni. 2019. "Data Protection Is More Than Privacy. *EDPL*. http://digifolio.me/elliott/wp-content/uploads/sites/41/2019/03/19-01-Data-Protection-is-More-than-Privacy.pdf.

Gehman, Chuck. 2019. "How to Use Open Source Code in Proprietary Software." *Perforce*.

Kulkarni, Ajit. 2018. "What to Watch Out for Before Using Open-Source Software in Your Product." *Hackernoon*. https://hackernoon.com/what-to-watch-out-for-before-using-open-source-software-in-your-product-32a822e3a60b.

Stallman, Richard. 1996–2018. www.gnu.org/licenses/copyleft.en.html.

Resources

Berne Convention www.wipo.int/treaties/en/ip/berne/summary_berne.html.

Copyright www.copyright.gov/circs/circ01.pdf. and www.copyright.gov/circs/circ38a.pdf.

Creative Commons. https://creativecommons.org/licenses/ https://creativecommons.org/choose/.

Ethical Digital Media Literacy (Canadian Centre for Digital and Media Literacy) https://mediasmarts.ca/sites/mediasmarts/files/pdfs/tipsheet/TipSheet_Getting_Goods_Ethically.pdf. and (Britannica) https://www.britannica.com/topic/intellectual-property-law/Economic-and-ethical-issues.

Fair Use. (Stanford) https://fairuse.stanford.edu/overview/fair-use/four-factors/ and (Harvard, Berkman Center) www.dmlp.org/legal-guide/fair-use.

Open Source. https://opensource.org/.

Plagiarism (MIT Center for Comparative Media Studies and Writing) https://cmsw.mit.edu/writing-and-communication-center/avoiding-plagiarism/.

Right to Privacy https://definitions.uslegal.com/r/right-to-privacy/.

World Intellectual Property Organization www.wipo.int/portal/en/.

Coda

A note on advanced topics in digital humanities

Advanced topics

A number of topics that are part of long-term or higher-level project development will be touched very briefly here since they are part of the larger landscape of digital scholarship but require specialized professional or technical knowledge.

Legacy data and re-use

Legacy data is material shaped by someone else and preserved for future use or re-use. Permissions to use the data and considerations of privacy and intellectual property are essential. The hazard of legacy data is that it is very difficult to recover the context in which it was made, the model on which it is based, and design decisions that led to its having the shape or specific content in which it is discovered. The other difficulty—and it is a problem with all data—is that it is often impossible to tell what is missing. Is the data representative, exhaustive, or merely a small sample?

Integrating legacy systems

Systems as well as data can be a legacy of past information technology and infrastructure. Many cultural institutions have back-end collections or administrative management systems that were custom built or created in platforms or programs that no longer exist or are not supported. Replicating their functionality in an updated system can be time consuming. Migrating data and workflows into new systems is also a challenge. But in addition to their role in remediation projects, these legacy systems are themselves objects of study. The history of knowledge organization and management is integral to the design specifics of these projects and they deserve their own place in the research agenda of cultural historians.

Silos and consortia

An earlier section examined the work of researchers involved in the Linked Open Data project and other approaches to creating consortia or frameworks for integrating previously siloed data or repositories. Because considerable work in electronic record keeping occurred before the Web, the process of integrating siloed data (and legacy projects) continues. This is clearly an advanced topic, since figuring out how to make this material useful without destroying its specificity and semantic content is often a non-trivial matter.

An index or directory of digital research

No single register of digital humanities projects exists. Projects are created and hosted constantly on local servers, within small and large institutional contexts. They do not get listed in WorldCat or other online library catalogs, and to find these projects is often a matter of following a random search engine result or a trail of specialized in-crowd references. The hesitation about having library catalog entries for digital projects comes in part from their ephemerality, but also, their iterative quality. However, a complete index or directory, though a major undertaking, would serve a broad community interested in the contents of these projects, their intellectual labor and contributions, but also, their role in building a knowledge-base for how to think conceptually within the frameworks of digital platforms and tools.

Designing custom platforms and tools

Another area of advanced topics is the development of custom tools or platforms for doing the work of digital humanities. Such work might include more specialized or sophisticated versions of an existing program for analysis, visualization, or data mining. But it might also involve creating an entire platform or a new tool. For this, collaboration with a programmer with expertise is recommended.

Critical issues

The multiple volumes of "debates" and "companions" in the field of digital humanities testify to the ongoing vitality of discussion around critical issues. [See Recommended readings.] In the earlier decades, struggles for definition—"what is digital humanities?"—were prominent. These were also accompanied by fairly straightforward assertions about the value of digital methods, which in turn, provoked a backlash. Digital humanities was criticized from various sides—for making no intellectual contributions of substance, for promoting an entrepreneurial approach to scholarship, for monopolizing resources. It seemed exclusive, masculinist, and even elitist to some. But other questions continued to inform its development, many grounded in a better understanding of its methods and either their contribution or their need to expand into speculative modes. More recently, questions of whiteness and diversity among practitioners, hegemonic values imprinted in technological systems, practices of inclusivity and exclusivity in access, and expertise across a range of communities have become current topics within the field.

Programming knowledge

To code or not to code? This perpetual question continues within digital humanities. Clearly, the more you are capable of, the more you can work effectively—within reason. Most humanities scholars will not become expert programmers. Their knowledge of their disciplinary field forms the core of their contribution to any project. But having a working knowledge of the role of programming and types of relevant programs will elevate fundamental literacy in this area. Having an ability to at least *read* lines of code and understand how they are produced, what their syntax is, how they specify variables, and so on, is a useful skill for communicating effectively with those members of a team who will have expert coding experience.

The programs most likely to be used by humanists are either scripting or object-oriented programs. The difference between these is that scripting languages compose instructions for how to do something while object-oriented languages are composed in modules that contain information and behaviors. Scripting languages act on existing data and files. Two of the most popular computer languages are JavaScript (its name immediately identifies it as a *scripting* language) and Python (a general-purpose language that can write object-oriented code). These are both used to develop customized applications. JavaScript is used more often to create modifications of web applications. Python is more likely to be used to prototype project operations. Other programs are designed to suit specific communities, like the program R, which is the foundation of statistical work, broadly used in the social sciences. SQL (Structured Query Language) is the programming language for working with data bases, and SPARQL is the query language designed to work with data stored in RDF (Resource Description Framework). A look at the W3 School tutorials will give a good sense of currently useful programming and scripting languages: from HTML, CSS, and JavaScript, to SQL, Python, PHP, jQUery, JavaScript, C++, and C#. The general wisdom is that learning *any* programming language (JavaScript and Python are considered "easy" to learn) will provide a solid introduction to concepts and practices.

Conclusion

In many ways, the core of digital work remains the task of modeling—of thinking about how the abstraction of complex or ambiguous analog artifacts experienced within an interpretative activity can be effected in an ethical and self-conscious manner. Something is lost as well as gained in the multiple mediations and re-mediations of artifacts and experience into a digital framework. We should remain aware of the effects of concealing those very processes whose operations transform the source materials into computational form—leaving much of the richness of these artifacts aside in the outcome. Digital storytelling can provide a synthesis and narrative of a project—but it can also conceal the models and evidence on which a consumable version of research is being produced. The ethical issues of property, appropriation, privacy are all crucial considerations, but so are the pressing problems of sustainability in ecological terms.

The myth of the "immaterial" character of digital platforms was just that, and the high costs of high tech should be kept in mind. What justifies expenditures and the many elements of abuse and exploitation of human rights and labor as well as environmental conditions in making a project? Sustainability within the sphere of digital work can be understood as part of immediate and ongoing challenges to the ecological survival of the planet. But the intellectual frameworks within which the work is conceived also have date stamps, though that does not guarantee the obsolescence of ideas.

The historical richness of human culture does not diminish with time, and though platforms may look outdated and functionality may be compromised, the same has always been true. For thousands of years, we have managed to "migrate forward" the cultural materials that have been part of our long history. Cave art, ritual sites, monuments, and works of art, law, history, and every other form of human expression have been preserved through these efforts. Digital methods and scholarship are one phase of this process, but we should not lose sight of the need to preserve the analog world and its precious legacy as well.

Digital assets are not archival, and the work done in this medium is more fleeting and vulnerable than in any previous format. Our investment in its production should be tempered by that realization. The real work of preserving a *living* environment might well be kept foremost in mind in this as in every other aspect of our ongoing commitment to humanistic research, scholarship, and pedagogy.

Recommended readings

Berry, David M., ed. 2012. *Understanding Digital Humanities*. London: Palgrave Macmillan.

Berry, David M., and Anders Fagerjord. 2017. *Digital Humanities: Knowledge and Critique in a Digital Age*. Cambridge: Polity Press.

Gitelman, Lisa, ed. 2013. *Raw Data is an Oxymoron*. Cambridge, MA and London: MIT Press.

Gold, Matthew K., ed. 2016. *Debates in Digital Humanities*. Minneapolis, MN: University of Minnesota Press.

Gold, Matthew K., and Lauren F. Klein, eds. 2019. *Debates in Digital Humanities*. Minneapolis, MN: University of Minnesota Press.

Losh, Elizabeth, and Jacqueline Wernimont. 2018. *Bodies of Information: Intersectional Feminism and Digital Humanities*. Minneapolis, MN: University of Minnesota Press.

Risam, Roopika. 2018. *New Digital Worlds: Postcolonial Digital Humanities in Teory, Praxis, and Pedagogy*. Evanston, IL: Northwestern University Press.
Schreibman, Susan, Ray Siemens, and John Unsworth. 2016. *A New Companion to Digital Humanities*. Hoboken, NJ: Wiley-Blackwell.
Smithies, James. 2017. *The Digital Humanities and the Digital Modern*. London: Palgrave Macmillan.

Resources

Or www.cambridgesemantics.com/blog/semantic-university/learn-sparql/sparql-vs-sql/.
Python vs. Javascript https://skillcrush.com/blog/python-vs-javascript/.
SPARQL tutorial, see: https://jena.apache.org/tutorials/sparql_data.html.

Index

Note: Page numbers in *italics* indicate a figure and page numbers in **bold** indicate a table on the corresponding page